£2.99

④

A Field Guide in Colour to

WOODS & FORESTS

A Field Guide in Colour to

WOODS & FORESTS

by
M. Poruba, J. Pokorný,
O. Rabšteinek and R. Hrabák

Fig. 1 — Deciduous trees in the early summer (page 2)

PICTURE ACKNOWLEDGEMENTS

265 photographs by
Bárta (2), Bellmann (6), Bluďovský (2), Brchel (1), Breburda (1), Chroust (5), Danegger (5), Diffené (3), Eichhorn (5), Formánek (2), Harz (1), Hrabák (35), Hoch (5), Humpál (1), Jurzitza (9), Kahl (2), König (10), Kricnar (1), Kunc (1), Limbrunner (7), Moosrainer (2), Pavlík (27), Pfletschinger (18), Pradáč (18), Rabšteinek (5), Reinhard (23), Rödl (4), Rohdich (1), Rudert (1), Rys (5), Schrempp (14), Studnička (5), Vlasák (1), Weber (9), Zeininger (25), Zepf (3)

Colour illustrations by Květoslav Hísek
Line drawings by Michal Skalník

Text by Rudolf Hrabák, Jaromír Pokorný, Miroslav Poruba, Otomar Rabšteinek
Translated by Margot Schierlová and Marie Hejlová
Graphic design by Stanislav Seifert

English version first published 1982 by Octopus Books Limited
59, Grosvenor Street,
London W1

ISBN 0 7064 1485 3
Printed in Czechoslovakia
3/07/04/51-01

Contents

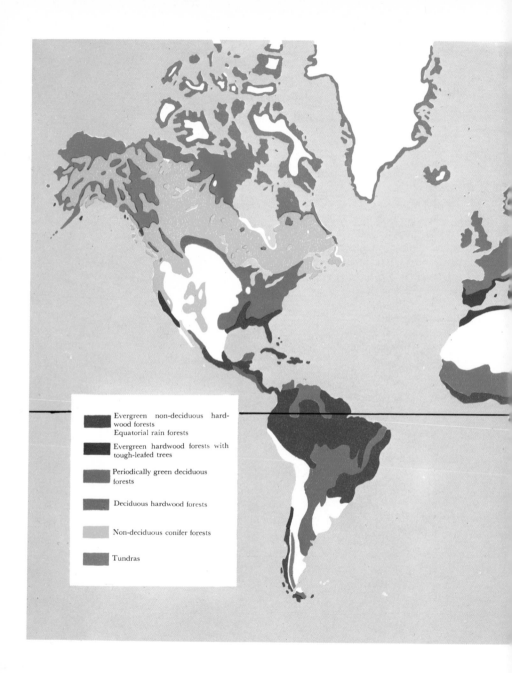

Evergreen non-deciduous hardwood forests
Equatorial rain forests

Evergreen hardwood forests with
tough-leafed trees

Periodically green deciduous
forests

Deciduous hardwood forests

Non-deciduous conifer forests

Tundras

The distribution of forests on the Earth

After 'Lehrbuch der Botanik' by
E. Strasburger

The distribution of the world's forests

Today forests cover about 29 % of our planet's land surface, but the proportion used to be far greater. This decrease has been caused by natural factors such as changes in climate and environmental catastrophes as well as by the exploitation by man in pursuit of his need for timber. According to the statistics of the Food and Agricultural Organization, the distribution of forests on the various continents is roughly as follows:

	Forest area (x10⁶ ha)	Percentage of whole area covered by forests
Europe excluding the USSR	169	30.4
USSR	910	40.6
North America	750	38.6
Central America	76	27
South America	795	54
Africa	763	25.4
Asia excluding the USSR	548	20
Oceania	218	27

For comparison, agricultural land occupies some 23 % of the Earth's land surface.

There are therefore 4,229 million ha of forest on the Earth. If they were to be concentrated in a single place they would cover the whole of North and South America. This might create the impression that we are more than well supplied with forests, but on closer examination we find that, owing to extreme climatic conditions, one third of the world's wooded areas consist of only shrubs and stunted trees of no value as timber. (These woods are however important for soil conservation, although the countries where they occur all too often fail to appreciate this fact.) In addition, some 500 million ha of forest have been devastated by reckless exploitation, while half the world's forests cannot be economically utilized at all using contemporary technology. We can thus say that of every 1,000 ha of forest, only 75 ha are properly cultivated and a further 225 are simply exploited for timber, while over 70 % of forested areas are not — or cannot be — utilized at all. Today the average area of forest per person is 16,000 m², but local differences are enormous. For instance, the area per person in Alaska is 50,000 m², whereas in Holland it is only 2,000 m². The world's timber reserves are estimated at 192,000,000,000 m³ — an enormous quantity. In fact, mankind cannot even consume the annual increment. The world's timber supplies are not evenly distributed, however, and the above figure includes the reserves of inaccesssible forests. The world's yearly timber consumption amounts to 1,400,000,000 m³, which would fill 1,285,000 railway trucks: if these were arranged one behind the other, the track would go 26 times round the equator. Annual wood consumption is constantly increasing, however, and in future the production of cultivated wood will have to be increased and various substitutes for wood will have to be found.

Fig. 2. — Cultivated forests composed of extensive spruce monocultures are today artificially distributed over large areas of Europe.

Forests can be classified into different types, according to whether they are composed mainly of softwoods (conifers) or hardwoods (broad-leaved trees). Hardwood forests can be subdivided into evergreen and periodically green (deciduous) types. Evergreen trees also shed their leaves, but not all at once. The times during which periodically green trees bear leaves and are leafless, are strictly defined and are associated with seasonal changes in the climate. Conifers are in general non-deciduous: they shed their old needles, but keep the younger ones, so that they are always green (hence the name 'evergreen'). The one exception are the larches, which lose their needles in the autumn and grow new ones in the spring. The main non-deciduous hardwood forests are the rain forests of tropical and subtropical regions, in particular the equatorial forests which grow where rains are heavy and temperatures high. In such regions there are no significant changes in rainfall and temperature during the course of the year. Abundant moisture and high temperatures promote luxuriant growth of many different species of plants. This type of forest is the most complex forest community and is characterized by high species diversity at all levels of development, as well as by the most intense competition for living space between the plants in it. One typical feature of the tropical forest is the number of trees which grow to different heights, so that their crowns fill most of the space above the ground. The number of species of trees in these forests is estimated at 10,000 (in central European forests there are only about 40 species). Since tropical trees grow the whole year round, their foliage is sparser than that of our own trees and their crowns have fewer branches. In consequence, tropical forests are less shady than our own woods and the lower vegetation layers are able to grow better. Unlike European trees, they do not have a thick layer of dead bark and their buds are not covered with protective scales. Tropical rain forests are also characterized by numerous epiphytes — orchids and ferns which are specially equipped for taking up water and minerals formed by decayed vegetation, so that they have no need of actual soil for growth. Twining lianas, which often grow to a length of hundreds of metres, are also typical of these forests. With such a wealth of plants, practically the whole of the space below the crowns of the trees is filled and fully utilized. The climatic conditions ensure that dead plant remains decay very quickly and are broken down to their constituent minerals, which are thus readily available to living plants. From the point of view of forestry, however, the tropical forests are of little use, as the production of commercially valuable wood is small. In the tropics, the distribution of rain forests is confined to coastal regions with a mean temperature of about 25°C and an average rainfall of 2,000 mm, i. e. to India and the Malay Peninsula, the Congo, Guinea and the Amazon basin.

Bay trees and other tough-leaved trees form a further group of evergreen hardwood forests. The leaves of these trees are hard, leathery, small and non-deciduous and are covered with a waxy or resinous substance protecting them from excessive loss of water by evaporation during the hot, dry summer. The trees themselves are mostly small, with knotted trunks, and often grow far apart. Unlike the trees in rain forests, their trunks are encased in thick bark or even cork. Their open crowns let in the light to a brushwood layer composed mainly of thorny shrubs, which usually contain a high concentration of volatile oils. This type of forest grows all around the Mediterranean, where the summer temperature averages 25°C, the winter temperatures 8−11°C and the rainfall up to 800 mm (Fig. 3). Deciduous hardwood forests, on the other hand, grow in regions having marked seasons and are composed of trees

Fig. 3 — Vegetation zones in Europe: 1 — pinewoods and moors, 2 — montane and subarctic spruce forests, 3 — beechwoods, 4 — oakwoods, 5 — forest steppes, 6 — Mediterranean evergreen forests, 7 — woodlands requiring warmth, 8 — tundras

with thin, bright green leaves. The appearance of these forests changes seasonally as they lose their leaves during the colder winter period. Their buds are protected by scales and often by hairs or sticky resin as well and they are mostly wind pollinated. As a rule, these forests tend to be of single species, or to show a preponderance of one particular species of tree. Deciduous hardwood forests are confined to the northern hemisphere and are adapted to the extreme conditions of successive summers and winters.

Non-deciduous conifer (softwood) forests grow chiefly in the colder regions, i. e. in the more northerly parts of Europe, Asia and North America, or at high altitudes. The trees in these forests have long, smooth trunks and therefore produce good timber. Conifers often form pure stands especially in climatically inclement regions. In such pure growths, undecayed plant remains, in the form of raw humus, tend to accumulate more than usual and have an adverse effect on the soil, making it acid. We shall have more to say about hardwood and softwood forests later, when the various types of European forest are discussed.

The forest as a natural community

The woods are always beautiful, whatever the time of year, but an ordinary visitor, who sees just the beauty, has no idea of the wonderful complexity of the life behind it, of the plants and animals which inhabit the forest and live there together in peaceful coexistence or fierce competition. The trees look down on the most diverse destinies, but the human eye sees little of the tragedies played out in accordance with nature's law — that of the survival of the fittest. One creature's death means prolongation of life for another and every birth conceals the germ of a future death. It is in this never-ending cycle, in the incessant fight for life, that the forest lives.

The distribution of the Earth's forests and of their various types is not fortuitous, but is the result of a whole series of external environmental factors, such as climate, the composition of the soil, the altitude, the animals and other plants, and of course Man's influence. The environment and the forest influence each other reciprocally. The forest is not a random collection of plants and animals, but is an ordered natural system. Where conditions are different, other natural communities, such as peat bog, steppe, desert, stagnant water and rock communities are found, but the forest community is the most distinctive, both as regards its manifestations and its effect on the environment. Wherever plant communities compete under natural conditions, the forest will always take over a denuded space as long as the soil and the climate permit. The forest is the dominant plant community and once it has occupied a locality it never leaves it. The only things that can cause the forest to retreat are interference by Man or a change of climate which makes the growth of trees impossible. The forest is thus the final and permanent stage in the colonization of the soil, whereas the other types of communities are temporary and through their development prepare a suitable environment for future forests. Let us follow the sequence of colonization of bare soil by plants. The first pioneers to settle are lichens, whose root fibres push their way into small cracks and secrete acids which break down the rock. This creates conditions enabling more advanced plants, such as mosses, ferns, grasses and herbaceous plants, to take root. With mechanical weathering of the soil, these plants spread and shrubs begin to appear. Then come modest pioneer trees, like the willows, birches and Aspen, which prepare conditions for more permanent and demanding trees such as Beech, spruces and oaks (Fig. 5a). The succession of communities can be followed best in deforested areas, i. e. in clearings, although here the activity of soil pioneers is not needed, since the soil of clearings already forms a suitable medium for germinating plants. The sequence of the successive communities remains the same, however, proceeding through herbaceous

Fig. 4 – Trees make use of every cleft in the rocks and colonize even the most inhospitable places.

plants and shrubs to a forest community. This process whereby a new plant community comes to replace an earlier one is called secondary succession. For example a pond silts up and is replaced by woodland (Fig. 5b) or a new woodland grows to replace felled trees (Fig. 5c).

Competition for living space can be seen in the forest at any and every stage of community development, but is most fierce at the time of the plants' maximum growth. Favourable environmental conditions accelerate and intensify such competition. The outcome of all these complex relationships between plant organisms is that given species group together into communities within which they interfere with each other as little as possible. Forest vegetation is divided into several more or less distinct layers formed by plants which grow to much the same height above the ground, or whose roots go down to roughly the same depth (Figs. 6, 7). The highest is the tree layer, followed by the shrub, herbaceous, moss and upper, middle and lower root layers. This stratification of the forest is very important, as it enables a large number of different plants to grow in the same place and makes the best possible use of the space above and below the ground. The more conducive the environmental conditions to an abundance of species and to luxuriant growth, the more pronounced the stratification of the forest vegetation and the greater the interdependence of the forest's various components. When we examine different types of woods, we find that where conditions are not very favourable, the forest has fewer species and is more

13

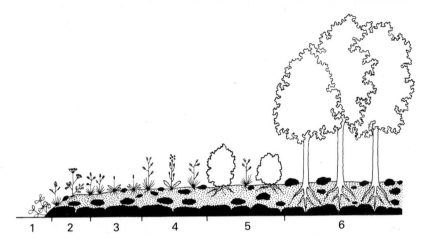

Fig. 5a — Natural succession of communities on a rocky substrate: 1 — pioneer species, 2 — hard grasses (fescues), 3 and 4 — reed grasses and other tall grasses, 5 — shrubs, 6 — mature oak woodland

simply organized; at the same time the various species are less dependent upon each other. Loosening of these relationships can be best observed in thinly forested mountain areas, where the herbaceous layer is hardly any different from the flora of the adjacent meadows. If different plant species are to co-exist, they must not interfere with each other too severely. For example, trees differ in the amount of light they require. Some, such as larches, oaks and birches, need plenty of light, while others, e. g. Beech and the firs, can tolerate, or may even need, shady conditions, especially while they are young. Such shade-tolerant trees are well equipped to form an understory or to grow up through an existing canopy. The structure of a species crown is also related to its light requirements: trees needing a lot of light having loose crowns and those tolerating shade having dense crowns. The stratification of a forest community is thus also influenced by whether the uppermost layer is composed of trees with a loose or a dense crown. Forests consisting of photophilic (light-loving) trees are therefore richer in undergrowth and in herbaceous species.

The soil is another major factor influencing the forest community. Its effects on forest structure and type are so great that some knowledge of how soils are formed and the processes that occur within them are vital if we are to fully understand their importance. Soil is formed slowly, over hundreds of years, through the interaction of parent rock, climate, plants, animals and time. It is thus a kind of link between living and non-living nature. Its formation is primarily a biological process. The weathering action of rain, frost and plant roots causes the rocks to disintegrate and these fragments mingle with the dead parts of plants and animals, which are broken down by fungi, bacteria and small animals to simple, water-soluble substances suitable as nutrients for plants. The activity of living organisms is thus mainly responsible for the enrichment of mineral soil with nutrients. Organic plant and animal remains are decomposed by two basic processes. The first is humification, in which organic matter is converted to raw humus, composed of substances which plants are unable

14

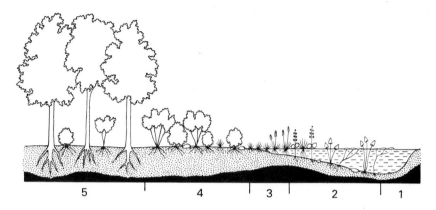

Fig. 5b — Secondary successsion of communities in and beside overgrown ponds: 1 — free-floating plants, 2 — plants anchored to the bottom, 3 — Reed Grass and rushes, 4 — hardy shrubs, willows and alders, 5 — oakwood with birches.

to take up. In raw humus the structure of the original organic matter is still discernible. The other decomposition process, in which this organic matter is completely decomposed to gaseous products, water and inorganic minerals, which the plants can assimilate, is called mineralization. The converted organic substances — nutrient humus — are dark-coloured and the original structure of the crude humus from which they were formed can no longer be distinguished.

Humification and mineralization must take place in a given ratio if the fertility of the soil is not to be adversely affected. If mineralization predominates (e. g. as in many newly formed clearings), organic matter is quickly decomposed to substances

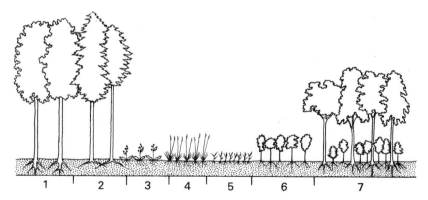

Fig. 5c — Secondary succession of felled beechwoods: Beech and spruce growths (1 and 2) prior to felling: small willows and knotgrasses (3) in the clearing are soon succeeded by reeds (4) and finally by heather (5): pine and birch seeds are deposited in the heather (6), where they pave the way for the main species — Beech and firs together with spruces (7).

Fig. 6 — Vertical stratification of species in a forest community helps the plants to make better use of the space above and below the ground.

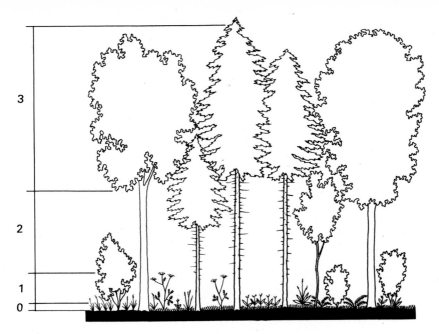

Fig. 7 — The layers of the forest community: 0 — the moss and lichen layer (up to a height of 5 cm), 1 — the herbaceous layer (up to 1 m), 2 — the shrub layer (1—3 m), 3 — the tree layer (over 3 m).

readily available to plants, but since more mineral substances are formed than the plants are able to utilize, they are therefore wasted. If humification is dominant, the result is nutrient deficiency. In addition, dead waste accumulates forming a layer of raw humus which prevents seeds from germinating and hinders natural regeneration of the forest. The ideal situation is when all organic remains are decomposed to humus during the year. Plants and soil create a dynamic balance in which nutrients are cycled back and forth between them (Fig. 8). Ideally this cycling is such that nutrients do not accumulate in any part of the system. One of the main differences between forest soil and other soils, e. g. agricultural soils, is their capacity to produce large amounts of humus, since the forest is rich in vegetable waste in the form of fallen leaves. Among European deciduous trees, Beech yields the largest amount of humus and birches the smallest, while among conifers most comes from the firs and least from the larches. Conifer needles take longer to decompose than the leaves of deciduous trees. The amount of leaf material that falls is considerable. Spruce woodlands shed about 3,000 kg/ha of needles each year, while in beechwoods the amount may be as much as 4,000 kg (Fig. 9).

A tremendous number of soil plants and animals — mostly microscopic — participate in the decomposition of organic remains. They include bacteria, algae, fungi, various protozoans, arthropods, worms and even certain vertebrates which live within the soil. Spore-bearing plants form the largest contingent; animals are represented by a larger number of species, but by a far smaller number of individuals. All types of soil organisms take part in the process of organic decomposi-

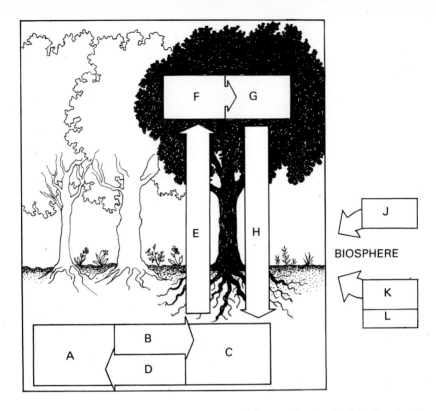

Fig. 8 — The calcium cycle in a deciduous woodland. A — calcium stored in soil and rock-forming minerals. B — calcium made available through weathering. C — amount of calcium available in the soil. D — calcium incorporated into new minerals. E — calcium consumed by vegetation. F — calcium contained in living vegetation. G — calcium contained in dead parts of vegetation. H — calcium returned to the soil through decay of dead plant material. J — calcium in rainfall. K — calcium leached out of soil in solution. L — calcium washed out of soil as soil particles. About one quarter of the available calcium participates in the cycle each year.

tion, each modifying certain substances to produce simpler ones, which in turn can be utilized and decomposed by other organisms. Some of the animals essential to humus formation are relatively large. In almost every type of soil we can find earthworms, various parasitic worms, crustaceans, centipedes, ants, spiders and insect larvae and it is these which feed on the millions of minute organisms present in soil, returning them to the never-ending organic cycle. Earthworms are extremely important for the circulation of substances in the soil, but their numbers vary; in favourable, loose soils they average about 1,000/m³. By tunnelling the soil in all directions they let in air and moisture, while during the night they come to the surface to drag down plant remains for food. They swallow quite large amounts of soil a day, which, when passed out with the undigested portion of their food, forms small granules and promotes good soil structure.

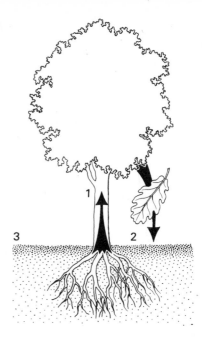

Fig. 9 — The role of trees in the circulation of nutrients and the accumulation of certain elements in the upper humus: 1 — uptake of nutrients from the soil, 2′ — shedding of the leaves (return of nutrients), 3 — accumulation of humus with nutrients.

The number of organisms in a given soil sample is vast. It has been estimated that one hectare has an average population of 500 million animals, but the bacterial population cannot possibly be expressed in figures, although their weight has been put at several hundred kilograms. These creatures disturb and aerate the soil with their movements and fertilize it with their nitrogen rich excreta. The outcome of the combined activity of this underground community is forest humus and a soil with good structure and an abundance of available nutrients to support plant growth. Every living organism plays its part in this cycle and even the tiniest are an integral part of the forest community.

However, under certain circumstances the balance of a soil can be upset and we might almost say that the soil has become diseased. Particular combinations of climate, tree species and human interference can ruin the natural fertility of a soil. As an example, we shall take a simplified look at what can happen to the soil under a pure stand of spruce. Colloids (substances insoluble in water) are an important component of soil. They can be either organic (originating from humus) or mineral (derived mainly from silicic acid or from aluminium and iron salts). Colloids are carried through the spaces in the soil by rainwater and as soon as they come into contact with some substance giving an alkaline reaction, they are precipitated into an amorphous or structureless form. In this precipitated state they have an important function, however, since they retain nutrients on their surface and prevent them from being washed into the deeper layers of the soil, where the roots of the plants would be unable to reach them. The depth at which colloids encounter alkaline substances is, of course, very important. In places where the rainfall is relatively low and the soil is poor, colloids quickly come into contact with alkalis and are precipitated at depths of a metre or less. A dense colloid-rich layer forms, which, in particularly unfavourable circumstances, may become impermeable. In this case, the passage of water is restricted, with the result that in the rainy season the soil turns to mud, while in the dry season it dries up because water cannot rise from the deeper layers. In such soils, therefore, colloids have a negative effect.

Plants in the forest

Our definition of a forest, therefore, might be a plant community dominated by trees in which there is a balanced relationship between the organic and inorganic components of the environment. What, then, are the environmental components which affect the forest's growth and development? They can be divided into non-living natural factors determined by the locality in which the forest grows, such as the climate and the soil, and into living factors, such as plants, animals and Man. Finally, we must consider the feedback effect of the forest on the environment and the intricate inter- and intra-specific relationships between the various organisms within it.

The aerial parts of plants, the stems and leaves, are subject to the effects of climate and the gaseous composition of the atmosphere. We shall look in turn at these factors – light, temperature, humidity, oxygen concentration and wind.

Light is essential to all green plants; they need it for photosynthesis, in which the plant takes up carbon dioxide from the air and water from the soil, and using solar energy trapped in chlorophyll (the green pigment of the leaves) converts these to the sugars essential for growth. Together with water, light thus plays an important role in the formation of organic matter. The more light the plant utilizes, the more such matter it is able to synthesize. The greater the leaf area, the more light a tree can trap, so that the rate of growth depends on leaf area as well as the amount of sunlight available. The optimum size of a tree crown is at least one third the length of its trunk. The light supply depends on the length of the day, which varies with latitude, and strongly influences the growth of plants and hence their distribution. We recognize long-day plants (growing in northern latitudes) and short-day plants (in the tropics and subtropics). Light also affects the germination of seeds. In some species it stimulates germination, in others it retards, or even prevents it.

In most plants the leaves face the source of light in such a way that they can utilize it to the maximum, but not keep it from the others. We can observe how leaves turn to follow the light, or how their petioles are twisted. Not all plants react to light in the same way, however. In some cases the leaves face incident light directly, while in others they shun direct sunlight or do not react to it at all and are distributed in all directions, as on the pines, for example. In fact, they may even react differently on the same plant. For instance, the leaves at the top of a Beech are turned away from the main direction of incident light (they use only dispersed light), whereas inside the crown and on the lower branches they face the light directly. Like herbaceous plants, different species of tree have different light requirements. The density of the foliage of a tree is a good guide to its needs for light. If the crown is dense, then relatively little light will reach the lower leaves, and we can conclude that the species is shade tolerant. Conversely, where the crown is sparse it is apparent that the tree requires more light. Larches, pines, birches and acacias are examples of heliophilic (sun-loving) trees. The light requirements of some trees change as they grow older; they usually become less shade tolerant. For example, young Ash do not need a great deal of light in contrast to the mature tree; the same is true of the Rowan and others.

The shape of the crown and the way the tree is constructed is also influenced by light. Conifers in the far north usually have narrow, tapering crowns, but as we approach the equator, the crowns of the trees become flatter. This phenomenon is related to the position of the sun. The conical trees of the far north utilize the rays of a low-lying sun, which fall on them from the side, whereas in the tropics, where the sun is usually overhead, the upper surface of the flat-crowned trees intercepts direct sunlight and the under surface, light reflected from the ground. In Europe, the crown shape typical of each species is also modified by the light environment. For example, at high altitudes or further north, pines and spruces have slimmer, more conical crowns, while the rounded crowns of deciduous trees (oaks, Sycamore, Beech) are better suited to light conditions in flat country and low hills (Fig. 11).

The trees species in our latitudes have a typical form, which in the case of deciduous trees can be seen best in the winter, when they have shed their leaves. In general, conifers have one straight, central trunk, as can clearly be seen in larches and spruces. The side branches radiate from this in whorls, or in the case of larches, in a spiral. Broad-leaved trees branch in a quite different manner and their crowns have a different structure. With few exceptions, (e. g. Beech) they do not possess an apex and their branches grow from several places. They generally have a slender crown when young and only when they are older does the crown acquire its typical

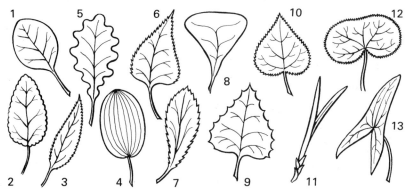

Fig. 10a — Shapes of simple leaves: 1 — elliptic, 2 — ovate, 3 — lanceolate, 4 — oval, 5 — crenate, 6 — acuminate, 7 — obovate, 8 — cuneiform, 9 — triangular, 10 — cordate, 11 — acicular, 12 — reniform, 13 — sagittate

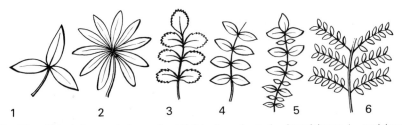

Fig. 10b — Shapes of composite leaves: 1 — trifoliate, 2 — palmate, 3 — imparipinnate, 4 — paripinnate, 5 — pinnate with interjected leaflets, 6 — bipinnate

21

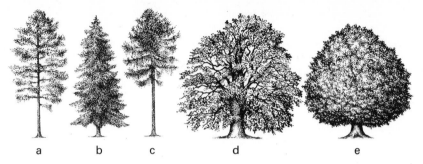

Fig. 11 — Typical tree forms: a — fir, b — spruce, c — larch, d — oak, e — lime

form. The crown of the Beech becomes conical, for example, and the crowns of limes ovoid, while those of the elm are goblet-shaped. The extent to which trees are dependent on light is also evident from the pattern of their growth. This dependence is particularly marked in the case of broad-leaved trees, which need more light and, when mixed with conifers, find it by growing into spaces in the canopy. This gives rise to trees with one-sided crowns and/or twisted trunks. In properly tended forests, therefore, an adequate light supply is assured by regulating the canopy. We distinguish between the horizontal canopy — the distance between the crowns — and the vertical canopy — the differences in the heights of the various crowns. Correct trimming of the canopy in both these dimensions encourages trees with the optimum length and form of crown, ensuring the best possible use of the available light. Obviously a good canopy has a beneficial effect on the life of the vegetation as a whole. An inadequate supply of light not only reduces photosynthetic production, but also lowers the temperature of the soil and thus limits the activity of soil microorganisms: this impairs the decomposition of humus and causes the physical properties of the soil to deteriorate.

Temperature is another important factor influencing the forest through its effects on photosynthesis, transpiration and respiration. While every species has a different optimum environmental temperature, the minimum required by most European plants is 0—5°C, the optimum 20—30°C and the maximum 40—50°C. Some arctic plants can survive temperatures as low as −60°C, while certain tropical species die at below +3°C. Organs which contain little water, such as roots and, in particular, seeds, can tolerate lower temperatures than the more juicy parts of the plant without coming to harm. Woody parts are the most resistant. Plant life therefore is closely regulated by ambient temperature.

In the forest, temperature influences the distribution and the type of trees present. Species which tolerate large temperature differences, like birches and Aspen, are widely distributed. The period during which growth is possible is taken as the number of days each year with an average temperature of over 10°C. Even if this is less than two months, spruces, pines and larches may survive, but Beech and oaks require 3—4 months at least. This period also determines roughly the highest altitude at which a tree can grow. With every 100 m increase in altitude, it shortens by an average of 8—9 days, while the winter, i. e. the period with average daily temperatures of less than 0°C, becomes 7 days longer. The summer period, i. e. with average daily temperatures of over 15°C, loses 14 days with every 100 m. The distribution of the most important European trees with increasing altitudes (i. e. with falling temperatures) follows approximately the sequence: Sweet Chestnut, Sessile Oak, Black Alder, Hornbeam, Pedunculate Oak, limes, Ash, Beech, Sycamore, firs, spruces, pines, birches and Aspen.

It is not average temperatures, but temperature extremes which are the most important, however, since it is extremely hot summers or extremely cold winters which decide whether a plant will live or die, even though they may occur only once in several decades. In the case of extreme cold, it is important whether it comes during the trees' rest period or when they are actively growing. Extremely low temperatures cause cracks at the bottom of the sunny side of the trunk and form frost wounds which spoil the wood or cause the top of the tree to dry up. Damage caused by heat, such as blistering of the bark, is rarer; the main trees to suffer are those with a smooth bark, such as the spruces, firs, Beech and Hornbeam, i. e. trees which prefer shade. The sun-loving Silver Birch is protected by its white bark, which absorbs very little heat, and when older by a thick bark.

All changes in our atmosphere are influenced — directly or indirectly — by temperature and it is therefore not surprising that temperature is the main criterion for delimiting the various climatic zones and the corresponding types of forest. The tropical or torrid zone has an average annual temperature of over 20°C and a tropical flora. In some areas tropical forests are replaced by savannah. The subtropical zone, which is characterized by evergreen broad-leaved forests has an average temperature of up to 20°C for 1—8 months of the year; the mean temperature in the cold months does not fall below 10°C and the long-term minimum temperature below −5°C. The inland regions of this zone are characterized by deserts and semi-deserts. The temperate zone, which is characterized by deciduous broad-leaved forests and grassy inland steppes, has a year with four distinct seasons. Further north is a cooler zone, where the forests are composed mainly of conifers. The vegetation growth period lasts for not more than four months and the mean temperature in the warmest months is over 10°C. Last of all comes the polar or tundra zone, which possesses no coherent forests and merges with the extreme zone of eternal snow and ice.

All plants require water. The hydrogen it contains is an essential structural element of all the carbohydrates and proteins needed for growth and metabolism. It moves from the roots to the leaves in a continuous stream, carrying nutrients taken up by the roots from the soil. When it reaches the leaves it vaporizes into the atmosphere, through small openings in the leaves known as stomata; the process is called transpiration. The uptake of water from the soil and its evaporation must be in balance, since water pervades the whole body of the plant, crosses cell membranes and passes through plasma. If the water content of the plant drops, the stomata must be closed to reduce further loss. The leaves can no longer breathe and photosynthesis and respiration rates fall, inhibiting the plant's ability to grow. In addition to the importance of the water balance for growth, if the water content of the plant falls too low, it will die completely. The amount of water required varies not only with the species of plant or with the type of plant organ, but also changes with the time of year. A plant consumes more water in the flowering period than during ripening of the seeds. If water loss by transpiration exceeds the water intake, the plant withers.

It is able, to some extent, to adapt itself to a variable state of hydration, however, by regulating the rates of transpiration, of respiration and photosynthesis. Such adaptations influence the anatomical structure of plants. According to their water requirements, plants can be classified as xerophytes (liking a dry climate), hydrophytes (liking moisture) and mesophytes (with moderate water requirement).

In regions where dry and rainy periods alternate, as in steppes, for example, the period of rest in the plants' life cycle coincides with the dry period, which their organs of regeneration — seeds, tubers or bulbs — can easily survive without coming to harm. If such a cycle is impossible, plants growing in dry spots have various external and internal devices enabling them to exist there. One such device for regulating hydration in dry regions is to be found in certain succulent plants, whose aerial parts are very poorly developed compared with their unusually elaborate and deep root systems. Another way in which plants can protect themselves from excessive water loss is by shedding their leaves. Broom, for instance, which grows in dry places, has small trifoliate leaves in the spring, but in summer, when the shrub's water consumption increases, it sheds them and the green stalks are responsible for photosynthesis. Plants which do not form leaves at all and whose green stalk is the only photosynthetic organ are extreme forms of xerophytes. The classic examples are the cactuses, whose spherical or cylindrical bodies present the smallest possible exposed area and hence enjoys the smallest evaporation rate.

A thickened cuticle and a reduced number of stomata are other ways of limiting evaporation. The stomata of hydrophytes are located on the surface of the leaves, in the epidermis, whereas in xerophytes they lie below the epidermis, in pits out of the way of drying winds. These pits are sometimes also equipped with hairs, which impede evaporation still further. Some plants have leaves which curl up to protect the stomata from coming into contact with the movements of the air, while in others, such as Mullein, evaporation is limited by various types of hairs. Similarly, the leaves of many xerophilous plants have a coating of wax or resin to protect the epidermal cells against loss of water. The various movements of leaves mentioned in the section on the effect of light likewise provide protection against excessive evaporation. If conifers need to limit transpiration, they can partly block their stomata with resin. The very structure of their needles prevents increased evaporation in windy weather. In the summer the needles transpire; in the winter, when the stomata are choked with wax and resin, transpiration stops. The frozen ground makes the intake of water impossible, so that water losses must be reduced as much as possible.

Mesophytes have moderate water requirements and can adapt themselves to conditions in a wide range of climatic zones. They cannot tolerate extreme conditions, however. Practically all European deciduous trees and cultivated plants are mesophytes. Because of their adaptability mesophytes have no special structural adaptations; they are bare and hairless and are always bright green.

In Europe, hydrophytes grow mostly in the lower forest layers, or beside streams, in the shadow of other species. Since they grow in a damp environment, they have a very high transpiration rate. Otherwise they are typical of wet tropical forests. As a rule they have large, thin, divided leaves (to increase their surface area) and large numbers of stomata; their stems are also usually juicy. Another way in which plants can get rid of excessive water is by active secretion of fluid through various types of apertures. Cuckoo-pint is a good European example of this phenomenon.

Fig. 12 — Seedlings, fruits and seeds of some forest trees: a — Large-leaved Lime, b — Sycamore, c — Sessile Oak, d — Common Alder, e — Beech, f — Ash, g — Silver Fir, h — Norway Spruce.

For European conifers and deciduous trees the winter is the dry period. As the temperature falls the roots of conifers stop functioning sooner than the roots of broad-leaved trees and larches (which are deciduous). This is associated with the xerophilous character of conifers and with their protective adaptations against evaporation. Deciduous trees prepare for the winter by shedding their leaves because they are unable to replace from the frozen soil the water which would be lost from the leaves by transpiration; otherwise they would dry up during the winter. The tree prepares for leaffall in a careful sequence. First, it limits its entire growth and concentrates all the nutrients contained in the leaves in the trunk (these would otherwise be wasted when the leaves were shed). The array of colours acquired by leaves in the autumn is a sign that this process is under way. The next step is the formation of a fine layer of cork at the place where the leaf joins the twig, so that the connection is eventually severed and the leaf simply drops off. The cork actually forms large numbers of little stoppers blocking the vessels transporting nutrients to the leaves and back again. The 'wounds' are thus 'dressed' and the tree is protected against infection. Such a precaution is essential in view of the countless holes that would be left each autumn. In addition the cork scars prevent the loss of precious water. The pattern and form of the scars is typical for each tree species.

European trees can be classified according to their water requirements as follows: the pines, acacias, birches and Aspen are satisfied with very little moisture, the Black Alder, Ash, poplars, willows, spruces and the Sessile Oak have high water requirements and the rest have moderate demands.

Water also plays an important role in germination. Seeds usually ripen in the autumn and have to survive the winter without coming to harm. During its autumn maturation a seed loses practically all its water, dehydrating its nutrient supply. For the seed to be able to germinate, this process must be reversed. When the spring rains come, water infiltrates below the outer coat of the seed until it reaches the germ of the future new plant. The seed swells and as it takes in more water its metabolic rate increases. Lastly, water can help to disperse certain seeds — usually seeds equipped with a kind of air cushion enabling them to float, as in the case of the alders (Fig. 12).

If we take a closer look at the forest's moisture requirements, we find that, of all natural communities, the forest consumes the most water for the synthesis of organic substances, of which it produces far more per unit area than any other plant community. Despite this, only a small proportion of the rainfall may determine a forest's characteristics. It has been estimated that a forest requires about 50 mm rainfall in each of the four growing months, i. e. from May to August, making a total of 200 mm, with moderate humidity. It is thus not the mean annual rainfall which dictates the occurrence and characteristics of a forest, but the distribution of the rainfall during the year. The cause of the anomalous vegetation in the Mediterranean region is thus not an inadequate rainfall, but its unfavourable distribution, since the maximum rainfall occurs in the winter.

The relationships between trees and the air movements that comprise the wind, are many and varied. Wind is beneficial to the forest and is indispensable to its existence, but can sometimes be destructive. It spreads pollen and helps to distribute seeds and fruits. Seeds borne by the wind are usually winged or have silky 'parachutes', enabling them to be carried long distances on the breeze. The wind is less beneficial when it affects the growth of trees, as may be seen on the edges of forests or at high altitudes where wind velocities are high. In the mountains we find spruces like pennants, with dried and withered branches on the windward side and the rest of their crown streamed in the direction of the wind. Similar misshapen crowns can be seen beside the sea. In such cases the mechanical effect of the wind is not only to blame: increased evaporation caused by the wind, dries and stunts growth of the branches to windward. Whole forests can be affected by the wind in this way. Wind may also affect tree form in areas with heavy snowfalls. Here shrubs and trees may not grow higher than the level of the winter snows. Any shoots that protrude are blasted by the strong winter winds, and die off. The effect of the wind is not only physiological but physical as well; it is loaded with sharp ice crystals that cut the shoots like a sandblaster.

The movement of the air stimulates transpiration and thus causes faster transport of nutrients within the plants. If there is not an adequate water supply, the effect is the same as after a severe drought, i. e. the plant dries up. Wind also dries the soil and blows dead leaves and fine humus away, thereby impoverishing the soil and contributing to the formation of raw humus. It likewise modifies the shape of the trunk. The greater the onslaught of the wind, the more tapering the trunk, which loses its cylindrical form and much of its commercial value.

The best known and the most obvious effects of severe winds are uprooted and broken trees, occasionally over extremely large areas. The resistance of trees to the wind depends mainly on their root system. The shallow-rooted spruces suffer the most, while firs and larches, like Beech, oaks and Maple, have deep roots and are more resistant to uprooting (Figs. 13, 14).

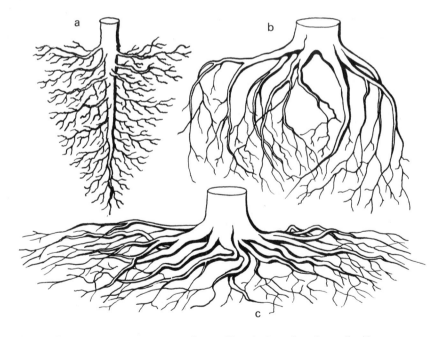

Fig. 13 — Types of root system: a — taproot, b — cordiform (or heart-shaped), c — discoid

Fig. 14 — Where soils are shallow and the depth of root systems is restricted, gales may cause windthrow over extensive areas.

The last abiotic environmental factor to exert an effect on the forest is the air itself. Air is composed of 78.03 % nitrogen, 21 % oxygen, 0.94 % inert gases, such as argon, krypton and xenon, and 0.03 % carbon dioxide, by volume. In addition to the chemical properties of the air, its physical properties are also important, since they influence the amount of light and heat which passes through it. The air supplies plants with oxygen for respiration, carbon dioxide for photosynthesis and sometimes with nitrogen, in association with the activity of certain bacteria. Air also contains a mixture of varying amounts of hydrogen, water vapour, ammonia and other gases of volcanic origin. Fine, light dust, soot and various minute particles are likewise suspended in the atmosphere.

Waste gases are today a very urgent problem. Pollutants are an abnormal component of the atmosphere and present at levels such that their danger cannot be ignored. The most harmful waste gases for plants are the sulphur oxides. They do physiological damage by being absorbed into plant tissues, where they act as assimilatory poisons. When mixed with water, they cause physical damage to the surface of leaves through their corrosive effect. The degree of damage depends on the length of exposure and the gas concentration. Large doses (e. g. about 0.2 % by volume sulphur dioxide) acting for a short time produce acute damage. Chronic damage may result from long-term exposure to low concentrations (e. g. 0.001 % sulphur dioxide by volume or less). Different species of trees differ in their susceptibility to smoke damage. Broad-leaved trees are generally more resistant than conifers, mainly because they shed their leaves and thus get rid of the poisoned tissues; the same applies to the larches. The most easily damaged are the firs, Ash, spruces and limes. Lichens are also very sensitive to waste gases and are practically never seen in polluted areas. The overall damage is increased by rain, which washes industrial waste gases into the soil, thereby damaging its chemical composition.

Having discussed the environmental factors influencing the existence and growth of plants, let us now examine the forest community as a whole. Every plant requires a given type of habitat, but many species have the same or similar requirements and compete for living space. This competition is hence most acute between individuals of the same species. For example, one hectare of forest growing naturally from wind borne seeds may initially comprise some one million seedlings; in the space of 100 years this number will have fallen to about 600. The more favourable the conditions for growth, the more rapidly will this reduction of numbers through competition take place. The strongest individuals will benefit most and oust their weaker competitors. Competition is not restricted to the aerial parts of the trees; below ground the roots usually come into competition for space and nutrients before the leaves of one tree begin to rob those of another of light.

Plant communities are not built on competition alone, however. Beneficial relationships of mutual aid and advantage also exist, such as the coexistence (symbiosis) of fungi known as mycorrhiza with the roots of various plants and of practically all trees. Roots on which these fungi occur have a somewhat anomalous shape; they have short branches and are often covered with bulbous nodules. The fungus either clings to the surface of the root, or penetrates into its tissues. Many diverse groups of fungi form mycorrhizal associations. Some are specific to a given type of tree — as mushroom gatherers know from practice — while others grow on the roots of more than one species. The symbiosis keeps the tree supplied with nutrients which its roots would not normally be able to obtain, chiefly complex nitrogen compounds, which only these fungi can extract from acid soils. The mycorrhizae are also a substitute for the poorly developed root hairs of conifers. These relationships are thus of the greatest significance in soils with raw humus; in soils with well decomposed humus their significance diminishes and the fungi can actually become parasites.

There are other plant relationships in the forest also. With few exceptions, green (autotrophic), photosynthesizing plants can lead a completely independent existence. Conversely, heterotrophic plants, which have no chlorophyll, are dependent upon organic matter produced by other organisms. They take their sustenance either from dead material, in which case they are known as saprophytes, or from living organisms, when they are called parasites. Heterotrophic organisms secrete enzymes which break down the substrate on which they live and thus make available certain substances not normally accessible to autotrophic plants. Saprophytic nutrition is extremely important for the circulation of nutrients in nature, since it brings substances which have been discarded back into circulation again. Saprophytes thus enrich the soil and break down humus and dead material. The processes involved are complex and the successive action of a number of organisms, each metabolising the waste products of the previous saprophyte, may be necessary to complete the cycling process. Only a very few seed-bearing plants are saprophytic, such as the Bird's-nest Orchid *(Neottia nidus-avis)* and the Yellow Bird's-nest *(Monotropa hypopitys)*.

There are many intermediates between saprophytes and parasites, which draw sustenance from living organisms. Their special secretions interfere with the host's metabolism to their own benefit. They often cause deformities in the host, such as tumours and dense tufts of twigs. Parasites either live in their host's body, or covering its surface, send suckered fibres known as haustoria down into its tissues in search of nourishment. The host plant combats the parasite by forming antibodies, or by producing special tissues aimed at localizing the intruder and preventing it from spreading. Mistletoe *(Viscum album)* and the related species *Loranthus europaeus* are exceptional among European tree parasites, since they are autotrophic, i. e. green plants. They do not draw photosynthetic products such as sugars from their host, but merely dissolved nutrients which the host obtains from the soil. Such plants are known as hemiparasites.

Epiphytes are a special group of plants. Their characteristic feature is that they spend the whole of their life, from germination of the seed to ripening of the fruit, on another plant, without coming into contact with the soil, and despite this are not parasites. They generally settle on trunks or branches. Actually they could be described as 'space parasites' since they only deprive their host of a little sunlight. Epiphytes are to be found amongst every group of plants. At the lowest level they include algae, lichens and mosses, which grow on the bark of trees and shrubs. They absorb water over the whole of their body surface; nutrients are taken in from airborne dust and from substances formed by the decomposition of the bark. In the forests of the temperate belt, lichens constitute the dominant epiphytic flora, while in the tropics many ferns and even seed-bearing plants are epiphytic. They often have two types of roots — sucker roots with which they cling to the tree and aerial roots with which they absorb water from the atmosphere. The aerial roots often contain chlorophyll, so that they are also able to take up carbon dioxide from the air and produce sugar by photosynthesis. Epiphytes also often have two types of leaves — funnel-shaped leaves in which they collect the decomposing substances on which they live, and true photosynthetic leaves, which are usually quite differently shaped. Epiphytes are most numerous in tropical forests, where inadequate penetration of light through the canopy, excessive humidity and easy formation of humus associated with rapid decomposition promote the evolution of a large number and variety of such species.

The life of a forest is therefore extremely complex. On the one hand, competition forces the species present to diversify and to exploit a variety of different life-styles, so that the forest becomes ever more varied. On the other, the forest community as a whole modifies its environment and develops within the constraints laid upon it by factors such as the altitude, latitude, rainfall and the mineral content of the soil.

Animals in the forest

The other living component of the forest community — the fauna — likewise plays an important role. About half of all the species of animals living in central Europe, i. e. about 40,000, live in forests. The majority — some 70 % — are insects. The forest provides suitable conditions for shelter, nutrition and reproduction for a wide variety of animals, many of which could not exist without it and whose life in turn influences the development of individual trees and even of whole communities.

The most important effects of animals on the forest are through their requirements for food. Herbivores act directly, by actually eating the plants, but carnivorous animals are important also. Though they can rarely control the numbers of the herbivourous species they eat, they do reduce them and hence their impact on the

Fig. 15 — The Wild Boar and other animals are an inseparable part of the forest community.

plant community. Of the European trees, the species which provide the greatest number of animals with food are the oaks, followed by elms, willows and pines. Yew and Acacia are used by the least number of species. The forest is also important for animals in providing a habitat for reproduction and a refuge from enemies. Trees and shrubs provide material and suitable sites for building nests, and burrows and underground shelters may be dug in the forest floor. Hollow trees furnish excellent nesting sites for woodpeckers and innumerable species of insects and spiders hide away behind the bark. Dense brushwood provides safe shelter for many species of birds and mammals, especially in the winter, when the open country is stripped bare. Of all plant communities, the forest thus provides animals with the most diverse conditions for finding food and shelter and for reproduction.

The relationships between animals and plants are interesting and complex. They may be close, loose or merely fortuitous. Some animals are bound to the forest for the whole of their lives, such as the Capercaillie or the bark beetle *Ips typographus* (Fig. 16), others only for a given length of time (mainly while caring for their young), such as the Crow or Badger. In other cases they merely prefer the forest to other plant communities, as in the case of the woodpeckers or the Roe Deer. Lastly, some animals, such as fieldmice, may simply stray into the forest. In general, the role played by an animal in the forest community is directly related to how much of its time it spends there.

Some animals are confined to given forest communities, or their dependence on a particular plant species may be so strong that they occur only on one type of tree (e. g. the Black Arches on spruce growths). Some plants are likewise dependent on insects for their pollination, although the majority of forest trees are pollinated by the wind. Insects do not carry pollen from the male to the female parts of the flower consciously, but because the flowers provide them with food. The role which insects

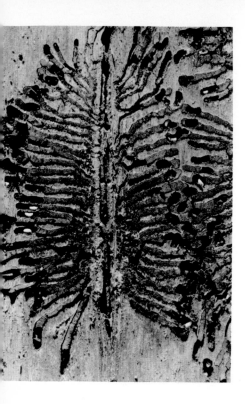

Fig. 16 — The gallery design of the most dangerous spruce pest — the bark beetle *Ips typographus*. The pupal cells, containing pupae, can be seen at the end of the larval furrows.

play in this process is nevertheless tremendously important: a bee, for instance, visits about 10,000 flowers in a day. Most flowers have special glands emitting various odours, some of them pleasing to the human nose, some of them very disagreeable. These odours are meant to attract insects; they hold out a promise of abundant food, or of a suitable medium for the development of offspring. For example, evil-smelling plants attract insects which lay their eggs in carrion and although the insects soon realize their mistake, they have done their good deed for the day and have pollinated the plant, whose odour has thus fulfilled its function.

Animals are important to the forest as agents of seed dispersal. For example, birds eat seeds and then may fly considerable distances before passing them out in their excreta. The Rowan, for instance, is dependent on thrushes for spreading its seeds, which will not germinate until they have passed through the birds' alimentary tract. Such trees usually have brightly coloured or otherwise conspicuous berries to attract the birds, such as the pinkish mauve seed capsules of the Spindle Tree, which are shaped like a priest's biretta. When they ripen, the capsules split open and the seeds, encased in a bright orange, fleshy covering, can be seen hanging by a stalk. Other seeds or fruits are equipped with hooks and cling to animals' coats (e. g. Burdock, bedstraws). Ants also help to spread seeds which have fleshy processes (e. g. Snowdrop and the celandines). In general, however, animals are more dependent on plants than plants on animals.

The forest fauna is composed of a large number of the most diverse species. Some forest inhabitants are so small that they usually escape our notice until their numbers become excessive. Others attract our attention by their voice, size or colouring. Some forest animals are useful, but others are exceedingly harmful, threatening the very existence of individual trees or whole stands. Some, like game, are actually included in forest management plans. Although the forest species are constantly engaged in a tenacious fight for life, in general a state of dynamic balance prevails, since one component always prevents another from gaining the upper hand. If — as sometimes happens in natural forests — a given species becomes unduly numerous, the population of its predators increases soon after and balance is restored. In commercially utilized forests, however, Man's reckless interference with the natural development of the plant community has also altered (sometimes very substantially) the composition of the forest fauna by wiping out or severely reducing the number of large animals, in particular beasts and birds of prey. As a result, the forester is today faced with the task of renewing the biological balance of the forest. The first step is to introduce measures which will limit the proliferation of certain forest pests, or to set their natural enemies against them. This biological method of combating pests is a very complicated matter and to be successful must mimic natural processes as closely as possible.

Birds play an important part in biological protection of the forest. In general, where there is a flourishing plant community providing a variety of different foods, we shall also find a large number of different birds (Figs. 17a,b). It is therefore important for the forester to protect species which will prove useful in maintaining bird diversity. Unfortunately, the numbers of birds — and mainly insectivorous birds — are constantly diminishing because Man deprives them of their natural nesting places. He cuts down hollow trees, drains swamps, burns brushwood and regulates the course of rivers. The maze of wires which criss-cross our modern countryside causes the death of many birds after dusk and in fogs. Birds are also killed on the roads. In West Germany alone, the number of birds killed by cars each year is estimated at one million. Only 100 years ago, the eagles, falcons, Hoopoe, Nightingale and Kingfisher were still familiar in Europe, but today they are fast disappearing. The International Union for the Conservation of Nature has therefore published a list of 383 endangered bird species which are to be given every possible protection. It is a depressing thought that migrating songbirds are still regularly shot and trapped in southern Europe. In this way, millions of Swallows, thrushes, Starlings, larks and quails end their life as delicacies on a market stall.

About 200 species of birds live in the forests of central Europe. The size of their populations is very varied, being smallest in artificially planted spruce woods (about 6 birds/ha) and largest in mixed forests with brushwood undergrowth (40/ha and over). It is easily possible to increase bird populations many times over without call for complicated measures. For instance, it is sufficient to leave hollow trees standing, to hang up nesting boxes of different sizes for different species of birds, to limit the cutting and burning of brushwood or to plant it in suitable places. In winter, extra food, such as sunflower seeds, may be provided, and in summer care should be taken to ensure that drinking water is available. During the breeding season freedom from disturbance is most important since many birds will desert their eggs or young if repeatedly disturbed.

The statistics on the usefulness of insectivorous birds are encouraging. Some tits

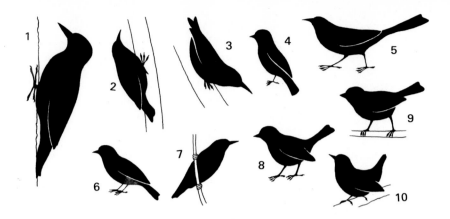

Fig. 17a — Characteristic silhouettes of some groups of forest birds: 1 — woodpeckers, 2 — treecreepers, 3 — nuthatches, 4 — flycatchers, 5 — wagtails and larks, 6 — finches, 7 — warblers, 8 — thrushes, 9 — tits, 10 — Wren

consume their own body weight in insects in a day. The Great Tit weighs 17 g and every day consumes 17 g of insects. The Wren, which weighs only 5 g, has a daily consumption of 7.5 g. To give some idea of what this means, 2,000 butterfly eggs weigh only one gram and 400 caterpillars of the extremely destructive Pine Looper Moth *(Bupalus piniarius)* weigh 12 g. When we consider that a pair of tits produces 6—10 young, sometimes twice in a year, we start to appreciate the work they do to keep the forest healthy. The physical feats of small birds also merit our admiration. Observations on a Great Tit showed that in 19 days it carried food to its nine young 6,786 times and during this period the young consumed 0.75 kg food. It is thus not surprising to discover that a pair of tits, together with their young, destroy a total of 75 kg of insects in a year. Another interesting feature of tit feeding is that every species catches a different type of food, or searches for it on different parts of the same plant. This diverse utilization of food sources enables tits to survive the winter months, when up to six species can live side by side without endangering the others' food supply.

Insects can boast the largest number of species among the forest fauna. Some of them are dangerous pests, while others combat pests and are therefore a fundamental component of biological protection of the forest. Predacious insects in general, and ants in particular, play an important role, since together with other food they also consume large quantities of harmful insects. Ants build nests in hollow trees, below roots and in holes in the ground, but best known are the wood ants with their large anthills built of conifer needles and small stones. The number of ants in a colony varies. Some colonies have only a few hundred members, while others number tens of thousands. The colony is organized on the basis of a division of labour amongst the different castes. The sexual individuals devote their lives to the production of offspring, while the asexual workers (actually females whose sexual organs remain undeveloped) forage and care for the young. Male ants have a very brief life, since they die soon after fertilizing the females. Once the eggs are laid the

Fig. 17b — Silhouettes of birds of prey in flight: 1 — Golden Eagle, 2 — Rough-legged Buzzard, 3 — Peregrine Falcon, 4 — Kestrel, 5 — Goshawk, 6 — Sparrowhawk, 7 — Buzzard

female pays them no further attention (except when founding a new colony) and they are taken care of by the workers. They constantly clean and feed the larvae, transferring pre-digested food from their own stomachs straight into the larvae's mouths.

Newly hatched ants are winged and the majority of them are workers. The females begin to show signs of restlessness as instinct urges them to fly away somewhere else and found a new colony. But the workers hold them back and hang on to their wings by their jaws. Most of the females fly away, however, together with the males, and mating takes place during flight. When they return to earth they rub their wings off and the fertilized female lays her eggs in a suitable sheltered spot. She cares for this first brood herself and feeds the larvae on juices, rich in protein, produced from oral glands. These larvae develop into the first workers and a new ant colony is formed to gladden the forester's heart.

Grasshoppers, dragonflies, damselflies and ladybirds are no less predacious than ants. Ladybirds are particularly useful, since the adults feed on aphids. Wasps and hornets are active predators, which attack their prey in the air and hurl it to the ground, where they tear off its legs and wings to render it helpless. Ground beetles are likewise predacious insects. Both the adult insects and the larvae are predacious. Although the period of larval development is relatively short (only about two weeks), the larvae manage to consume some 40 caterpillars in that time.

For one insect to devour another is a relatively simple means of obtaining food, but nature has more subtle methods also. For example, the body of one species of insect may act as a source of nutrition for the development of another species. The various forms of parasitism — which is far more complex in animals than in plants — are numerous. The most widespread and undoubtedly the most useful parasitic insects are the ichneumon flies, which lay their eggs in other insects' bodies. It is amazing to watch the attack of an ichneumon fly upon its prey, hidden under the bark. It knows exactly where to stop and where to stab its needle-sharp ovipositor, through the

35

wood, into the unsuspecting larva gnawing away below. The passage of the egg along the thin ovipositor held tight in the wood is one of the technical miracles of nature. The egg is flexible and is 'shot' into the victim, the tapering end of the ovipositor increasing its velocity. Once it is safely embedded in its host, it reassumes its original form. The larva is assured of safe shelter and of an adequate food supply inside the host's body, which it steadily eats away, although the host does not actually die until the larva's development has been completed. Some species of ichneumon flies specialize in a particular insect, others attack several species. In addition to the ichneumon flies there are species whose larvae develop inside the caterpillars, pupae and eggs of insects. Sand wasps attack various types of caterpillars, paralyse them by stinging with nerve poisons and then bury them in a pit where they lay their eggs. When the larvae hatch out, they find a plentiful supply of fresh food awaiting them. Tachinid flies, some species of which are specialized feeders on insects damaging to forests, form a smaller group of parasitic insects. They look like flesh-flies and are often mistaken for them.

Different species attack their hosts in different ways. Either the eggs or the larvae (equipped with keen sensory organs) are placed on the caterpillar host's body, below its cuticle or on the food on which it lives. Once inside the host's body, the larvae first merely devour the contents of the body cavity and do not attack the other organs until just before their development is completed, when the host dies naturally. Tachinid larvae possess a special tooth for boring, but digest their host's tissues by dissolving them with their saliva. The larvae pupate in or on the host and sometimes in the ground. Like all flies, they pupate in tub-shaped capsules.

It would be too much to hope that animals which help us to combat insect pests would themselves have no enemies. Tachinids have an enemy in the Bee-fly *(Hemipenthes morio)*, which is easily identified by its black-tipped wings. Bee-fly larvae develop in the larvae of tachinids and quite often attack as many as 80 % of the population. This phenomenon, in which a parasite has a parasite of its own, complicates the relationships between forest animals still further.

Another interesting and important role performed by a number of forest animals, is the work they do in removing the dead remains of others. Carrion is eaten by a wide variety of creatures from the smallest microorganisms to the largest mammals, such as the Red Fox and Wild Boar. Amongst the insects, sexton and carrion beetles, and to a lesser extent rove beetles are the main removers of carrion. They have a special olfactory organ enabling them to scent prey over long distances and can thus fly to it directly in the shortest possible time. They crawl under the dead animal, loosen the earth to form a 'grave' and literally bury the body. When they have thus assured a supply of food for their offspring, they lay their eggs. In this way they efface all traces of the gloomier side of nature.

Game, which has always been of interest to Man, occupies a special position in the forest fauna. Game provided prehistoric hunters with skins for clothing as well as with food. When Man hunted simply for his own needs, only the numbers of game animals were affected. For the modern forester, game has commercial potentials, however, and consequently, he influences the state of game populations far more than his prehistoric predecessor. This interference with the forest community is naturally not without consequences and today we are faced with the seemingly paradoxical question: The forest or the game? Let us take a closer look at the problem as a whole. In Man's relationship to game and in the relationship of game

Fig. 18 — Deer cause tremendous damage to the forests by repeatedly stripping the bark from spruces.

to the forest there have been two decisive factors. Apart from minor exceptions, Man has wiped out the large predators, such as bears, the Lynx, Wolf and Wild Cat, which were the natural enemies of game animals. On the one hand, these predators helped keep the game population balanced and prevented it from becoming too large, while on the other they kept the population healthy, since their victims were mostly sick and weak animals. The second — and no less important — factor has been the mass cultivation of pure spruce and pine forests during the last two centuries at the expense of mixed forest. Mixed forests with a rich brushwood layer assured game of an adequate and varied supply of food during the winter, while spruce and pine forests are dry and the food supply is poor and less diverse. Foresters have tried to make good this deficiency by providing animals with additional food and at first glance there do not appear to be any problems. It is known how much food the animals require in a day and care is taken to see that they receive it. One thing was forgotten, however, and that was the effect of natural selection. Additional feeding reduces the number of deaths during the winter months, but it also means that weak and unhealthy animals, which would not survive the winter under natural conditions, are also kept alive. In the summer or the autumn, these animals mate and the inevitable outcome is degeneration of the stock. In theory, of course, the forester ought to take over the role of natural selection by shooting such animals.

As we have seen, the problems of a forest community are highly complex and any interference with its processes produces a reaction. The changed environment in which game — in particular Red Deer — live today must therefore have had some effect on their relationship to the forest. The original mixed forests, with their abundance of food, were not imperilled by game in any way. It must also be borne in mind that the number of game animals in these forests was substantially smaller than it is today in artificially cultivated forests in which, apart from clearings, the animals have no pasture. In consequence, deer make good deficiencies in their diet by gnawing bark and stripping it from the trees (Fig. 18). The results are catastrophic. The damaged part of the tree is invaded by fungi, which spread both upwards and downwards, so that the most valuable part of the tree is virtually ruined. Wind and snow complete the devastation, since the tree snaps off at the spot where the wood has rotted. The extent of damage caused in this manner is tremendous and in recent years there have been many attempts to resolve this problem. The forest and game are inseparable and it is our duty to preserve game and the other forest animals for future generations. To do this, however, we must introduce measures to ensure biological balance between forest and game, even where unnatural conditions exist.

The history of the forest

The contemporary state of our forests is the result of a long evolutionary development. The forest has asserted its supremacy over other plant communities ever since the first trees made their appearance. The evolution of the forest can be traced back for millions of years in fossil imprints and in coal. There would be no point in describing the various species of plants which grew in the earliest forests, since recent plants stem from the flora of the Tertiary period. At that time the climate was approximately the same over the whole of the globe and tropical forests grew in Europe. During the Tertiary period, the temperature steadily fell and tropical and subtropical plants began to disappear from the European flora. On the other hand, cooling provided favourable conditions for the spread of most broad-leaved trees, which today are an important component of European forests. At the end of the Tertiary, therefore, some one million years ago, the composition of the forests was similar to that of natural forests today. In those days the climate was still relatively warm.

The decisive factor influencing the development and structure of our forests was the Ice Age, when, at the beginning of the Quaternary period, our climate changed radically. A continuous ice sheet formed in Scandinavia and moved progressively further south until it reached central Europe, while an Alpine ice sheet moved across from the southwest. We should not imagine the Ice Age as a period of continuous cold, since it was characterized by a series of pronounced climatic changes. Several times the ice sheets receded and the climate temporarily became warmer. We therefore divide the Ice Age into cold periods (glacials), which were interspersed with warmer periods (interglacials). During the glacials the climate was so inclement that, except for small oases of warmth, no trees were able to grow at all and the whole of Europe was covered with tundra.

Some members of the Arctic and Alpine flora have survived in central Europe down to the present day. Since they settled there during the Ice Age, they are known as glacial relicts and we shall make their acquaintance when describing individual species of plants later in this book.

Evolution of the forests in continental Europe

Period	Dominant trees	Other trees
Pre-Boreal (10,000–8,500 years ago)	pines, birches	Aspen, willows; in warm areas Hazel and oaks
Boreal (8,500–7,000 years ago)	pines, Hazel	oaks, elms, Ash; in mountains spruces
Atlantic (about 7,000–4,500 years ago)	oaks, firs, spruces	alders, Hazel, Beech; on sandy ground pines
Sub-Boreal (4,500–2,800 years ago)	Beech, firs, spruces,	oaks, limes, elms Ash, Hornbeam
Sub-Atlantic (2,800 years ago to the present)	at first firs and Beech; latterly spruces and pines	in warm areas oaks, birches, Aspen, Hazel; in damp spots alders

At the end of the Ice Age, as the ice sheets receded, forest trees began to invade the European tundras, in particular the birches together with pines, Aspen and the willows — that is to say, the hardiest trees, which weathered the Ice Age close to the edge of the ice sheet. Eventually, the pines and birches became the dominant trees throughout the whole of Europe. This period, known as the Pre-Boreal period, goes back some 10,000 years and corresponds to the early Stone Age (Palaeolithic). Other trees naturally also appeared at the same time but for the time being did not play an important role.

The warmer period which followed the Ice Age was characterized by the preponderance of Hazel, showing that the woods were of a steppe type, even in the mountains, because the climate was dry and the summers long and warm. This period, known as the Boreal, goes back some 8,500–7,000 years and coincides with the middle Stone Age (Mesolithic). It was followed, at the beginning of the late Stone Age (Neolithic), by the Atlantic Period, which dates back to some 7,000–4,500 years ago. Mixed oakwoods were the dominant type of community. The oaks spread at the expense of the Hazel and pines, and the chief tees in the mountains were the firs and the spruces. At the beginning of this period the climate was warm and damp, but in time it became drier and somewhat cooler. Then the Beech made its appearance, fir populations increased and the pines were relegated to dry, sandy grounds.

In the next period, known as the Sub-Boreal, which coincided with the end of the late Stone Age and the beginning of the Bronze Age and dates back to some 4,500–2,800 years ago, the climate continued to grow colder and the rainfall increased, while the Beech, spruce and fir populations grew larger and completely dominated mountainous regions. Mixed oakwoods declined and the Hornbeam appeared in them with increasing frequency. This is roughly what the forests looked like at the beginning of historic times.

The last period, extending down to the present, is known as the Sub-Atlantic. The dominant trees were at first the firs and the Beech, and in warm regions oaks, birches and the Aspen, but then a new and powerful factor — Man — appeared on the scene in earnest. Man's interference with the general development of European forests has not only reduced their original extent, but in recent centuries has brought about far-reaching changes in their structure, with the result that today pines and spruces are the dominant species.

Man's influence on the forests first began to make itself felt in the late Stone Age, i. e. some 7,000 years ago, but in those days it did not seriously affect their extent because the human population was still very small. All that Man actually did was to take what the forest offered; that is to say, he hunted, gathered fruit and berries and found shelter there. It was not until later that he began to cut down whole tracts of forest and change the forest soil into pasture or arable land and it was not until the eleventh century that the first really marked changes appeared in the character of the forest. The population was growing apace, space was needed for new settlements, and at that time large numbers of villages were springing up, especially in central Europe. The growth of society was also accompanied by a greater demand for wood, which during the Middle Ages increased still further as towns were built and crafts and later industry developed. Wood was used for building, as firewood and to make tools. Mining also had a negative effect on the extent of the forests, while ironworks, glassworks, breweries and other forms of production all needed wood as fuel. This continuous plundering of the forests could have only one possible outcome and their condition already gave cause for anxiety by the end of the eighteenth century. The woods around industrial centres were practically laid waste and in warmer, more densely populated agricultural areas they had been destroyed to provide pasture. Since the demand for wood was constantly increasing, the need for controlled management of the forest became evident. This can be regarded as a turning point in the development of forestry. The first forestry schools, forestry experiments and forestry museums made their appearance, Man began to seek ways and means of protecting the forest and byelaws embodying all the principles of forest management and protection, including protection against theft, were issued.

At the same time the reforestation of empty spaces was started, the main trees used being spruces and pines. The fast growth of these trees made them very popular and at the beginning of the nineteenth century masses of them were planted. Another reason why these two trees were given priority was that the Beech had lost its importance as fuel owing to the advent of large scale coal mining. The existence of vast clearings and the desire to fill them as quickly as possible was a further reason for the appearance of large, even age stands of a single species. It is said that the road to hell is paved with good intentions and in this case we can say with perfect truth that in the short space of 150 years, Man, with the best intentions in the world, but with insufficient knowledge, managed to alter the structure of European forests beyond all recognition, without realizing how drastically he was upsetting the biological balance of nature.

Arrangement of the illustrated sections

The following part of the book contains 113 colour plates divided among six chapters, each dealing with one of the main types of European forest. The most characteristic members of the flora and fauna of each have been chosen, although it should not be forgotten that most of the species described have a very wide area of distribution and occur in several, or even all, types of forest. Each chapter is divided into a botanical part — which includes the most typical spore- and seed-bearing plants of the forest ground layer, and shrubs and trees of the upper layers — and a zoological part describing representative insects, amphibians, reptiles, birds and mammals.

The colour plates, each of which illustrates 2—4 plants or animals, are accompanied by brief written descriptions of each species. Since these were chosen according to the environment in which they are most common, they have not been classified in detail and apart from the genus and species, are assigned to family only.

The metric (S.I.) system of units is used throughout this book, the following abbreviations being used where appropriate:

grams: g
kilograms: kg (1,000 kg = 1 tonne)
millimetres: mm
centimetres: cm
metres: m
hectares: ha
litres: l

Riparian forests

Deciduous riparian forests occur in low-lying country beside rivers and streams. They are characterized by annual or occasional floods, when the river overflows its banks in spring. Whenever it is flooded, the forest soil receives extra nutrients, with the result that it is extremely rich in minerals. The water table is very close to the surface. The main trees in regularly flooded areas are poplars, willows and alders. Such assemblages are to be found in low country where the water subsides quickly. Trees standing beside the water are often damaged by ice. The Stinging Nettle *(Urtica dioica)* is the dominant plant in the rich herbaceous layer.

At higher altitudes (up to 300 m), where flooding occurs only occasionally, the soil contains an almost inexhaustible supply of minerals. The commonest trees here are oaks, limes, Ash, *(Fraxinus excelsior)* and Sycamore *(Acer pseudoplatanus)*. This type of riparian forest has the best soil of all. Trees, shrubs and undergrowth are all present and the better the conditions, the more fully is each layer developed. This system of layers allows a larger number of different types of plants to grow in the same area without hindering each other and enables them to fully utilize the space above and below the ground. These rich plant communities have a very variable appearance, which alters during the course of the year. They are generally most striking and beautiful in the spring; the still leafless crowns let through the sunlight, which quickly warms the soil, while the undergrowth prevents it from being cooled again by the wind. The heliophilic plants are at their best at this time; when the trees put out their leaves, they make way for species which prefer more shade. The dominant tree in these woods is the Pedunculate Oak *(Quercus robur)*, a heliophilic species with a spreading crown which enables it to intercept the maximum amount of light. It forms open stands, leaving room for other trees, such as the White Poplar *(Populus alba)*, Black Poplar *(Populus nigra)*, Ash and elms around it. These trees all have a flood resistant root system.

Where the ground-water comes near the surface we find willows (as trees or shrubs), alders and abundant swamp vegetation. In higher and drier places, Hornbeam *(Carpinus betulus)* and birches grow, while Bird Cherry *(Prunus padus)*, Alder Buckthorn *(Frangula alnus)*, Guelder Rose *(Viburnum opulus)*, Privet *(Ligustrum vulgare)*, Dogwood *(Cornus sanguinea)*, Cornelian Cherry *(Cornus mas)* and Hazel *(Corylus avellana)* abound in the shrub layer. Riparian forests are also characterized by forest pools and creeks with a well-developed aquatic and swamp vegetation.

The fauna of riparian forests likewise comprises a tremendous variety of species, despite the regular floods. We find large numbers of game animals, including the Red Deer *(Cervus elaphus)*, Roe Deer *(Capreolus capreolus)* and Wild Boar *(Sus scrofa)*, which, when the floods come, retire to higher ground to wait until the water subsides. Typical representatives of the bird population are the warblers, the Penduline Tit *(Remiz pendulinus)*, the Golden Oriole *(Oriolus oriolus)* and beside rivers, various aquatic birds and the Marsh Harrier *(Circus aeruginosus)*. Among the insects are several pests whose food requirements confine them to the tree layers, such as spruce and satin moths, various longicorn beetles and (in tree stumps) the larvae of the Stag Beetle *(Lucanus cervus)*.

Riparian Forests

Liverwort *Pellia epyphylla* (Hepaticae)   ❶

The liverworts (Hepaticae) comprise a vast group of spore-bearing plants, represented in Europe by about 300 species. They belong to the phylum Bryophyta and are regarded as the most primitive of the higher plants. The body of the plant, called the thallus, is flattened and has neither roots, stems nor leaves. It is attached to the substrate by adhesive filaments called rhizoids. With some exceptions, liverworts grow on permanently damp substrates. *Pellia epyphylla* has, as a rule, a dark green thallus with an easily discernible midrib. The plant is conspicuous mainly in spring due to its vitreous setae, several centimetres long, bearing dark, globular capsules full of spores. It is common at lower elevation in the vicinity of streams and in ditches beside woodland roads and trails, often covering such places with conspicuous dark green carpets.

Mnium punctatum (Mniaceae)   ❷

The second basic group of bryophytes are the mosses (Musci). Their thallus consists of a leafy stem terminated at its lower end with rhizoids. Typical of mosses are their spore-bearing capsules borne on a stalk or seta. As a rule, these capsules split open by the separation of variously shaped lids. In the European forests, mosses often form extensive carpets wherever they find favourable conditions; hence they are more conspicuous than liverworts. Since mosses do not possess true roots, they deprive the soil of a negligible amount of water, often actually protecting it from excessive evaporation. *Mnium punctatum* is one of the most beautiful mosses. It grows to a height of about 5 cm and has dark green leaves. Its stems are dark brown and covered with white down up to about half their length. The leaves are rounded (2a, left), gradually decreasing in size in the lower part of the stem. They end with a short, spinose tip and have a clearly visible midrib. The seta is 2—4 cm long and purple-coloured. The capsules (2a, right) are horizontal or drooping and have a long lid. This moss usually grows in moist positions with moving water, yet can also grow in stagnate bogs. It does not thrive in lime-rich soils.

Slime mould *Fuligo septica* (Myxomycetes)   ❸

The so-called slime moulds (Myxomycetes) are a most interesting group of lower fungi, showing affinities with the amoeboid Protozoa. In the initial stage of their development, their vegetative body has no stable form due to the absence of cellular membranes. They are, to all intents and purposes, clusters of protozoans, which move by means of pseudopodia. It is only later that they become organized into a fungus. Their entire developmental cycle is suggestive of animals rather than of plants. During their reproductive phase the cells are organized into chrome yellow, fleshy masses and are commonly found on rotting wood.

Tremella foliacea (Tremellaceae)   ❹

Representatives of this fungus family have gelatinous bodies which become hard in a dry environment. In wet weather, however, they rapidly swell up again. The thallus of this fungus is convoluted and folded and is cinnamon-brown with a pinky hue. It grows from June to August on trunks, branches and stumps of deciduous trees — mainly on oaks, Beech and birches.

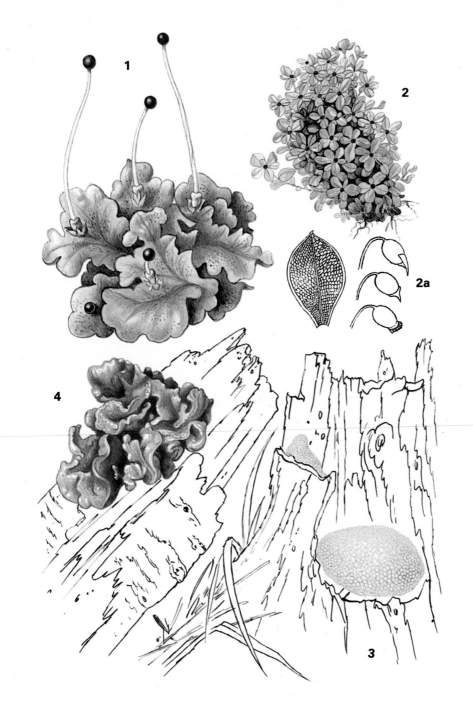

Riparian Forests

Cuckoo-pint, Wild Arum, Jack-in-the-pulpit, Lords-and-ladies ❶
Arum maculatum (Araceae)

An interesting plant — the Cuckoo-pint — flowers in moist, shady places towards the end of April and at the beginning of May. Its greenish flowers have a peculiar funnel shape, swollen at the bottom, around the reproductive organs. When the funnel opens, an unpleasant smelling, dark violet spadix appears. Its purpose is to lure insects, especially small flies, which come flying to it in swarms and enter the funnel. Below the spadix there is a ring of projections closing the entrance into the swelling which act as a mouse trap, allowing small flies to enter but preventing their escape. Male (1a) organs with red pollen sacks are gathered beneath this ring, while female organs with short stigmas are situated under them. In its efforts to escape a trapped insect rubs against the minute female stigmas and, if it has previously visited another Arum flower, the pollen grains sticking to its body effect the pollination. The insect is compelled to stay in the flower until the evening. In its confinement, however, it is even supplied with food; as soon as the stigmas are pollinated, they start secreting drops of sweet nectar. Moreover, the inside of the chamber is lined with thin-walled cells which also serve the insect as food. In the evening the pollen sacks begin to burst and a shower of golden pollen falls on the insect's body. The closing filaments of the ring subsequently fade, liberating the insect which then carries the pollen to another flower.

Dragonroot, Marsh Calla, Water Arum *Calla palustris* (Araceae) ❷

The Dragonroot is closely related to Wild Arum and is typical of swamps. Its flower consists of a membraneous spathe and a spadix which at first is enclosed within it. It is only later that the spathe unfolds setting the whole spadix free. The flower neither produces nectar nor a sweet smell but emits a disagreeable odour and is pollinated mainly by flies. As in the preceding Wild Arum its fruits are red berries which are dispersed mostly by water.

Marsh Marigold, Kingcup *Caltha palustris* (Ranunculaceae) ❸

From April to June — and often for a second time in September — flowers of the Marsh Marigold decorate the edges of forest streams and pools. In order to secure sufficient light, the basal leaves have long petioles, while the upper ones are sessile. They are pollinated by insects. Each fruit contains a number of seeds. The whole plant has a bitter taste; no animal takes Marsh Marigold as food.

Water Crowfoot *Ranunculus peltatus* (Ranunculaceae) ❹

Its small white flowers bloom from June until August on the surface of sheltered forest pools or slow running brooks and streams, often in large numbers. It is interesting in having leaves of two types: floating reniform ones holding the plant on the surface, and thin filamentous ones growing in water, or on dry ground if the pool or swamp dries out.

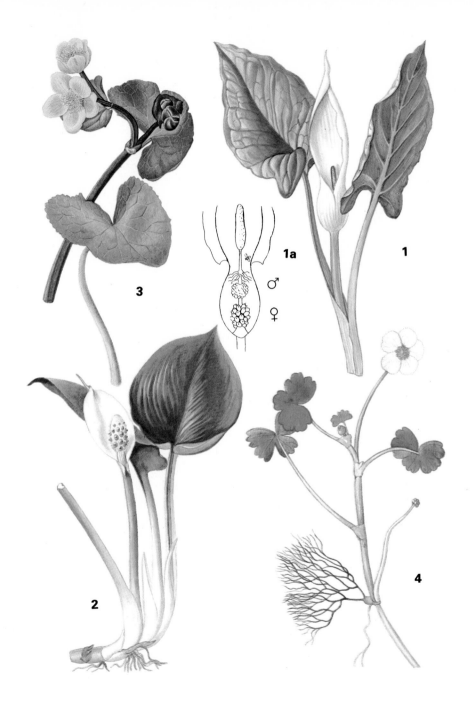

1a

♂

♀

1

3

2

4

Riparian Forests

Yellow Flag   *Iris pseudacorus*   (Iridaceae)   ❶
This 0.5–1 m high perennial, whose yellow flowers appear in May and June, grows in riparian forests, reed beds and moist meadows. It requires permanently wet, or flooded soils rich in nutrients. It is relatively abundant at lower elevations. It is anchored in the soil by a powerful rhizome bearing lateral roots from its lower parts. The flowers are wonderful: their outer petals bearing a comb of hairs are deflexed, while the inner petals are rolled to form a kind of helmet. The style is divided into three structures which bear the stigmas beneath. Like a little roof they cover and protect the anthers below. The nectar is deposited in the bottom part of the flower, and is accessible only from below the stigma bearers. After an insect lands on the outer petals, it catches at the comb of hairs along which it enters the flower. In doing so, it underruns the stigma bearers to which the so-called stigmatic tongue is attached; this subsequently bends out like a knife blade, barring the insect's way with its papillae. The insect rubs its back against it, thus wiping off the pollen from previously visited flowers. Since it is only the front surface of the stigma that bears papillae, the insect creeping out of the flower, rear first, cannot pollinize the stigma by conveying pollen from the same flower. The resulting fruit is shaped like a capsule.

Spring Snowflake   *Leucojum vernum*   (Amaryllidaceae)   ❷
A small globular bulb sends out a bunch of linear leaves with a single white flower bearing a greenish stain. This companion of moist woods, grasslands and wet meadows blooms in March and April. Bad weather halts the development of the bud, and the already blooming flower closes in case unfavourable weather sets in. The flower hangs downward, and this prevents it from being damaged by the rain. The insect that comes flying to the flower from below to suck nectar first strikes against the stigma, wiping off the pollen brought from another flower. The same motion, however, simultaneously shakes the stamens which drop new pollen on the insects. In bad weather, when no insects fly, the Spring Snowflake is pollinated by the wind: this sets the flower swaying and pollen is shed on the stigma. The fruit is a capsule.

Lesser Celandine   *Ranunculus ficaria*   (Ranunculaceae)   ❸
The Lesser Celandine is most commonly found in riparian and deciduous forests, and is an indicator of good soils. Its yellow, star-shaped flowers, protruding from the mosaic of glossy, oval leaves, appear from March to May. As is the case with many plants flowering in early spring, pollination by insects cannot be relied upon – and this is why the Lesser Celandine multiplies not only by seeds but also by special tubers formed in the leaf axils. In June, simultaneously with the shedding leaves, these little tubers also fall off – usually after rain – to give rise to new plants.

Yellow Star-of-Bethlehem   *Gagea lutea*   (Liliaceae)   ❹
This is a 10–20 cm high herb whose linear leaves grow from a bulb. The flowers, yellow inside and yellowish-green outside, bloom in March and April. Their self-pollination usually takes place when the flowers are closing for the night, as the crown presses the stamens against the stigmas. The Yellow Star-of-Bethlehem requires a great deal of nutrients and is an indicator of good, clayey, deep, moist soils.

Coltsfoot *Tussilago farfara* (Compositae)   ❶

Like the other representatives of this family, Coltsfoot bears its flowers in clusters or inflorescences called a capitulum. This is borne on a dilated axis, the so-called peduncle. The bracts surrounding it serve to protect the florets, as the individual flowers are called. These florets are of two types — the tubular and the ligulate. The tubular flowers are located in the centre and form a yellow disc — such as in the Ox-eye Daisy, while the marginal white ray florets are of the ligulate type. Tubular flowers are usually bisexual or male only, ligulate flowers are predominantly female. Very early in spring, frequently as early as the end of February, the creeping rhizomes of the Coltsfoot shoot forth stems covered with cobweb-like down and bearing a single golden-yellow capitulum. Its disk consists of about 30—40 male tubular flowers differing from the bisexual ones in having a stunted style which, in this case, serves as a device for sweeping pollen from the tube, not unlike a syringe piston. The ligulate ray florets are about 200—300 in number. They consist of a short tube containing one stigma only, and of a large, outward curved, petal-like ligule adapted to lure insects. These female flowers contain no nectar whatsoever, while male flowers secrete it in large quantities. In the Coltsfoot the male disc florets ripen later than the marginal female flowers. This is the case in all Compositae. After flowering, circular cordate leaves whose underside is covered with white down, start to develop from the rhizome. The Coltsfoot is one of the first plants to appear on barren soils and banks, and is an indicator of heavy, insufficiently aerated soils relatively rich in nutrients. It is abundant at all altitudes. Its multiple fruits are downy and of the single seeded type called achenes.

Rhizome with stems and flowers (1a), leaf (1b).

Butterbur *Petasites hybridus* (Compositae)   ❷

The Butterbur, another member of the Compositae, grows at watersides, in moist forests, and in occasionally inundated meadows. As early as the beginning of March its rhizomes put forth thick, scaly, flesh-coloured spadices covered with grey down and terminating in a raceme of pale pink capitula. Leaves do not appear before the end of flowering; their blade is remarkably large, deltoid-cordate, shallowly serrate and covered on the underside with grey down. Often attaining as much as 50 cm across, they are in fact the largest leaves in the central European flora.

Alternate-leaved Golden Saxifrage *Chrysosplenium alternifolium*   ❸
(Saxifragaceae)

This flowers in April in moist places with a permanently high water table. The flower itself consists of a small inconspicuous disc, which is seated on yellow leaflets whose purpose is to attract insects. It is only by clustering more leaves of this kind together that the little plant becomes showy.

Common Hop *Humulus lupulus* (Cannabaceae)   ❹

The Common Hop is a liana of bushes and coastal thickets. By lianas we mean plants with a weak axis which twine around neighbouring plants with the help of various devices. The creeping rhizome of the Common Hop produces an angular, spiral stem, up to 10 m long, clinging to its support by hooked hairs. The leaves are palmate, three- to five-lobed and coarse. The Common Hop is dioecious — male and female flowers develop on separate individuals. It grows at lower elevations.

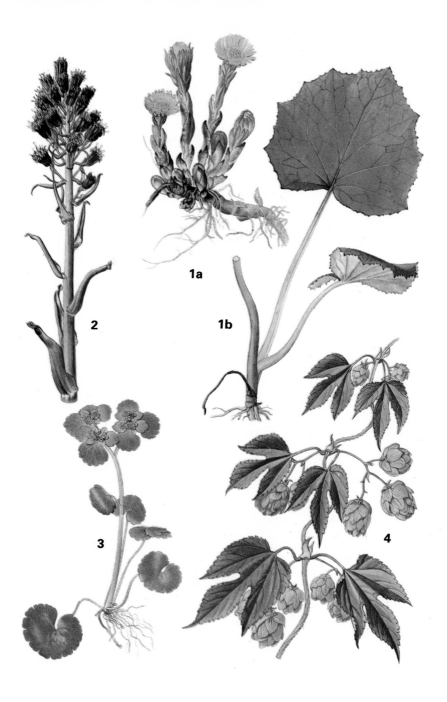

1a

1b

2

3

4

Riparian Forests

Pedunculate Oak *Quercus robur* (Fagaceae) ❶

Pedunculate Oak is an important tree of the European lowland forests. Its range extends from Spain northward to Great Britain and southern Sweden and eastward as far as the Ural Mountains. It attains huge dimensions and may grow to be 600−1,000 years old. It is a robust tree, 30−40 m high, and as much as 2 m in diameter. The trunk is covered with a blackish grey, deeply furrowed bark. The leaves are obovate, lobate, short-stalked and about 12 cm long. At the base the blade juts out in two auriculate extensions. Pedunculate Oak starts flowering and bearing fruit at the relatively advanced age of about 40−50 years. Male flowers appear in the form of pendent catkins; minute female flowers are attached to a 1−2 cm long stalk. Its fruit, the acorn, is 2 cm long, borne in a shallow cup on a 1−3 cm long stalk. It is by these stalks that the fruits of the Pedunculate Oak are distinguished from those of the Sessile Oak whose acorns are directly attached to the twig. The acorns mature and fall off at the beginning of October. The oak does not shed its leaves in autumn − they become brown and dry but still remain on the tree, in part until the spring months. The Pedunculate Oak has deep roots and produces numerous stump suckers. It prefers soils with high humidity and fertility, thriving best in the deep and heavy soils of alluvial deposits along river banks. It yields very valuable hard wood suitable for furniture, barrels, boats, parquet flooring, etc. Due to its stateliness and longevity, the oak was worshipped by our ancestors as a sacred tree. Also the abundant fall of acorns was greatly appreciated: swine were driven into oak forests to feed. Even now, acorns are a delicacy for game such as Red Deer, Wild Boar, pheasants, jays, and other animals.

Male flowers (1a above and below), female flowers (1a above and in the middle).

Smooth-leaved Elm *Ulmus carpinifolia* (Ulmaceae) ❷

This is another important lowland forest tree growing in western, southern and central Europe, whose northernmost limit reaches up to the Baltic Sea. It never forms pure stands but occurs in mixed growths with other deciduous trees, in particular with oaks, maples and limes. It attains a height of 30 m and develops a strong trunk covered with dark brown, furrowed outer bark. In early spring, towards the end of March, its inconspicuous flowers make their appearance on the bare branches. The fruits have a rounded seed surrounded by a membraneous, 1.5 cm long wing. The fruits ripen and fall off towards the end of May. The leaves are ovate, 5−10 cm long, with a coarsely serrate margin, asymmetrical at the base. The Smooth-leaved Elm has a massive root system and is often planted to reinforce stream banks. For its successful growth it requires moist and fertile soils.

Dry slopes are the home of a variety of the Smooth-leaved Elm − *Ulmus carpinifolia* var. *suberosa,* which bears corky wings on its twigs. In the past decades, elms have been exposed to the danger of 'Dutch Elm Disease', a fungus disease causing the desiccation of the elm and finally its death.

The closely related Fluttering Elm *(Ulmus laevis)* is less common in the riparian forests of central and eastern Europe. It is distinguished from the Smooth-leaved Elm by profuse trunk suckers, petiolate flowers, and rather small petiolate fruits. The brownish elm wood is highly appreciated and used in producing furniture, railway carriages, rifle butts, etc.

Flowers (2a on the right), fruits (2a on the left), flowers and fruits of the Fluttering Elm (3, 3a).

1

1a

3

3a

2

2a

Riparian Forests

Common Ash *Fraxinus excelsior* (Oleaceae) ❶

The Common Ash is frequent on alluvial river deposits in riparian forests. Its range extends from England over southern Sweden as far as Leningrad and the Volga and southwards to southern Europe and the Ukraine. It attains a height of 30−35 m, developing an upright bole with a high set crown. In winter it can be identified by its black round buds, which burst in summer to produce 20−35 cm long odd-pinnate leaves composed of 9−13 lanceolate, serrate leaflets. Its male and female flowers, lacking floral envelopes, come into bloom before the leaves appear and are pollinated by wind. The fruits are oval and winged, about 3 cm long, hanging on the tree in pendulous panicles long into the winter. The rich root system of the Common Ash fortifies the banks of streams and protects them against erosion. It is common in lowland forests, and also along brooks high up into the mountains as well as among broken rocks. It is fairly shade-tolerant when young, and its seedlings appear in great quantities even below the undergrowth. Old trees require full sunlight and lay relatively high demands on the fertility and humidity of the soil. The Ash is a tree suitable for avenues, particularly in foothill areas. Its light, elastic wood is used in the production of sporting equipment, railway carriages and furniture.

Female flowers (1a).

Black Poplar *Populus nigra* (Salicaceae) ❷

Other trees common in riparian forests near riverbeds are poplars, in particular the Black Poplar, growing on sand and gravel deposits. It is a robust tree with a spreading crown, which may grow up to 30 m. The long-stalked, rhomboid leaves, 4−10 cm long, are alternately arranged on the twigs. The male and female flowers bloom separately on male and female trees, before the leaves appear. Minute pubescent seeds mature in June and flutter through the air like snow. Poplars require moist localities with an easily reached underground water level, and an abundance of light. In commercially exploited woods the Black Poplar is nowadays being replaced by a more rapidly growing hybrid − the Carolina Poplar *(P. canadensis)*, obtained by crossbreeding the European Black Poplar with the American Eastern Cottonwood *(P. deltoides)*. Their soft wood is used mainly in plywood and cellulose production. A columnar form of the Black Poplar − the Lombardy Poplar *(P. nigra* var. *italica)* is widely planted along roadsides. It is more sensitive to frost than the normal Black Poplar.

Male flowers (2a), female flowers (2b).

White Poplar *Populus alba* (Salicaceae) ❸

The White Poplar is relatively abundant in large river valleys from the Rhine to the Yenisei. It is a robust tree with strong, grey branches and a widespreading crown. Its leaves are palmately lobed, 6−12 cm in length, covered on the underside with whitish down. Its massively developed root system produces root suckers often springing up at a distance of as much as 15−20 m from the trunk. This tree is a heliophyte requiring a high humidity level − not even spring floods can unfavourably affect it. It often stands as a solitary tree in valley meadows, while its cultivation in commercial woods has become relatively rare.

Male flowers (3a), female flowers (3b).

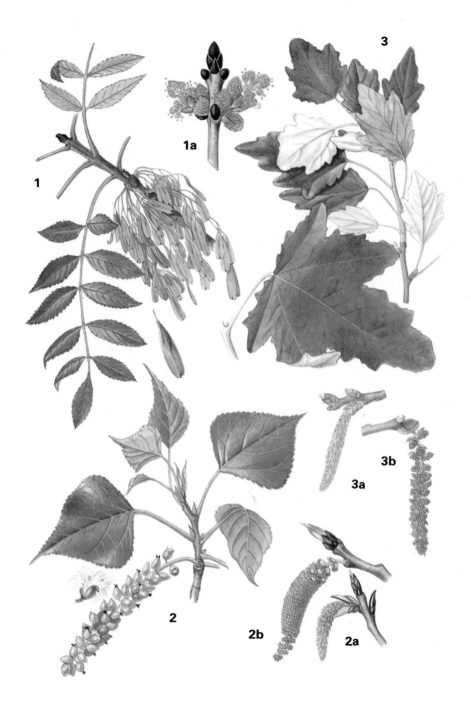

Riparian Forests

White Willow *Salix alba* (Salicaceae) ❶

Willows are typical trees of the waterside and riparian forests. The largest is the White Willow growing to a height of as much as 25 m and developing a powerful trunk covered with a longitudinally cracked outer bark. It is dioecious, with male and female flowers on separate trees. The seed capsules on female trees mature in June and release seeds covered in white down. The leaves are lanceolate, 7—10 cm long, with serrate margins and silky down on the underside. The White Willow is commonly found in large river valleys. It is able to withstand spring floods, tolerates more acid soils that the poplars, and prefers sunny habitats. It is capable of vegetative reproduction: its cuttings readily take root when stuck into the ground. Pollarded willows are a common sight alongside streams, in the vicinity of villages. These result from topping the trunks and repeatedly cutting off osiers for use in basketry and wickerwork. The soft and elastic wood of the White Willow is used in making boats, sabots, cricket bats and cellulose. It hybridizes with the Babylon Willow *(S. babylonica)* to produce a hybrid cultivated under the name of Weeping Willow *(S. sepulcralis),* an ornamental tree with a widespread crown and long, slender, pendulous branches. It is planted along watersides, river embankments, and so on.

Crack Willow *Salix fragilis* (Salicaceae) ❷

Another of the willow trees is the Crack Willow, though it does not grow higher than 10—15 m and usually develops crooked trunks. It frequents localities similar to those of the White Willow, but also grows at higher elevations up to about 500—600 m. Its name is derived from the ease with which its brittle lateral branches break off at the nodes. Its leaves, about twice as broad as those of the White Willow, are without hairs and bluish green on the underside. It is planted in rows alongside brooks and rivers to reinforce the banks. The wood mostly serves as fuel. Osiers are used in basketry and wickerwork.

Common Osier *Salix viminalis* (Salicaceae) ❸

This is one of the shrubby willows common alongside rivers and brooks at low elevations. It is a 2—6 m high shrub producing broom-like, extremely flexible osiers. Each male flower bears two stamens. The leaves are oblong-lanceolate, 11—20 cm long, 1—2 cm across, with a sinuate, deflexed margin. Their underside is covered with silvery grey hairs. The Common Osier is a heliophyte, in shade it dies away. Its long, flexible osiers are excellently suited for wickerwork and basketry.

Purple Osier *Salix purpurea* (Salicaceae) ❹

This is another shrubby willow occurring in great abundance. It thrives both in lowlands and in hills, and also at very high altitudes where it often forms thickets on gravel alluvia. It has the shape of a sparsely branched, broom-like shrub reaching a height of 2—5 m. The buds are alternate, but at least one opposite pair can be found on almost every shoot. Male flowers have a single stamen with red anthers. The leaves of the Purple Osier are invert-lanceolate, 4—9 cm long, bluish-green on the underside. The flexible osiers are very suitable for basket-making. Its cultivated forms are grown in willow plantations called osieries.

Riparian Forests

Common Alder *Alnus glutinosa* (Betulaceae) ❶

Common Alder prefers moist localities in or near riparian forests, swamps and pond banks. It is distributed over nearly the whole of Europe, from Spain to Scandinavia and east to Siberia. It grows to a height of 20—30 m and forms an erect bole covered with shallowly fissured bark. In winter it can easily be identified by its ovate, stalked buds. Its leaves are obovate to circular, notched at the apex, 5—9 cm in size, and sticky in spring. The flowers appear in March, prior to leaf emergence, and by autumn they develop into woody cones containing minute winged seeds. The seed is equipped with air cavities, enabling it to float on the water surface; thus it can float great distances. The Alder is characterized by an immense sprouting capacity even at an advanced age, so that the coppice method is often applied in cultivating it — that is, trees are propagated from stump sprouts, without planting new seedlings. Small nodules of nitrogen-fixing bacteria are situated on the roots, and so the Alder enriches the soil with nitrogen from the air. Consequently, nitriphile (nitrogen-demanding) plants, such as nettles, grow under it in great abundance. The Common Alder is a fast-growing heliophyte. Its orange wood is suitable for water constructions as well as for the production of plywood, matches and pencils.

Pendent male flowers and erect female flowers (1a), fruiting cones (1b).

Purging Buckthorn *Rhamnus frangula* (Rhamnaceae) ❷

The Purging Buckthorn often accompanies the alders in moist, swampy localities. This tree-like shrub grows to a height of 3—7 m. When young it is recognizable in winter by its violet-brown bark with whitish lenticels (tubercular excrescences on the bark) and naked, rusty-coloured, pubescent buds. Its leaves are broadly elliptical, 4—7 cm long, with entire margins. Small whitish flowers appear continuously from May to August and since the fruits ripen and change their colour in turns, in late summer the shrubs are covered with flowers as well as with green, red or black fruits, according to their developmental stage. Mature fruits are about 8 cm across. The Purging Buckthorn favours semishady habitats, is able to endure extreme frosts, and makes no great demands on soil fertility. The ashes of its wood were used in gunpowder production and the bark is still used in pharmacy.

Bird Cherry *Prunus padus* (Rosaceae) ❸

This is another shrub — sometimes a tree — growing in damp or swampy localities and ascending up to the mountains along brooks. It attains a height of 5—8 m, and usually has a large crown with drooping branches. The trunk and branches are covered with greyish black bark which, when peeled, emits an unpleasant scent reminiscent of bitter almonds. Its leaves, 6—12 cm in length, resemble those of the Cherry, yet their serration is finer and sharper. White, fragrant flowers arranged in pendent racemes bloom in May and June; they ripen into small black drupes (about 8 mm across) in August. Though astringent in taste, they are not poisonous. The seeds are spread throughout the wood by birds who have a particular liking for these fruits. Thanks to the fragrance of its flowers, the Bird Cherry is nowadays planted in gardens and parks.

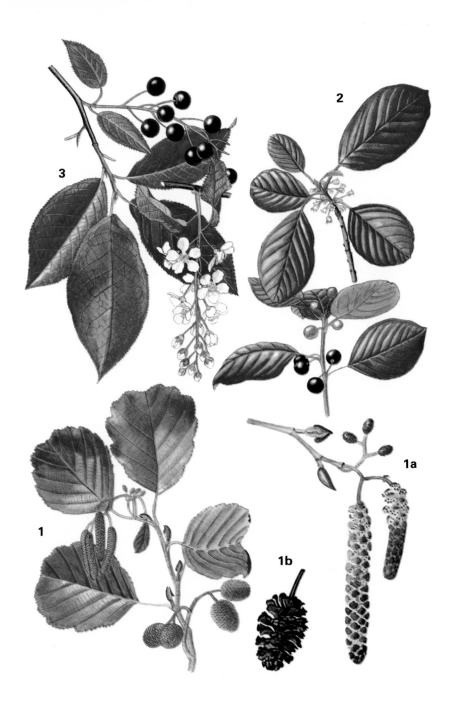

1

1a

1b

2

3

Riparian Forests

Tortrix viridana   (Tortricidae)
This tiny butterfly, with a wingspan of 18—23 mm, is characterized by bright green rectangular forewings and light grey hindwings. As a rule, the adult insects pair at the end of May and in June, usually in the evening. The females lay their eggs in depressions in the bark of twigs and the caterpillars do not hatch until the end of April of the following year. At first, the grey-green, black-headed caterpillars live on young oak leaves. They wrap these round themselves, joining them together with silken threads to make a place to live, and poke their heads out only to bite off more food. They pupate in a dark brown or black cocoon between two leaves. This butterfly occurs throughout the whole of Europe and primarily attacks oaks in riparian woods.

Southern Festoon   *Zerynthia polyxena*   (Papilionidae)
This moderately large butterfly (wingspan 44—60 mm) is very brightly and strikingly coloured. It is to be found chiefly on bushy hillsides or in open woods in southern Europe and as far north as the southeastern parts of Czechoslovakia and Austria. It is quite common in the Balkans. The butterfly is to be seen from the end of April to May, fluttering short distances before alighting. The caterpillars, which hatch after about a month, can be seen on different types of birthwort from May to July. They are yellow and have six rows of reddish-brown, black-tipped processes. If disturbed, they protrude a fleshy, forked gland (osmaterium) from behind their head, which emits a typical odour. The caterpillars pupate in dry plant débris or shrubs close to the ground. The chrysalis is brownish-grey, with fine dark markings. Large numbers die when the outskirts of forests are burnt down.

Great Peacock Moth   *Saturnia pyri*   (Saturniidae)
This saturnid is the largest European moth. It has a wingspan of 120—130 mm and is one of the most handsome and striking moths there is. It occurs chiefly in low-lying forests in southern Europe. The adult insect (imago) emerges in April or May, after spending one or two winters in the chrysalis stage. The females lay groups of relatively large eggs on elms, walnuts and Sloe bushes and — in cultivated steppe regions — on fruit trees. The full-grown caterpillar measures up to 120 mm and weighs about 15 g. It is green, with blue tubercles, and has a yellow stripe along its sides. It pupates as a solid brown chrysalis, usually at the foot of a tree.

Winter Moth   *Operophtera brumata*   (Geometridae)
This is one of the smaller species of moth (wingspan 23—25 mm), but is well-known for its sexual dimorphism. Only the male can fly, the female's wings being rudimentary and incapable of flight. The moth is to be seen in the autumn, in October and November. The fertilized female crawls up the trunk of a tree into the crown, where it lays small groups of eggs at the base of buds. The green caterpillars hatch out the following spring and when fully grown measure 25—30 mm. In addition to fruit trees, they inhabit oaks, Beech, Hornbeam, maples and various other deciduous trees. The caterpillars generally pupate in a loose cocoon, in or on the ground. In years when their populations are high they strip trees in deciduous woods and orchards bare.

Riparian Forests

Eyed Hawk *Smerinthus ocellata* (Sphingidae)

This hawk moth appears from May to the end of June, and in southern European countries also has a second generation between the middle of July and October. It is moderately large with a wingspan of 65—90 mm. Its forewings are greenish-grey, sometimes with a mauvish tinge, while the colouring of its hindwings is designed to frighten predators. They are pinkish-red, and are marked with large blue, black-rimmed ocelli (eye marks), which the moth uncovers when in danger. The green, white-spotted caterpillar has whitish stripes along its sides and a blue spine on its dorsal surface. It spends the summer in willows, poplars, apple and a number of other deciduous trees. The caterpillar's development takes 4—7 weeks: it pupates in the ground as a glossy brown chrysalis. Although lowland forests are its favourite habitat, this species is also found in the foothills of mountains. It is distributed over the greater part of Europe, including England and Ireland, and in the east extends as far as Turkey and Transcaucasia.

Pale Tussock Moth *Dasychira pudibunda* (Lymantriidae)

This moderately large, thick-bodied moth (wingspan 45—55 mm) has neutral grey or brown-tinged wings, marked with darker and gently undulating stripes, especially in the middle. The moths fly between April and July and in some places they occur in large numbers. The females lay flat piles of greyish eggs (50 or more in a pile) on the bark of deciduous trees. The hairy caterpillars live on the leaves of practically all the main trees in hardwood forests. If present in excessively large numbers they may strip the trees bare. The development of the caterpillars takes 2—3 months and they are still to be seen at the end of October. Their colouring is very variable; their ground colour may be yellow, brown, pink or grey. In the autumn they pupate in a yellowish cocoon among dry leaves and the imago does not emerge until the following year.

Eupsilia transversa (Noctuidae)

This moth, which has a wingspan of 34—40 mm, has reddish-brown (sometimes greyish) forewings and brownish-grey hindwings. Its characteristic markings are three white, yellowish or sometimes orange spots on the forewings, the largest of which is situated near the wing joint. This moth can be seen from the autumn to the spring: if the winter is not too severe, it is roused by thaws and often comes out during the daytime. The caterpillar lives on the leaves of a variety of deciduous trees, chiefly oaks. At the end of June it wraps itself in a loose cocoon in the ground and turns into a yellowish-brown chrysalis.

Catocala electa (Noctuidae)

This large moth, with a wingspan of about 70 mm, belongs to the underwings, which have crimson hindwings, and is one of the rarer species. Its range of distribution stretches from the Scandinavian peninsula over the whole of Europe and across Siberia as far as Japan; it is more abundant in warmer countries. The moths fly from July to September and are to be seen in the meadows between lowland forests, at forest margins, and in damp places (beside ponds and streams). In the autumn the female lays its flat-bottomed, domed, radially grooved eggs on the bark of willows. The caterpillars hatch out the following spring and grow to maturity during May and June. They are mainly yellowish-brown or yellowish-grey. When they measure about 80—90 mm, they look for a convenient spot to pupate and turn into brown, blue-sheened chrysalises.

Cerambyx cerdo   (Cerambycidae)

This is a large beetle 24—53 mm long, the females being larger than the males. It is almost black, but for the tip of its wing-case, which is reddish-brown. The male's antennae are much longer than its body. The adult beetle (the imago) pairs in May, but it is most often seen during June and July, coming out chiefly in the evening and at night. In living trees its metamorphosis takes 3 years, but if the tree is felled it may take up to 5. The female lays its eggs in cracks in the bark of living trees (usually solitary oaks), but the larvae are to be found on chestnuts, walnuts, Beech, Hornbeam, elms and Ash. In their first year the larvae live on dead bark, but in their second year they attack the bast and cause the sap to escape. After their second winter, when they measure about 70—90 mm and are full-grown, they tunnel deep into the wood, where they gnaw out a roomy chamber for themselves and pupate. The pupal stage lasts some 5—6 weeks. The beetle spends the winter in the chamber and does not leave it until the following year. The tunnels made by the larvae lower the commercial value of the wood and seriously damage living trees. In some regions this beetle is already rare, but its range of distribution covers the whole of Europe and in the east it extends to the western Ukraine.

Lesser Stag Beetle   *Dorcus parallelopipedus*   (Lucanidae)

This moderately large beetle (19—32 mm) has a flatly domed, dull-black body; the females are a little more glossy. It is a lethargic insect, but is more agile in the evening, when it often flies. It usually spends the daytime resting in the branches, and sometimes behind the bark. The larvae develop in the mould of a variety of deciduous trees, chiefly oaks and Beech. The imago appears between may and July. This species occurs in Europe and Asia Minor.

Stag Beetle   *Lucanus cervus*   (Lucanidae)

This is one of the most striking beetles and due to its size, it is also one of the best known. The male is up to 75 mm long, whereas some females do not measure more than 25 mm. In addition, the males have paired jaws which are used not for catching food, but as weapons for dealing with rivals in fights over females. The adult beetles have a predilection for sweet juices and escaping sap. They mate in oakwoods in June and July. They are most active in the evening, when the males fly low in search of still unfertilized females. The larvae develop in old oak stumps, or at the foot of old oaks. They are white, have powerful jaws and their development takes several years, after which they pupate in a chamber made of wood débris. The Stag Beetle helps to break down old tree stumps and enriches the forest soil with humus substances and should therefore be strictly protected. It occurs chiefly in lowlands and in the warmer parts of Europe.

Hermit Beetle   *Osmoderma eremita*   (Scarabaeidae)

This is a comparatively rare European beetle. The adult insect has a glossy, somewhat flattened back and emits a typical odour of Russia leather. Hermit Beetles pair in June and July, but otherwise lead a retiring existence in hollow trees. The larvae develop over several years in hollows in old deciduous trees, particularly in the débris of rotting willows. They are distributed throughout European hardwood forests.

Fire Salamander   *Salamandra salamandra*   (Salamandridae)
The Fire Salamander is a strikingly marked amphibian whose colouring is a warning to other animals to keep away, since its skin contains poison glands. It is completely black, with yellow or orange spots on its head, back, sides and legs and sometimes on its belly. This basic form lives in central Europe, but numerous colour variants occur in other parts of Europe. The west European type has two yellow dorsal stripes. One third of the animal's length (150−230 mm) is accounted for by its tail This salamander inhabits damp, forest areas with gently flowing streams with muddy beds; here it finds adequate shelter and food − mainly insects, worms and gastropods − beneath the boulders. The Fire Salamander is viviparous and the female deposits her larvae in springs of clean water or in gentle streams. The larvae have four legs and paired, feathery gills. The young salamanders acquire their typical colouring when they leave the water for the dry land.

Common Tree Frog   *Hyla arborea*   (Hylidae)
This is one of the best-known frogs and also one of the smallest, since it seldom measures more than 45 mm. The green of its back and sides is sharply separated from the yellowish white of its belly by a 'seam' in the skin. Its characteristic club-tipped toes enable it to hold firm on smooth surfaces; the toes of the hind limbs are slightly webbed. The males have an ochre-coloured throat, whose folds cover the vocal organ. Another feature of the Common Tree Frog is its ability to change colour from light green and yellowish to dark green or brown, with dark spots. The males have a metallic, tinkling call. The adult frogs live high up in trees and come down at mating time or during inclement weather. The eggs are laid in water and the 5 mm long tadpoles leave the water the same year as small frogs. Tree Frogs live on small insects, which they catch by leaping on them.

Green Toad   *Bufo viridis*   (Bufonidae)
After the Common Toad, the Green Toad, which is about 70 mm long, is the commonest member of the genus *Bufo*. It occurs in central and southern Europe and also as far as north Africa and parts of Asia. It generally inhabits open country and is even found at considerable distances from water. In woods it prefers the margins and often settles in the burrows of various rodents. Its basic green colouring is broken up by large, irregular patches of grey. Some of the many warts on its skin are reddish in young specimens. It lives mainly on insects and worms.

Common Frog   *Rana temporaria*   (Ranidae)
This frog, which measures 80−100 mm, is characterized by brown colouring, a smooth, moist skin and long hind limbs with well-developed webbing between the digits. Its eyes are covered with a dark nictitating membrane. In forests, the Common Frog frequents damp spots, but may be found quite a long way away from water. It also occurs at quite high altitudes. Its diet consists of insects and molluscs. It reproduces in stagnant water, in which it lays groups of eggs in the spring.

Riparian Forests

Common Toad *Bufo bufo* (Bufonidae)

One of the commonest tailless amphibians in Europe, this toad lives both in open country and in forests, from the lowlands to the foothills of high mountains. It is one of the largest toads; the female grows to a length of up to 120 mm, and is brown, with a light belly, and rough, warty, dry skin. Young specimens are more brightly coloured and some of their warts are red. The eyes have a red iris. In spring, the animals pair and lay their eggs in water; the eggs are joined in jelly-like strings formed of 3—4 rows of eggs side by side. The tadpoles are almost black, and at the end of the summer turn into small toads, which disperse all over the surrounding area, especially after rain. They live mainly on earthworms, slugs, spiders, harvestmen and large insects. They are therefore an important factor in the maintenance of biological balance and are extremely useful animals which deserve our protection.

Sand Lizard *Lacerta agilis* (Lacertidae)

The Sand Lizard is one of the commonest lizard species. It lives chiefly in dry habitats, but does not avoid water. It finds its way into woods mainly along roads and footpaths; it usually lives on the outskirts of the forest and in clearings, where it may more easily bask in the sun. It occurs mainly in low-lying country, but quite often occurs at altitudes of up to 700 m, and in southern Europe even higher. It is 160—180 mm long and more robust in appearance than other European species. The male is green with a brown stripe, while the female is brown and has rows of light spots along its sides and down its back. It is oviparous and usually lays 3—15 eggs in shallow holes between May and July. In southern Europe in particular grass-green subspecies occur, resembling the Green Lizard *(Lacerta viridis)*, which is common in the south of Europe and is to be found in only the warmest parts of central Europe.

Slow-worm, Blind-worm *Anguis fragilis* (Anguidae)

Slow-worms are actually lizards without limbs and with a snake-like body. This species is covered with large, smooth, glistening and tightly overlapping scales. It attains a length of up to 50 cm, especially in the south of its range. When young it has a markedly dark belly and a light bronze-brown back, but as it grows older this difference is partly obliterated. Some of the scales of very old specimens are a vivid blue, giving rise to irregular, variegated markings. The female is viviparous and gives birth to about 20—25 young, which hide under tree trunks and leaves. Slow-worms live on earthworms and slugs.

Dice Snake, Tessellated Water Snake *Natrix tessellata* (Colubridae)

The Dice Snake requires large rivers and ponds and therefore occurs mainly in low-lying country. It lives chiefly on fish, but also eats frogs, tadpoles and newts. Its length rarely exceeds 1 m, but specimens measuring up to 2 m are known. It is yellowish-brown, with dark spots on its back, but no characteristic marks on its head; its body is covered with ridged scales.

Riparian Forests

European Teal *Anas crecca* (Anatidae)

This small duck, which nests everywhere in Europe except the most southerly parts, is another dabbling duck. In the water it can be recognized from the drake's brightly coloured wings and from its size, since it is about a third smaller than any other duck. At the beginning of April the Teal returns to central Europe from its winter haunts in western and southern Europe and settles beside rivers, where the female builds a nest of dry grass on the ground and lays 8—10 light green eggs. It broods for over 3 weeks and when the young are able to leave the nest escorts them for about a month, until they learn to fly and group together in large flocks. Teal live on insects and in the autumn eat seeds and plants.

Pochard *Aythya ferina* (Anatidae)

This is the commonest diving duck, easily identified by its deeper 'draught' when swimming, its tail, which barely shows above the surface, and the black and white spots on its wings. Diving ducks look for their food on the bottom. The Pochard is distributed throughout eastern, central and northwestern Europe and from here migrates in the autumn to the Mediterranean region, though not regularly. It spends most of its life in the water and only builds its nest on dry land — near water, of course. The nest is lined with plant fragments and down. The young hatch from the greenish eggs in about 24 days and immediately leave the nest accompanied by the female. Like all ducks, the Pochard lives on aquatic plants and various insects.

Mallard *Anas platyrhynchos* (Anatidae)

The Mallard, which is the best-known and commonest dabbling duck, can be identified in the water from its turned-up tail and bright blue patches on its wings. It seldom dives but prefers to look for food in shallow water or just below the surface. It inhabits the whole of Europe, Asia and North America and is generally sedentary, only its northern populations (or others in severe winters) migrating to southern or western Europe or to north Africa. The drake is brightly coloured from the autumn to the spring; the female is brown, with a blue patch on each wing, the whole year round. The ducks arrive at their nesting site at the end of February and the beginning of March. In April the female begins to lay 8—10 (sometimes more) light green eggs. It builds the nest itself, usually in dense undergrowth close to the water, though sometimes on a low tree quite a long way away from the water. When the ducklings are hatched 22—25 days later, the female immediately escorts them to the water and cares for them diligently for several weeks. Mallards live on aquatic insects, worms, seeds and shoots, and in towns, where they spend the winter on ice-free ponds, they may even eat refuse. They are hunted everywhere for food, so that in recent years their numbers have seriously diminished; it would therefore be a good thing to show them a little more consideration and care.

Goosander *Mergus merganser* (Anatidae)

The Goosander belongs to a third group of ducks, which differ from dabbling and diving ducks chiefly in their slimmer bodies, their larger, crested heads and their long, hook-tipped bills. It is a very good diver and can remain under water — looking mainly for animal food — for a long time. The Goosander primarily inhabits northern Europe, where it nests in old, hollow trees, sometimes far from water; it usually lays 8—10 eggs. In the autumn it migrates to central and western Europe, where it spends the winter on ice-free water. It is easy to distinguish from other ducks in the water because of its size (it is over 60 cm long), its black head, which has a green lustre, and its long, red bill.

Riparian Forests

Great Crested Grebe   *Podiceps cristatus*   (Podicipedidae)

Of all five European grebes, this is the best-known species, because of its striking appearance and its style of swimming and diving. All that can be seen above water is part of its back, its long, ruffed neck and tapering head with two tufts of feathers. It is fairly common on ponds and on stagnant water overgrown with reeds, where it builds a floating nest of aquatic plants, often over 50 cm high. Its 3–4 eggs are white at first, but later become darker; the young hatch out in succession, after 25 days. They immediately tuck themselves under the parent birds' wings and the adult birds swim with them and often even dive with them in this position. Grebes live chiefly on small fish, disgorging the remains together with balls of feathers which they swallow as an aid to digestion. They inhabit the whole of Europe except northern Scandinavia and also occur in Asia and Africa.

Coot   *Fulica atra*   (Rallidae)

This aquatic bird is very common everywhere in Europe. Occasionally it will remain on ice-free water during the winter, but in autumn it generally migrates to the south and to northern Africa. It is always to be found on ponds and creeks, where it builds a floating nest, made from the stems of aquatic plants, among the reeds at the water's edge. The nest is generally attached to the stems of the plants, which form a kind of roof over it. In March the female lays 10 or more greyish-yellow, spotted eggs, which are incubated by both birds in turn for about 3 weeks. The newly hatched young are very active and are able to dive if in danger. They are fed by the parents on a vegetable and insect diet. Coots sometimes nest again in June, but the second clutch is usually smaller. The young are black like their parents, but do not acquire the bare white patch above the beak until the autumn.

Moorhen   *Gallinula chloropus*   (Rallidae)

This aquatic bird is common throughout Europe, Asia und Africa, except in the most northerly regions. It primarily frequents rushy ponds, creeks and forest pools, where it builds a nest of interwoven stems in the aquatic vegetation at the water's edge. It nests in April, a second time in June and sometimes again in August, each time laying 6–8 eggs, which the parents take turns in incubating. The young hatch after about 3 weeks. They soon leave the nest and take to the water, where they gather the seeds of aquatic plants and catch aquatic insects. The Moorhen is browner than the Coot, and has a reddish-yellow beak and twitches its tail as it swims. It migrates to the south of Europe in October and returns to its nesting places at the end of March.

Woodcock   *Scolopax rusticola*   (Scolopacidae)

The Woodcock, which is about the size of a pigeon, is essentially an inhabitant of lowland deciduous and mixed woods. It nests throughout the whole of Europe with the exception of northern Scandinavia. Those breeding in central and eastern Europe migrate to southwestern Europe at the end of September and in October. They return in March and April and on the way perform courtship ceremonies in wooded valleys. The female, sitting on the ground, calls to the male, which flies just above the tops of the trees. The male answers by alighting at once beside the female and hopping around her. The 4 round, light brown, spotted eggs are laid in a small depression lined with moss and dry leaves. When the young hatch out, 3 weeks later, they immediately leave the nest together with the female. Woodcock live on a variety of insects and worms, which they hunt on the ground; they often stab their long beak, which is equipped with sensitive tactile corpuscles, into the soft soil, looking for hidden insects. Throughout practically the whole of Europe the Woodcock is regarded as game, but its significance as a gamebird is comparatively small.

Riparian Forests

Penduline Tit *Remiz pendulinus* (Paridae)

The Penduline Tit is a small tit inhabiting southern, southeastern and parts of central Europe. It is usually a resident bird and only populations living near the northern limits of its range migrate further south in the winter. It chiefly inhabits dense riparian forests and the banks of rivers and ponds bordered by plenty of bushes, in which it weaves a hanging nest of grass blades and plant fibres over the water. Its pear-shaped nest is ingeniously constructed. It is about 15 cm high and 10 cm wide and has a tunnel-like entrance at the top. The female incubates up to 8 white, elongate eggs for 2 weeks. During this time the male begins to build a second nest and if it succeeds in luring another female, starts another family. The work of feeding the offspring devolves on the female, which keeps the young supplied with insects (mainly caterpillars, small beetles and mosquitoes) for about 18—20 days.

Roller *Coracias garrulus* (Coraciidae)

This is a typical bird of riparian forests, deciduous woods and rows of trees beside rivers and streams in central and southeastern Europe and the Mediterranean region. It also occurs in western Europe (except the British Isles), around the Baltic and in southern Scandinavia. Its bright colouring (which is the same in both sexes), its quick and almost acrobatic flight and its habit of sitting on elevated objects make it fairly conspicuous. When it arrives in Europe at the end of April (sometimes from as far afield as the south of Africa), the female lays its 4—5 polished eggs, one every other day, in a hollow tree. The young hatch out successively after 18—20 days. Both the parents feed them — chiefly with insects, but occasionally with lizards, frogs and small mammals. As early as the end of August, the Rollers fly south again.

Great Reed Warbler *Acrocephalus arundinaceus* (Sylviidae)

The Great Reed Warbler inhabits dense rushes and the brushwood layer beside rivers and ponds over the whole of Europe except Scandinavia and England. Reed warblers all have much the same inconspicuous colouring and the same retiring habits. Only their noisy song, which is more like a high-pitched screech, betrays their presence. The whole day, they climb untiringly up and down the stems of the rushes, gathering small insects, caterpillars and water snails. The nest — a neat little basket about 20 cm high, which is usually suspended between rush stems some 70 cm above the water — is a veritable work of art. Since the Great Reed Warbler does not return to Europe from its winter haunts in equatorial Africa until late in the spring (sometimes the end of June), it lays only one clutch of eggs (usually 5). These are incubated for 2 weeks, the parents taking turns to sit on the eggs. Both feed the young together for about 14 days.

Reed Warbler *Acrocephalus scirpaceus* (Sylviidae)

The Reed Warbler differs from the preceding species in its smaller size (it measures about 12 cm), its distribution and mode of life. It chiefly inhabits central Europe, the Balkans and Scandinavia and does not occur in southern and southeastern Europe. It also builds a smaller nest, which is often to be found in the brushwood layer of riparian forests. The female sits on the 5 eggs, which are white with olive-coloured spots, for about 12 days. The Reed Warbler arrives in Europe at the end of April and in the second half of September it migrates to northern or equatorial Africa.

Riparian Forests

Barred Warbler *Sylvia nisoria* (Sylviidae)

The Barred Warbler, which is about the size of a sparrow, lives in dense shrubs in the undergrowth of the hardwood forests of central and eastern Europe. It is differently coloured from other warblers, having a greyish-brown back, and white underside barred with grey ripple marks. After wintering in Africa it returns at the beginning of May and immediately builds a nest of neatly interwoven stems lined with fine fibres and hairs in dense bushes. The female incubates the 4—5 yellowish or greenish, grey-spotted eggs for 2 weeks. About 14 days after hatching the young are able to fly, but for a few weeks still roam about the undergrowth together with their parents. They live on small insects and insect larvae. The Garden Warbler *(Sylvia borin)*, which lives in hardwood and mixed forests all over Europe, except for the most northerly and most southerly parts, is slightly smaller.

Blackcap *Sylvia atricapilla* (Sylviidae)

Blackcaps are numerous in lowland hardwood forests and montane conifer woods throughout the whole of Europe, northern Africa and western Siberia. They return from their winter haunts in equatorial Africa in April and immediately build a solid nest made of grass blades and thin twigs on a forked branch in the brushwood undergrowth, close to the ground. The young hatch from the 4—6 brown-spotted eggs after about 2 weeks and for some 12—14 days both the parents feed them on insects (chiefly small caterpillars). The Blackcap usually nests a second time in May. The adult birds live mainly on insects, caterpillars, larvae and spiders and in the autumn on berries. In September they migrate southwards in small flocks.

Golden Oriole *Oriolus oriolus* (Oriolidae)

In May, if you catch sight of a yellow, black-winged bird about the size of a Blackbird in a deciduous wood or a large park, you may consider yourself very fortunate. You have seen a Golden Oriole, a bird which inhabits the whole of Europe except the most northerly parts. Although quite common in some places, it remains so well hidden among the branches of the trees that it easily escapes notice. Its nest, which is made of bast and grass blades, is suspended from a forked branch and forms a hanging cradle for the 3—5 white, finely spotted eggs. The young hatch in 14 days and are fed by both the parents on insects for a further 14. Orioles live mainly on caterpillars and beetles and their larvae, but also eat Diptera (two-winged flies), which they catch on the wing. During August they migrate to their winter haunts in tropical Africa.

Black Kite *Milvus migrans* (Accipitridae)

In some parts of Europe this bird is still quite common, but in others it is already rare. It occurs more in lowlands and foothills, but only where there is water, as it lives mainly on small (and often dead or diseased) fish, frogs, young birds and small birds of prey. It always nests in the crowns of trees, where it usually adapts the nest of some other bird of prey or large bird. As a rule it has only two young, which hatch out in about 4 weeks. Black Kites winter in the southern half of Africa and migrate there at the end of August.

Pine forests

Virgin pine stands hold a special position among the various forest communities, since, owing to their modest soil requirements, pines may survive in places where no other trees would be able to grow. Pines grow mainly on rocks, peat and sandy soils at all altitudes. These original pinewoods are the remains of the unbroken forest of pines, present after the end of the Ice Age. Even today, pine forests cover extensive areas over a large part of Europe. Most of them have been planted artificially, however, usually in impoverished regions. The shrub layer is often absent, while the herbaceous layer tends to be thin, and is generally composed only of lichens and various xerophilic plants. The only places where we are likely to find other trees (chiefly the Medlar *(Mespilus germanica)* and Whitebeam *(Sorbus aria)*) are on stony soils with a limestone base.

Native pinewoods in marginal areas, are important not only for the protection of the soil, but are of value to the environment in general. In rugged country, only pines can find a foothold in crevices in the steep rocky slopes. Here the trees are exposed both to the wind and to marked changes in temperature and their only source of water is from rain caught in cracks in the rocks. In such localities the forester's main task is to preserve a forest cover, since deforestation would devastate the environment as a whole, leaving only bare rock or a sterile sea of stones. Pine growths play an equally important role in forest conservation on badly drained, wet or boggy soils, where the water table is often almost level with the surface of the ground. In both the above cases pines show a different growth from the one we normally see; the trunk is often twisted and stunted and grows very little in girth.

The commonest sites for pine forests are acid, quick-drying, clayey-sandy to sandy soils with a layer of crude humus. In the undergrowth we often find Juniper *(Juniperus communis)*, Heather *(Calluna vulgaris)*, Cranberry *(Vaccinium oxycoccus)* and lichens.

The pine forests which cover extensive areas on sandy soils from central Europe to the Baltic, contain relatively few large forest animals. Only among the insects do we find typical pine pests, in particular the Pine Sawfly *(Diprion pini)* (which abounds in warm regions) and the Pine Looper Moth *(Bupalus piniarius)*, a well-known geometrid which occasionally does serious damage to pine stands. Among the more serious pests are the Pine Hawk *(Hyloicus pinastri)*, whose caterpillars nibble the needles, and the Pine Owlet *(Panolis flammea)*, whose over-proliferation can cause great damage. There are also some serious pests among the beetles, such as the large brown pine weevils or Elephant Beetle, which often destroys whole nurseries of pine seedlings, or the pine bark beetles, whose larvae live behind the bark. Pine forests have a fairly large and varied bird population, but have no typical species of their own. One can see relatively large numbers of various species of tits (in particular the Coal Tit *[Parus ater]*, and the Crested Tit *[Parus cristatus]*), large woodpeckers and − at the margin of clearings − Woodlarks *(Lullula arborea)* and Skylarks *(Alauda arvensis)*. In recent years, pinewoods on rugged rocks have become increasingly popular with the Eagle Owl *(Bubo bubo)* − the largest European owl − as a place of refuge. Underground rocky labyrinths are inhabited by Foxes *(Vulpes vulpes)* and Badgers *(Meles meles)*, while sandy soils provide a dwelling-place for Rabbits *(Oryctolagus cuniculus)*. In general, however, relatively few species are found in pine forests.

Pine Forests

Leucobryum glaucum   (Leucobryaceae)   ❶

Its thalli form thick, loaf-like cushions up to 50 cm in diameter and 15 cm in height, which, in dry weather, turn a whitish colour. It is common in the semishade of coniferous stands, and is an indicator of poor, insufficiently aerated soils, or of areas with dry, raw humus. At first the moss appears only sporadically. Its cushions rapidly grow in size, thicken and absorb water which they retain firmly. If fully saturated with water, this moss is capable of surviving even the longest droughts. It restricts the growth of all other mosses and plants and even the hardy Bilberry dies away if entrapped by it. Wherever it appears in continuous cushions, it interferes with the natural regeneration of the forest, for the fallen seed is completely stifled in its cushions.

Entodon schreberi   (Hypnaceae)   ❷

This extremely plentiful moss forms independent, discontinuous dark to pale green clumps. The stems or caulicles may grow to be 15 cm long, and are pinnately branched into two regular rows. The branch tips are recurved. The caulicle leaflets are hollow, broadly ovate, with a stunted rib; branch leaflets are similar to the preceding but smaller in size. The setae are red and tapering. The capsules are usually oblong-ovate and curved, with a tapering lid. This moss requires abundant light or slight semishade, and is restricted to coniferous stands — especially pine woods — in localities with raw humus. However, it can also be found on dry, sandy substrates where there is sporadic Heather. On suitable soils it attains a considerable height and forms loose, hollow cushions capable of retaining water for a long time. It ranges from lowlands to highlands.

Ceratodon purpureus   (Ditrichaceae)   ❸

Its fluffy little cushions are green, brown or red and 1–4 cm high. The caulicles are erect, forked and sparsely covered with leaflets which are ovate-lanceolate, pointed and deflexed almost all along the margin, with a strong rib. The capsule is held at an angle or horizontally and is reddish-brown, with a short, tapering lid. It is a strictly light-demanding species incapable of surviving the slightest shade or high levels of atmospheric or soil humidity. It is most abundant in dry clearings and heaths where it covers extensive areas, attracting attention by a multitude of glossy red setae. It is thus characteristic of dry to arid, poor soils devoid of humus.

Bracken   *Pteridium aquilinum*   (Polypodiaceae)   ❹

Each year, the stout creeping rhizome of this fern sends out a frond which frequently attains the height of 2 m. Its blade is bipinnate to tripinnate, tough, triangular in shape, with simple pinnate leaves. It is one of the most widely distributed ferns in the world. It is semishade-tolerant to sun-loving, most frequently found in pine woods, on soils poor to moderately rich in minerals, with the ground-water table at least 2 m below the surface. On sandy soils poor in humus it degenerates, becomes pale in colour, and does not exceed 15 cm in height. It is detrimental to the natural regeneration of the forest only when it forms continuous, dense growths. In clearings, however, it is always useful, being often the only plant to protect seedlings against frosts and desiccation. Yet its primary importance lies in that its rhizomes loosen the soil and, after dying off, raise its content of organic matter.

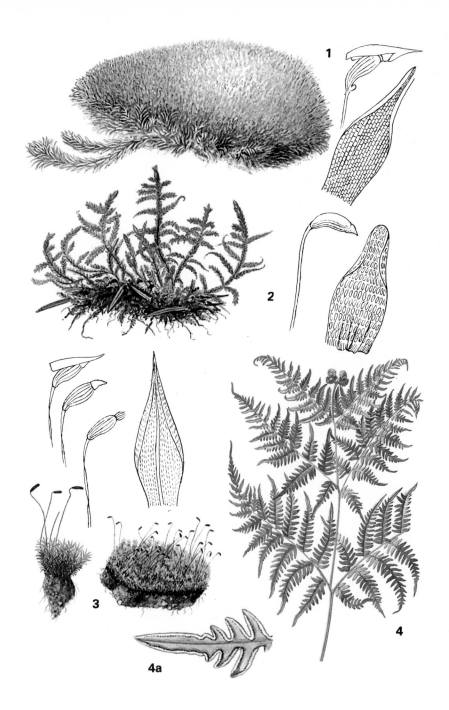

1

2

3

4

4a

Pine Forests

Xanthoria parietina (Theloschistaceae) ❶
The lichens are plant organisms consisting of a combination of a fungus and an alga. The symbiosis of both components gives rise to a new organism endowed with new properties. In the majority of cases the alga is subservient to the fungus. Though the latter provides the alga with moisture and the mineral substances dissolved therein, thus protecting it against desiccation, it draws in return all the remaining substances arising from photosynthesis. This pooling of abilities enables lichens to grow in places where no fungus and no alga could hold their ground separately — for instance, on a bare rock. Lichens are also capable of producing a number of acids helping them to corrode the substrate on which they have taken root. They are, in fact, pioneers of life on bare rocks, contributing to their decomposition and preparing a suitable environment for other plants. *Xanthoria parietina* is attached to the substrate by a thallus whose surface colour varies from yellowish to orange. Its rosettes may grow up to 10 cm across. It is one of the most abundant and variable lichens growing on substrates of all kinds — on rocks, walls, and the bark of old trees. Its distribution is practically world-wide.

Reindeer Moss *Cladonia rangiferina* (Cladoniaceae) ❷
Unlike the above species this lichen has a biform thallus composed of a lower corticate part adhering to the substrate and of an upper bushlike part. It may grow to as much as 15 cm high and is greyish-white, its curled twigs ending in brownish tips. It grows in great profusion on soils with a medium to high acidity level, from lowlands to the mountains. It is restricted to arid areas tolerating even long-lasting droughts, and is abundant in dry pine forests. Often it becomes so dehydrated that it breaks apart at the slightest touch. Although it rapidly absorbs water when rain comes, it cannot tolerate permanently high humidity. It is a characteristic indicator of dry, poor soils.

Iceland Moss *Cetraria islandica* (Parmeliaceae) ❸
The Iceland Moss has a foliaceous or foliaceous-fruticose thallus up to 13 cm high; its lobes are usually coiled into a cone, or tube, often with ciliate margins. The upper side of the thallus is glossy, olive-green to dark brown, while its underparts are usually paler and dotted with white. The Iceland Moss favours sandy soils and heaths but never appears in great abundance — in small groups at most; it prefers to grow singly, often in company with the preceding species. It is an indicator of dry and sandy sites.

Parmelia physodes (Parmeliaceae) ❹
Parmelia physodes is one of the most common European lichens. Its thallus is frondose, flatly clinging to the substrate. Its surface is grey or greyish-green, becoming white towards the margins and beneath it is dark and rugose. This lichen is most abundant on trees in the lowlands, particularly in places characterized by high atmospheric humidity and little wind — in such situations it may cover entire trunks and branch systems. It also grows on rotten wood, stones, rocks, and even on bare, dry soils.

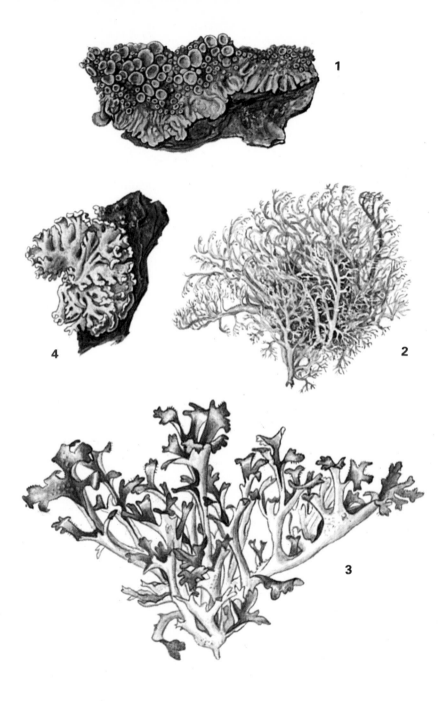

Bilberry, Whortleberry, Blueberry *Vaccinium myrtillus* (Ericaceae) ❶
Representatives of the family Ericaceae are most commonly found in peat bogs or high moorlands. Their symbiotic relationship with fungi living on their roots helps them to overcome the unfavourable conditions they encounter. The Bilberry is a low shrub which, under favourable conditions, reaches a height of 50 cm. The leaves are ovate, finely serrate, and shed before winter. The crown of solitary pendent flowers changes from green to red, and develops into the well-known black berries covered with a fine, bluish, powdery coating (1a). The flowering period is from May to June. The Bilberry needs abundant light but not warmth; it grows from lowlands up to the mountains. It requires rather high soil humidity and thus can be found also on peat soils. On the whole it characterizes acid soils, usually poor in nutrients. Since its growth produces raw humus, it impedes the natural regeneration of forests.

Cowberry, Red Whortleberry *Vaccinium vitis-idaea* (Ericaceae) ❷
The Cowberry is a low shrub growing to a height of 30 cm with leathery, non-deciduous leaves which are dark green and glossy above, light green and dotted with brown below. The flowers, arranged in unilateral racemes, have a bell-shaped, pink corolla. Its fruits are beautiful red berries (2a). Under favourable climatic conditions it flowers twice a year. The Cowberry requires lots of sun and poor, acid soils; if we were to replant it on richer soil, it would degenerate and die. This phenomenon is connected with the Cowberry's method of nutrient uptake via its symbiosis with a fungus capable of obtaining nutrients in forms inaccessible to higher plants. This fungus requires an acid soil, otherwise it deteriorates and the assimilation of the Cowberry is consequently impaired. This is why it favours woods where acid raw humus is being formed. Just like the Bilberry it hampers the sprouting of forest-tree seeds.

Heather, Ling *Calluna vulgaris* (Ericaceae) ❸
This is the well-known, broom-like little shrub with narrow triangular, evergreen leaves. Racemes of its ornamental rosy florets appear from August to September. The rosy four-sided calyx is often mistaken for the petals, though actually these are hidden within this calyx. Special processes situated on the stamen filaments act as levers. These are agitated by foraging insects, setting the stamens in motion, and shaking off the pollen. The style and the stigma are longer than the stamens and attain maturity after all the pollen has been shed. When the stigma dries and falls off after pollination by the insect, the hitherto drooping stamens, bearing the anthers at their upper end, straighten up and protrude above the flower; this facilitates the transfer of the remaining pollen to another plant. Thus Heather presents an example of plants insect-pollinated at first, wind-pollinated later on. Heather requires full exposure to sunlight. This typical companion of acid substrates, poor in minerals, itself contributes to the development of unfavourable forms of humus.

❹
Cypress Spurge *Euphorbia cyparissias* (Euphorbiaceae)
This is one of the plants having milky sap. All its organs contain tubes which exude milk when injured. Its stem is strewn thick with narrow, linear, hairless leaves. The Cypress Spurge requires ample light and grows on relatively dry, warm soils rich in minerals, its roots penetrating deep into the earth.

Pine Forests

Scots Pine *Pinus sylvestris* (Pinaceae) ❶
This tree has a vast distributional range extending across almost all of Europe, from Spain and Greece northwards beyond the Arctic Circle. In southern Europe it is a mountain tree, in the north it descends to the flat lowland plains. It grows to a height of 30—40 m, forming first a narrow, tapering, then a broad, wide-branched crown situated high up on a smooth trunk. The bark covering the lower part of the trunk is thick, deeply furrowed and dark reddish-brown or black, while in its upper part it is orange-brown. The needles are 4—7 cm long and sparsely arranged on the twigs in pairs. It flowers in May, clouds of its yellow pollen spreading by the wind. The cones ripen in autumn of the following second year and release winged seeds in the following spring. The cones are approximately 3 cm long, with dull grey scales. Vast numbers of cast cones may be observed under some trees: the result of Magpies' bringing the pine cones to suitable trees to insert them in crevices and extract the ripening seeds. The Scots Pine is an adaptable tree thriving on dry and sandy substrates as well as on overmoist soils. It is found both in the cold north and in warmer southern regions. The deep taproot anchors it firmly in the ground and enables it to grow in dry localities. The Scots Pine yields light wood suitable for the production of doors, shutters and cheap furniture. Its resin is gathered locally for the purposes of the chemical industry.
Male flowers (1), female flowers (1a), cone (1b).

Austrian Pine, European Black Pine *Pinus nigra* (Pinaceae) ❷
The alternative name comes from the dark grey bark. It is indigenous to countries bordering the Mediterranean, where it ranges from Spain through Corsica as far as Turkey. Today it is cultivated also in western and central Europe, particularly on dry, sunny slopes, in karst regions, and on coastal sand dunes. It attains a height of about 30 m, forming a rather large crown richly foliated with needles. These are arranged in pairs, dark green in colour and are 8—15 cm in length. The cones exceed those of the Scots Pine in length (5—8 cm) and have glossy, yellowish-brown scales. The Austrian Pine has no demands regarding the fertility and humidity of the soil, and improves the soil by its abundant needlecast. Not even sea winds manage to deform its crown, and so it is extensively planted on coastal dunes. It yields good resinous wood well suited for marine use and shipbuilding. It is also a significant source of turpentine.

Juniper *Juniperus communis* (Cupressaceae) ❸
Juniper usually grows as a shrub, less frequently as a small tree up to 10 m in height. Its prickly needles are about 10—15 mm long and arranged in whorls of three. Being a dioecious species, the Juniper produces some trees with only male flowers and others with female flowers. It is on the female trees that bluish, frosted-looking, globular berries, 5—8 mm across, ripen towards the end of the second year. They may be used as spices or for producing alcoholic drinks such as gin. The Juniper is a sun-loving woody plant making no demands on the fertility and humidity of the soil. It inhabits woodland margins, pastures, heather moors, or forms an undergrowth in sparse pine forests from lowlands to high mountain elevations. In the majority of cases, its occurrence gives evidence of cattle grazing in the woods.
Mature female twig with berries (3), male twig (3a), female twig with flowers (3b).

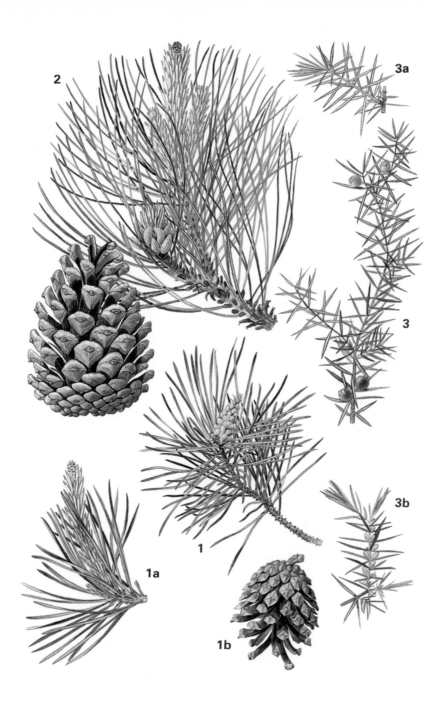

2

3a

3

1

1a

1b

3b

Whitebeam   *Sorbus aria*   (Rosaceae)   ❶

The Whitebeam appears as a constituent of pine woods and warmth-loving oak forests on sunny limestone hillsides with shallow, rapidly drying soils. It occurs mainly as a shrub but as a tree it may attain a maximum height of 15 m. It has broadly ovate leaves, 6—12 cm long, with serrate margins, their undersurface covered with white down. Whitish flowers appear in the first half of May and develop by autumn into globular, scarlet, berry-like fruits, about 15 mm across. The fruit stalks are also downy, as are the remainders of the calyx. The Whitebeam requires plenty of light and warmth, and is most common in warm, vine growing regions. On a calcareous substrate, however, it ascends to montane elevations above 1,000 m. It is of small economic significance but is used as a pioneer species in the afforestation of karst regions.

Southern Scandinavia is the home of the closely related *Sorbus intermedia*. This is a more robust tree, as much as 15 m in height, with broad, short-lobed leaves bearing greyish-green down on the underside. In central Europe it is extensively cultivated in parks for ornamental reasons.

Common Cotoneaster   *Cotoneaster integerrimus*   (Rosaceae)   ❷

This is a small, densely branched shrub about 1 m high with hanging branches. Its small ovate leaves, 2—3 cm in size, have a smooth margin and their undersurface is covered with grey down. Inconspicuous rosy flowers make their appearance in May and by August they develop into red, globular, pea-sized fruits resembling berries. The Cotoneaster is most common on dry, rocky hillsides in central Europe. On limestone substrates in the Alps it grows up to elevations above 1,500 m. It requires abundant light but can easily tolerate a low humidity level.

Broom   *Sarothamnus scoparius*   (Leguminosae)   ❸

This shrub reaches a height of 1—2 m. Its angular twigs are green and its leaves, divided into three in the lower parts of the shoots, are entire and stalkless near the twig tips. They do not exceed 1.5 cm in length and in drier years are shed as early as August. Towards the end of May and at the beginning of June, the shrub is adorned with an enormous number of yellow flowers about 2 cm in size, typical of those found on others of the pea family. These develop into brownish-black, 4—6 cm long pods containing numerous yellowish-brown seeds. Its taproot penetrates deep into the soil. Small tubers containing nitrogen fixing bacteria, situated on the roots, help to increase the amount of nitrogen in the soil. Broom grows in hilly regions, in dry and light woodlands or on their margins and on heaths and sandy substrates. Though exceedingly light-demanding, it does not require high fertility and humidity of the soil. It is absent from calcareous localities, and, owing to its low tolerance of frost, does not occur at higher mountain elevations either. In winter it is eagerly sought by hares and rabbits who like to eat its shoots and bark.

1

2

2a

3

Pine Forests

Emperor Moth *Saturnia pavonia* (Saturniidae)

The Emperor Moth is distributed over the whole of Europe. The females (wingspan about 80 mm), which generally have grey fore- and hindwings, are more robust than the males (wingspan about 45 mm). Males have grey forewings like the females, but bright ochre-yellow hindwings. In both sexes, all four wings have pronounced ocelli. Like other saturnids, the males have markedly pectinate antennae. Both the males and the females have only rudimentary jaws and the imagos take no sustenance. They pair from April to June, depending on the altitude. The females lay their eggs on a wide variety of plants in the middle and ground layer of the forest. The caterpillars live on Sloe, willows, birches, buckthorns and oaks, while in the undergrowth they are mostly to be found on Bilberry plants and Heather. At first they are entirely black and live on the host plant in groups: later they turn greener and become independent, while finally they are entirely green, with orange tubercles. The full-grown caterpillars measure about 6 cm. They pupate at the end of the summer near the ground, forming a brownish pear-shaped cocoon. The moths may emerge the following spring, but they may also spend several winters in the chrysalis stage. They are typical inhabitants of open, light pinewoods, but are also to be found at higher altitudes.

Pale Oak Beauty *Serraca punctinalis* (Geometridae)

This very common species is not entirely dependent upon any one tree. The adult insects have a wingspan of 30—40 mm, the females being slightly larger than the males. Their whitish grey ground colour is enhanced with small brown spots and dark brown lines. Dark and even black forms are also known. The greenish or red-brown caterpillars appear on birches and alders from June to the end of August. They pupate in the ground as reddish brown chrysalises and in this form they spend the winter. The moths fly from April to August.

Pine Owlet Moth *Panolis flammea* (Noctuidae)

The Pine Owlet Moth has a wingspan of 30—35 mm. The ground colour of its forewings and thorax grades from reddish-brown to greyish-brown and its abdomen and hindwings are yellowish-brown. During the day it remains seated on pine twigs or needles, although when it has just emerged it may be found clinging to the trunk. When at rest the moth keeps its wings held close together and their mottled colouring makes it very hard to see. If the weather is favourable, the moths may mate as early as the end of March, but April is more usual and they sometimes only appear at the beginning of May. They are active after dusk, when they fly round the crowns of the trees, where the females lay their eggs in rows on the needles. The caterpillars are green, with stripes of a darker green, and with brown lines down their sides. In July, when their development has been completed, they burrow in the loose needles on the ground, where they spend the winter as glossy black-brown chrysalises. At the tip of its abdomen the chrysalis has two very fine points, which often snap off. This moth mainly frequents European lowland pinewoods and in years when it is particularly numerous may become a serious forest pest.

Pine Looper Moth *Bupalus piniarius* (Geometridae)

The Pine Looper is a moderately large moth (wingspan 30—40 mm). The male is yellowish-white, with dark brown-edged wings, while the female is rusty-yellow, with light-edged wings. The interesting feature of this moth is that it holds its wings closed when it alights, like a butterfly, and does not keep them spread, like the other geometrids. The imagos mate between May and July. In some years they are particularly abundant, especially on the sunny outskirts of pinewoods, where hundreds and thousands can be seen flying about in the middle of the day. The female lays its eggs in rows on pine needles. The green caterpillars, which have three white lines running down their bodies, pupate in the ground. These moths may occasionally become over-abundant and their caterpillars do serious damage to pinewoods.

Pine Forests

Pine Hawk *Hyloicus pinastri* (Sphingidae)

This very common species is confined to conifer forests in general and to pinewoods in particular. The imago is a robust moth with a wingspan of 60—80 mm. Its ground colour is usually grey, but in some populations may be almost black. During the day the imagos rest on tree trunks, generally not more than one metre from the ground and, as a rule, on the northern side. In some years this moth is particularly abundant. It flies from May to July and is to be encountered at all altitudes, from the lowlands to the crooked timber zone in the mountains. The female lays its green eggs either singly or in small groups on conifer needles, and the green caterpillars, which have a black spine on their bodies, hatch after 14 days. By the time they reach the last stage of their development they are more brightly coloured. They have a brown head with black stripes on the sides and although green is still their usual ground colour, some populations are brown and only have green markings. They always have a brown stripe down their back, however, and two whitish parallel stripes on either side. Their spiracles are orange, with a black border. The caterpillars live on the needles of various pines and spruces and sometimes may be found on firs and larches. Their development takes 4—8 weeks, after which they pupate as shiny brown chrysalises under fallen needles near the foot of the tree on which they developed.

Tawny-barred Angle *Semiothisa liturata* (Geometridae)

Unlike the two preceding species, this moth is confined to pinewoods and less so to spruce stands. The caterpillar lives on pines, spruces, firs, Weymouth Pine and even Juniper needles. The imago's colouring matches the pine bark extremely closely, so that a moth resting there is hard to detect. More often it betrays itself by its zigzag flight as it escapes from the disturber of its peace. The moth has a wingspan of about 25—28 mm and is to be seen in European conifer forests from May to August.

Cicindela hybrida (Cicindelidae)

This beetle is a predator which relentlessly hunts small insects and thus helps to maintain biological balance in the forest. It measures 12—16 mm. It is particularly active in the midday sunshine and runs rapidly hither and thither in a constant search for food. The characteristic feature of the members of this family is their ability to take flight instantaneously without warning. The larvae, which are likewise predacious, live in the sand on the outskirts of pinewoods. This beetle occurs in Europe and Asia.

Ant Beetle *Thanasimus formicarius* (Cleridae)

The Ant Beetle, which measures only 7—10 mm, is a very useful species in European forests, since it destroys the larvae of bark beetles. This applies both to the adult beetle and to the larva, which lives behind bark. It mostly destroys pine bark beetles, but does not despise the pests of other conifers or even of deciduous trees. It is to be found the whole year round, but is somewhat rarer at the end of May and the beginning of June, when its larvae are more abundant.

Pine Forests

Phaenops cyanea (Buprestidae)

This blue or bluish-green beetle, which measures 8–11 mm, mates in June and July. It flies around the trunks of pines, particularly if the sun is shining, and settles on the sunwarmed trunks of trees already weakened, for example, by caterpillars. The larvae bore winding tunnels in the bast and, after hibernating there, pupate in a chamber gnawed in the thick bark. This beetle occurs all over Europe, as well as in north Africa, the Caucasus and Siberia.

Spondylis buprestoides (Cerambycidae)

This completely black longicorn beetle, which is 12–22 mm long, has relatively short antennae compared with the other members of its family. It swarms from June to September and is active during the evening, when it flies busily about seeking mates. In the daytime it remains motionless under piled timber, and is often found near timber-yards and sawmills, as well as in the forest. The female lays its eggs in the trunks of pines (though occasionally also spruces), where the larvae eat out tunnels. This species is considered a secondary pest, because it attacks dead trees, tree stumps and felled trees, not live, healthy ones. Its very wide range of distribution includes the whole of Europe and extends into eastern Asia.

Pine Weevil *Hylobius abietis* (Curculionidae)

This beetle, which measures 10–13 mm, is reddish-brown with a head produced into a 'snout'. The beetles mate repeatedly and from May to September the females lay approximately 120 eggs each in the roots of pine and spruce stumps. The larvae, which hatch 2–3 weeks later, form typical longitudinal tunnels in the bast of the roots. Most of the larvae hibernate and pupate in the bark, but about one fifth pupate in pupal chambers in the wood itself, carefully blocking up the entrance with minute splinters. The pupal stage lasts 1–4 weeks. The development of a whole generation usually takes 2 years. In the first year the larvae develop and in the second, the beetles hibernate in the loose needles on the ground. It is not the larvae which do the main damage, however, since they only attack stumps and thus hasten their decomposition. The beetles are most to blame, for in July and August they nibble conifer seedlings and in the following spring do even greater damage by attacking the bark and bast of completely healthy pine, Weymouth Pine, spruce, Douglas Fir, larch and fir seedlings. In June and July they also attack the branches of fully grown trees, though compared with their effect on seedlings, the damage they do to branches is insignificant. This beetle is distributed throughout Europe and across Siberia as far as Japan.

Six-toothed Engraver *Ips sexdentatus* (Scolytidae)

This is one of the largest bark beetles (length 6–8 mm) and behind the bark its larvae form short tunnels, each ending in a shallow chamber. The egg passages, burrowed by the females, usually have three arms and are 50–80 cm long. The beetle chiefly attacks the base of thick-barked pines. It is a secondary pest and spares healthy trees. Today it seems to be rarer than it used to be. Since it produces two generations each year, the beetles are to be found the whole year round, except at the end of May and the beginning of June, when the larvae are most common. It is distributed throughout the whole of Europe (where it occurs chiefly in low-lying country) and extends into Asia Minor and Siberia.

Pine Forests

Wood Lark *Lullula arborea* (Alaudidae)

If a plain grey bird a little larger than a sparrow suddenly soars upward in a clearing in a pinewood or on a moor, it is almost certainly a female Wood Lark, frightened from its nest, cleverly hidden under a low tree or bush or in the Heather. The Wood Lark generally nests twice — once early in the spring and again in June or July — and the female incubates the 4—5 finely spotted eggs for 14 days. The young are soon independent and leave the nest after 10—12 days, but the parents still feed them for a few days outside the nest, mostly on small insects. In the autumn they live mainly on the small seeds of field and forest plants. They spend the winter on the coast of northern Africa and return to Europe in March, when their melodious song can be heard, chiefly at night and in the early morning, until late into the summer.

Tree Pipit *Anthus trivialis* (Motacillidae)

The Tree Pipit occurs from the middle of April until the end of September in practically all clearings and on the outskirts of mixed and conifer forests (especially pinewoods) in uplands and mountainous regions all over Europe, except in the Iberian Peninsula. In the spring, the male can be identified by its typical flight: it soars a few metres from a tall tree and then, trilling and with spread wings, spirals down to the ground. The Tree Pipit always nests on the ground in dense, tangled grass. The 5—6 bluish eggs are laid in May and the female incubates them for 12—13 days. The young leave the nest at the age of 2 weeks, but the parents still feed them for a few days outside the nest on insects and spiders. Towards the end of the summer Tree Pipits invade the fields, where they destroy large numbers of insect pests, and at the end of September they migrate to northern Africa.

Nightjar *Caprimulgus europaeus* (Caprimulgidae)

This is the only European representative of the relatively large nightjar family, most of which live in the tropics. It is completely insectivorous and hunts at dusk or during the night. In the summer it has a preference for chafers, hawk moths and other nocturnal insects, on which it also feeds its young (of which there are generally two) for over 2 weeks. The young hatch after 17 days from grey-spotted eggs, laid in a primitive nest which is no more than a depression in a tree stump or dry grass. The Nightjar inhabits mixed woods with a preponderance of pine trees and its greyish-brown colouring provides perfect camouflage. At the end of August it migrates to northern Africa and returns again at the end of April.

Eagle Owl *Bubo bubo* (Strigidae)

The largest of the European owls has a wingspan of up to 160 cm and a body length of about 70 cm. It nests throughout the whole of Europe (except the British Isles and northern Scandinavia) and inner Asia and lives in dense mixed and conifer forests in lowlands and mountains. It nests on bare rock, in ruins, in tree hollows or in old nests of birds of prey. The female alone incubates the 2—4 white eggs for about 5 weeks and the young hatch in the middle of May. The male keeps the female supplied with food (jays, crows, acquatic birds, pheasants, hares and even Kestrels, for instance), while the female feeds the young for up to 2 months, inside and out of the nest. Eagle Owls attack their prey at night. At one time their numbers in central and western Europe fell very low, but strict protection has helped them recover in recent years.

Pine Forests

European Wild Rabbit *Oryctolagus cuniculus* (Leporidae)
This inhabitant of open pine and mixed woods in lowlands and uplands likes light, sandy soil for its intricate warrens. It lives on various herbaceous plants and the leaves of shrubs and gnaws the bark of trees, coming out to graze at dusk and during the night. In the woods it is something of a nuisance, owing largely to the size of its colonies, which do considerable damage in the immediate vicinity. After a gestation period of about 30 days the female gives birth, in a separate burrow, to 4—10 young. There may be from three to five litters a year. The young are blind for the first 10 days and do not leave the burrow for about a month. The female suckles them regularly twice a day and on leaving the burrow always covers up the entrance. When independent, the young live in the colony with the others and reach sexual maturity at about 6 months. The size of rabbit populations is very variable and for many years now they have been regularly decimated by infectious diseases and their numerous enemies. It is about 700 years since the rabbit spread from its original home in northern Africa and Spain to cover the whole of Europe, where its tasty flesh (a mature one weighs about 1.5 kg) has made it very popular as game.

Red Fox *Vulpes vulpes* (Canidae)
The Red Fox is the best-known European predator, but also lives in Asia and North America. It is numerous from the lowlands to the mountains, in forests, on bushy hillsides and in open country. It lives in deep underground dens, where the female, after a gestation period of 50 to 52 days, gives birth in April to 3—8 young, sometimes more. For the first 14 days the cubs are blind and the female suckles them for about a month. After they open their eyes, both parents begin to give them flesh and by the end of the summer they go hunting on their own. Despite the determined efforts of hunters and foresters (many Foxes are killed during the time that young are being reared), their numbers do not seem to have been seriously affected. They are useful to both forestry and agriculture, as they destroy murine rodents (which form up to 60 % of their diet), and are also useful in eating carrion and catching sick and weak game animals.

Badger *Meles meles* (Mustelidae)
The Badger, which in the autumn may occasionally weigh as much as 20 kg, is the largest mustelid in European forests. In some places it is relatively abundant, from the lowlands up into the mountains. It digs deep underground burrows with several lairs and large numbers of exits and quite often occupies deserted fox-holes. The Badger family stays together from March or April, when the 3—5 young are born, until December. The young are blind for 4—5 weeks and the female suckles them for 2 months; they become independent after 6 months. The Badger is omnivorous; it lives on tree fruits and seeds, berries and mushrooms, but also insects, voles, mice and carrion and even young birds, small pheasants and hares. It is therefore useful since it destroys insect pests and voles, but in pheasant and other small game preserves it can do considerable damage.

Wood Mouse, Long-tailed Field Mouse *Apodemus sylvaticus* (Muridae)
The Wood Mouse is found on the outskirts of dry pinewoods and in hedgerows, thickets and fields all over Europe and Asia. They can be distinguished from the House Mouse by their long tails and relatively large ears. They live mostly in burrows dug in soft soil, where they have up to three litters of 6—8 young each year. The young are blind for about 2 weeks. These mice live mainly on the seeds of forest trees, grain and sometimes insects and snails. In the winter they venture close to human dwellings, where they often raid granaries and larders. Although caught by birds of prey, owls, Weasels and Foxes, they remain fairly abundant.

Deciduous woods of lowlands and hills

This forest group includes hardwood forests, from the oak belt in the lowlands to the upper limit of the Beech belt in the uplands, growing in regions with a warm climate, mild winters and an annual rainfall of up to 700 mm. Here the dominant tree is the Sessile Oak *(Quercus petraea)* and in places the Pedunculate Oak *(Quercus robur)* and the Hornbeam *(Carpinus betulus)*, with an admixture of other deciduous trees. In uplands the Beech *(Fagus sylvatica)* is the most prominent tree. These forests usually have a very rich shrub layer.

Oakwoods were most highly developed during the warmest postglacial period, when Man first attempted to form settlements and started to develop agriculture. The demise of the oakwoods is thus closely associated with Man's activities, since he changed their natural structure by felling.

Oakwoods have a very wide range of distribution, within which they form several distinct types of forest determined by the local conditions.

On stony or rocky hillsides and on steep, dry slopes we find a specific type of oakwood composed of stunted trees like shrubs. Such growths are not dense and there is usually an admixture of birches. The undergrowth consists of species requiring a warm, dry environment. The chief benefit of forests in such localities is that they protect the soil.

In warm, dry lowlands, pure oakwoods grow on quickly drying soils poor in minerals, where other trees and shrubs with a surface root system would be unable to find sustenance. Grasses preponderate in the ground layer. This type of forest sometimes changes to mixed birches and oaks, with the Bilberry *(Vaccinium myrtillus)* as the typical plant in the undergrowth, indicating that the humus is not properly decomposed.

Oakwoods with an admixture of Hornbeam are encountered on moderately rich, deep and adequately moist clayey soils at low altitudes. Oaks and limes form the upper layer and the Hornbeam grows below them. The commonest plants in the brushwood layer are the Hawthorn *(Cretaegus monogyna)*, Hazel *(Corylus avellana)*, Sloe *(Prunus spinosa)*, Elder *(Sambucus nigra)* and Privet *(Ligustrum vulgare)*.

At higher altitudes Beech appears in the oakwoods and various grades of beech/oak forests are formed. Originally these stands also contained an admixture of firs.

Not unnaturally, it was mainly in the lowlands that this type of forest was damaged most severely by Neolithic Man. Both the climate and the open structure of the warmth-loving oakwoods suited him best, providing his cattle with pasture and other sources of rich nutrition without the need to clear large areas of trees. It was not until much later, at the end of the eighteenth and the beginning of the nineteenth century, that the further development of society led to deciduous forests being felled and the empty spaces being reforested with spruce monocultures.

The large variety of woody and herbaceous plants in oakwoods encourages the presence of numerous species of insects, birds and mammals. The largest number of insect pests appear on oaks; they include the spruce moths, the Oak Gall Fly *(Andricus kollari)* and the Oak Procession Moth, and we also find longicorn beetles, stag beetles and cockchafers there. Deciduous forests provide rich sources of food and shelter for insectivorous birds, among which, in addition to many species of tits, such as the Great Tit *(Parus major)*, Blue Tit *(Parus caeruleus)* and Coal Tit *(Parus ater)*, we also find hole nesting species, such as the Great Spotted Woodpecker *(Dendrocopus major)*, Green Woodpecker *(Picus viridis)*, Wood Pigeon *(Columba palumbus)* and Tree Creeper *(Certhia familiaris)*.

Among the mammals are species typical of a rich shrub and herb layer; chiefly the Common Shrew *(Sorex araneus)*, Dormouse *(Muscardinus avellanarius)* and Edible Dormouse *(Glis glis)*. The margins of deciduous forests are often visited by various game animals, in particular Hares *(Lepus europaeus)*, Roe Deer *(Capreolus capreolus)* and the Wild Boar *(Sus scrofa)*, which come there for shelter or in search of food. Most of the species mentioned above occur in other types of forest as well (especially riparian and mixed forests), but their populations are largest in oakwoods, where they find the most abundant supplies of suitable food.

Deciduous Woods of Lowlands and Hills

Daedalea quercina   (Polyporaceae)   **❶**

Fungi (Mycophyta) do not possess the plant pigment chlorophyll, essential for the production of sugars by photosynthesis, and consequently must obtain their nutrition from other organisms as do animals. Some 60 % of fungi (i. e. 42,000 species) parasitize living organisms; all but about 500 species prey on plants, the rest on animals. The remaining 28,000 species are saprophytes obtaining their nourishment from decaying organic matter. Some fungus species are microscopic, others attain a weight of several dozen kilograms. The main fungal body is the mass of threads called the mycelium, which, under favourable conditions, produces fruiting bodies which are often very conspicuous. In the higher fungi the fruiting bodies bear a spore-producing layer known as the hymenium; this is situated either among the gills or in tubes, or it may cover the whole surface of the fruiting body. Many fungi are crop pests, while others are Man's helpers. The latter are of importance especially in the food industry and medicine (many are active antibiotics). Some fungi live in symbiotic association with certain plants which they supply with materials necessary for growth, while, in return, they draw from the plants nutrients they are unable to obtain otherwise. Together with bacteria, fungi also help to decompose decaying organic matter, thus contributing to the circulation of nutrients.

The wood-destroying fungus *Daedalea quercina* has semicircular fruiting bodies up to 40 cm across. They are light brown to grey in colour, corky, tuberculate on the upper surface. The underside is conspicuous for its numerous tubes, forming labyrinthine galleries. It is abundant on oak stumps. For the most part it grows on rotten wood and only exceptionally appears on living trunks, generally only at the site of an injury. Its occurrence on limes, Hornbeam and Beech is relatively rare. It is one of the most serious pests of oaks which it attacks eagerly.

Boletus luridus   (Boletaceae)   **❷**

This species has a yellowish to dark brown velvet cap. The pores are yellow initially, orange later on and deep red when mature, and turn blue when exposed to pressure. The stipe is slightly ventricose, marked with a red reticulum on a yellow background. The flesh is pale yellow, though rapidly turns blue with a greenish tinge when cut. It can be found from July to October in both deciduous and coniferous forests. It is edible, provided that it has been thoroughly cooked.

Russula lepida   (Russulaceae)   **❸**

The genus *Russula* includes both edible and inedible fungi which can be easily distinguished: all *Russula* having palatable, sweet, non-acrid flesh are edible, while those whose flesh is bitter and acrid are inedible. This does not of course apply to fungi in general! The *Russula* species present a lavish display of colours. *Russula lepida* has a hard, vermilion, lustreless cap. It is edible and tastes excellent.

Russula aeruginea   (Russulaceae)   **❹**

This species has a slimy, grass-green cap 5—12 cm in diameter, convex when young, depressed in the centre later on. The flesh is slightly acrid. It is edible, but not good eating. It grows from June to October, very often in the vicinity of birches.

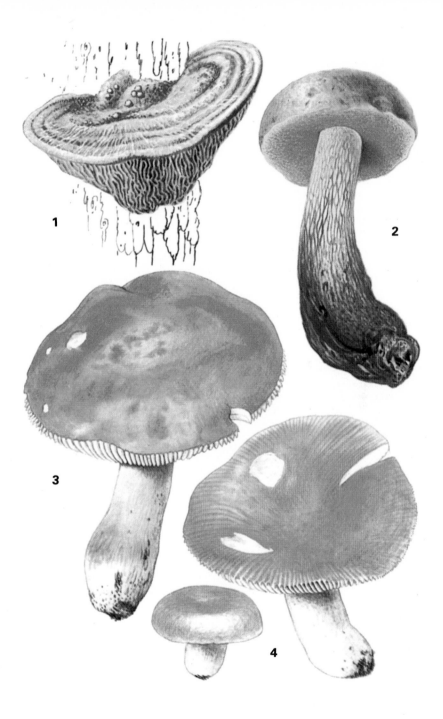

Deciduous Woods of Lowlands and Hills

Stinkhorn *Phallus impudicus* (Phallaceae) ❶

This peculiar fungus grows in deciduous woods, in orchards, and even among shrubs. Its foul smell carries for considerable distances. The young fungus has the shape of a pale, smooth egg. When cut open the thallus can be seen, concealed within and surrounded with gelatinous matter protecting it against dessication. Also rudiments of the stipe or stalk can be discerned. After warm rains the stipe starts growing rapidly and the cap perforates the egg cover. The remainder of the cover then forms a sheath wherein the stipe rests, yet it can easily be broken off. The stipe is white, with a dense network of grooves; the olive-green cap is conical. The surface of the cap is covered with a sporiferous layer which, after attaining maturity, turns into a foul-smelling liquid. The cadaverous odour attracts flies and other small insects which consequently ensure dispersion of the spores. After all the smelly liquid has run down the thallus, the stipe begins to soften and the entire thallus decomposes. At this time the fungus smells of honey.

Young egg-shaped thallus (1a).

Male Fern *Dryopteris filix-mas* (Polypodiaceae) ❷

In identifying ferns, particular attention should be paid to the frond undersurface where sporangia develop whose shape and position are characteristic of every species. The sporangia are small structures containing spores and are either naked or enclosed in a fine membranous covering − the indusium. The Male Fern is a common species of deciduous and mixed forests in Europe. It grows from a short rhizome covered with rusty hairs and may attain a height of 1.3 m. New frond rosettes develop every year. The convolution of fronds into a spiral affords an advantage: the youngest shoot, situated inside the spiral, is protected against frosts. In the course of the sprouting process, this spiral slowly unwinds. The frond blade tapers towards both ends and is dark above, lighter below. In this fern there is no difference between fruiting fronds bearing sporangia and vegetative fronds, as is the case in some other fern species. The sporangia on the underside of the fronds are arranged along the central vein and covered with kidney-shaped indusia. In central Europe the Male Fern is widespread from lowlands up to the mountains. Though preferring some sun, it is able to withstand deep shade. It is most usual in Beech stands, or in stands where other species mix with Beech, and serves to indicate rich, fresh, damp soils with an active decomposition of humus. It is hence absent from poor and dry soils.

Frond undersurface with sporangia (2a).

Common Horsetail *Equisetum arvense* (Equisetaceae) ❸

This perennial grows from a long subterranean, dark brown, segmented rhizome which enables it to spread vegetatively with ease. In spring the rhizome sends out a simple, waxy yellow stem ending in a sporiferous spikelet (3a) and bearing conspicuous sheaths formed by coalescent leaves. After all the spores have been shed the stem fades and dies off, giving way to new, branched, green, summer stems (3b) which grow out of the same rhizome. These, being infertile, serve exclusively for photosynthesis. They grow to a height of 10−50 cm. The Common Horsetail occurs from lowlands to the mountains and its wiry, deep-set rhizomes frequently make it an unpleasant weed of forest nurseries. It appears in great abundance on heavy soils. Being a heliophyte, it is found only on woodland margins and in ditches adjoining agricultural areas.

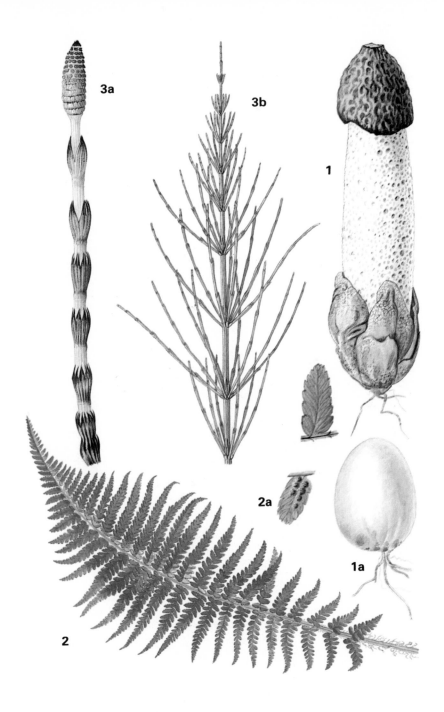

3a

3b

1

2a

1a

2

Deciduous Woods of Lowlands and Hills

Hollow Fumitory   *Corydalis cava*   (Papaveraceae)   ❶
In early spring, sometimes as early as March, the hibernating hollow tuber puts forth tripartite leaves (a simple blade divided into three segments of varying depth), together with a raceme of violet or reddish flowers. The ensuing fruit is a capsule. *Corydalis* favours fresh, humic soils rich in nutrients, and accompanies mixed deciduous lowland forests. As it often forms extensive carpets, it makes a major visual impact in early spring, when the canopy is still devoid of foliage. Despite these extensive, continuous growths, it is not detrimental to the natural regeneration of the forest since, in summer, its aerial parts die off and very quickly vanish, helping to enrich the forest humus.
Hollow tuber (1a).

Bats-in-the-belfry   *Campanula trachelium*   (Campanulaceae)   ❷
This is a perennial herb, 30—100 cm high, whose bright violet-blue flowers bloom from July to September. The basal leaves are broadly cordate, the others are ovately lanceolate and covered with hairs. The fruits are like capsules. This campanula occurs in both lowlands and mountains, accompanying deciduous forests of various types. It is an indicator of rich, rather moist soils in which active humus decomposition is taking place. The hanging habit of most campanula flowers is advantageous: the interior of the flower, in particular the pollen and the nectar, are thus protected against bad weather. The position of the bells also affects the pollination process — only insects capable of flying into the flower from below can pollinate it, and pollination is primarily by bees. In view of this fact, some campanula species which bear their flowers erect in the early stages, incline their stalks in maturity, so as to turn their flowers downward.

Sweet Woodruff   *Asperula odorata*   (Rubiaceae)   ❸
A long, creeping rhizome puts forth unbranched, erect, square-sectioned stems, 10—30 cm high, bearing whorls of hairless, oblong-lanceolate, light green 'leaves'. From a strictly botanical point of view the whorl is not entirely composed of leaves: there are only 2 true leaves among the 6—8 'leaflets' involved — the others are enlarged stipules. These, however, are identical to leaves, and even perform the same function. The stem ends in a cyme of minute white flowers which open from April to May and develop into globular dry seeds covered with hook-like bristles. These help to disperse the seeds since they easily get caught in animals' hairs. When withering, the entire plant sweetly smells of the alkaloid coumarin. It is most abundantly distributed in the Beech forest belt. Woodruff is extremely demanding as regards soil conditions — it requires moist, light, aerated soils rich in nutrients, and with active decomposition of humus. It grows from lowland to mountain elevations.

Ground Ivy   *Glechoma hederacea*   (Labiatae)   ❹
Ground Ivy is a perennial herb with a prostrate, 10—40 cm long stem. The leaves are reniform in the bottom part of the stem, while in its upper part they are rounded cordate and crenate. The leaf stalks are shorter than the internodes. From May till July, one to three violet-blue florets appear in the leaf axils. When rubbed, the whole plant gives off an agreeable smell. It requires moist soils rich in nutrients (especially in nitrogen), with a satisfactory humus turnover. On soils of this kind Ground Ivy may be found in forests of various types, but also in meadows, along roads, and in weed communities, from lowlands to the hills. It tolerates full sunlight.

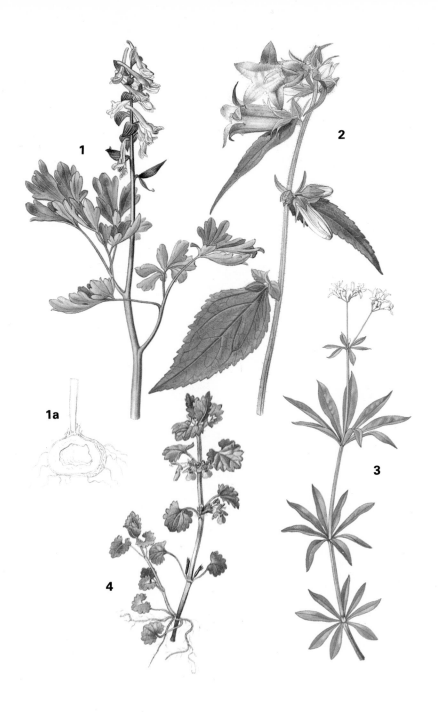

1

2

1a

4

3

Deciduous Woods of Lowlands and Hills

Wood Anemone   *Anemone nemorosa*   (Ranunculaceae)   ❶
Its rhizomes send forth stems ending in a white flower with a whorl of three petiole-like, trifid bracts situated underneath. The Anemone flowers in early spring, often as early as March and its aerial parts wither after the trees have come into leaf. Its fruits are achenes (small, dry single-seeded fruits). The anemone is not associated with any specific forest community, yet tends to appear more frequently in deciduous than in coniferous forests. Its occurrence both in meadows and in woods is proof of its great adaptability to various light conditions. It requires fresh, loose, moderately rich soils. Anemones are among those plants which can spread rapidly by vegetative means. They have an underground rhizome, about 30 cm long. A bud appears at one of its ends from which the rhizome grows, while the other end dies off. So the anemone moves along, securing a continuous supply of fresh, unexhausted soil. Moreover, the rhizome produces lateral buds giving rise to new shoots which proceed in the very same way. In the course of time, lateral rhizomes die off where they join the main rhizome, and the new plants become independent.

Sweet Violet   *Viola odorata*   (Violaceae)   ❷
Its sweet-smelling, dark violet flowers grow directly from the rhizome in March or in April, together with cordately ovate leaves. These first flowers only rarely develop into fruits. To make up for this, small, drooping flowers appear towards the end of summer, which do not even unfold and usually escape attention. Self-pollination takes place in these. The fruit is a multi-seeded capsule which opens by the abrupt separation of its three lids. This violet is most commonly found at lower elevations, among the hornbeam and oak forests; the soils it favours are fresh, loose and moderately rich in minerals. It is absent from soils with a large amount of humus.

Asarabacca   *Asarum europaeum*   (Aristolochiaceae)   ❸
The rootstock of this perennial herb puts forth stems with long-stalked, reniform, dark green, glossy, leathery leaves. The whole stem consists of annual internodes bearing four scales, one pair of leaves, and the terminal flower. During flowering, the present year's leaves remain small and do not attain full size until the flowers fade. A bud appears among the leaves from which a new, identical stem arises the following year; this pushes the old stem aside and itself grows in the direction of the maternal stem. The flowers open from March to May. The flowers which are bell-shaped, constricted at the mouth, and composed of three petals, are greenish-brown on the outside and dirty purple inside, and smell of pepper. They ripen into a hexagonal section capsule containing seeds with yellow, pulpy appendages. The seeds are dispersed by ants who seem to be attracted by the appendages. The Asarabacca is an exclusively shade-loving species intolerant of bright sun. It ranges from lowlands to mountains inhabiting deciduous forests growing on fresh, moderately rich soils, where there is active humus decomposition and turnover.

Hepatica   *Hepatica nobilis*   (Ranunculaceae)   ❹
Its well-known blue flowers appear in early spring. It has noticeable leathery, three-lobed leaves with an entire margin. Their undersurface is violet in colour, due to the presence of the pigment anthocyanin which can absorb sunlight to produce warmth. Thus the Hepatica has a kind of 'central heating', protecting it against frost. It occurs from lowland to submontane elevations, and is a typical component of spring in shady deciduous forests. It grows on fresh, moderately rich soils characterized by a favourable humus decomposition.

3

3a

1

4a

2

4

Deciduous Woods of Lowlands and Hills

Toothwort *Lathraea squamaria* (Orobanchaceae) ❶
In the bushy undergrowth of deciduous forests, its 10—25 cm high pink stems make their appearance in early spring. The flowers, too, have a rosy hue. This species is unusual among higher plants in that it lacks chlorophyll and is therefore not green. This phenomenon is relatively common in lower plants, especially in the fungi, which obtain nourishment in ways other than by photosynthesis — either as parasites or as saprophytes. The Toothwort is a parasite and lives at the expense of other plants. Most of the plant is up to 1 m underground: here its large rhizome, weighing as much as several kilograms, winds its way among the roots of various shrubs and trees. This rhizome shoots out fine filaments in all directions which end in adhesive tubercles which cling closely to the shrub roots. These gather nutrition from the host-plant's roots. The Toothwort rhizome is covered with numerous scales which provide a suitable shelter for insects; these often creep inside and not infrequently die there. Products of the decomposition of these insect bodies are subsequently absorbed by the plant. Indeed, the Toothwort was at one time considered a wholly insectivorous plant. It requires porous, damp soils rich in nutrients, and most frequently parasitizes the roots of alders and Hazel.

Lungwort *Pulmonaria officinalis* (Boraginaceae) ❷
This is a perennial herb with a 10—30 cm high stem bearing sessile leaves and a terminal cluster of flowers. The flowers are red at first but later on, after pollination, become violet and finally blue. This change in colour is due to a change in the composition of cellular sap whose originally acid reaction becomes alkaline. It is thought that these colour changes serve as a signal for insects, the colour indicating the presence or absence of nectar in a particular flower. Later on the rootstock also puts forth basal leaves with a cordate ovoid blade borne on a long petiole (stalk). The Lungwort is a shade-loving plant considered among the most demanding as regards both nutrients and water content of the soil. It grows in deciduous or mixed forests from lowlands to hills.

Spring Pea *Lathyrus vernus* (Leguminosae) ❸
The Spring Pea is a perennial with an upright, angular stem bearing 2—4 pairs of pinnate, lanceolate leaflets. The stem ends in a raceme of pink flowers which turn blue later on and ultimately develop into pods. It grows from lowlands to foothills, especially favouring deciduous woodlands on drier soils with an average mineral content.

Martagon Lily *Lilium martagon* (Liliaceae) ❹
The Martagon Lily adorns open groves, shrubby slopes and mountain meadows. An erect stem, up to 1 m in height, grows from a scaly bulb; it bears elliptically lanceolate, almost sessile leaves arranged in several whorls giving way to bracts in the upper part of the stem. Beginning in June, wonderful pendent flowers develop in their axils. These consist of six rosy, purple-spotted petals bent backwards, giving the flower a turban-like appearance. Their beauty is still further enhanced by protruding stamens with red anthers and by a long, curved style. They mature into capsules which open by the separation of three lids. The Martagon Lily occurs from lowlands to montane elevations on porous soils rich in nutrients, with an actively decomposing humus.

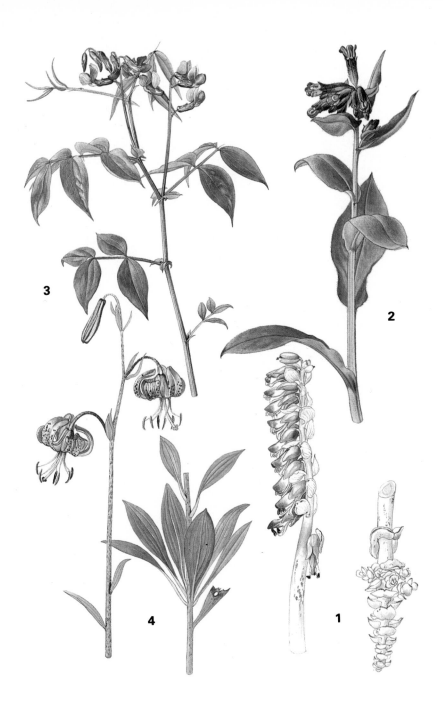

3

2

4

1

Deciduous Woods of Lowlands and Hills

Wild Strawberry *Fragaria vesca* (Rosaceae)   ❶
The Wild Strawberry is a well-known plant with sessile, trefoil leaves whose white flowers appear from April onward. The flowers develop into the familiar red berries. These interesting fruits are formed when the receptacle of the flower becomes pulpy, leaving the individual seeds (achenes) attached to the surface. The Wild Strawberry grows from lowlands to high mountain elevations. Making no specific demands on soil conditions, it appears on almost all types of soil, with the exception of extremely poor and strongly acid soils. It is common in forest clearings and glades in the initial stages of their development: later on, due to deterioration in the humification process, the Wild Strawberry gradually disappears from such localities.
   Longitudinal section through the fruit, showing the aggregation of achenes on the swollen receptacle (1a).

Dog's Mercury *Mercurialis perennis* (Euphorbiaceae)   ❷
The long rhizome produces a simple, 10—40 high stem with ovoid-lanceolate, serrate, dark green leaves. The flowers open from April to June — male flowers are arranged in spikes, female flowers appear in groups of two or three in the leaf axils. Both sexes of flower are very small and green. Owing to the poisonous substances it contains, eating Dog's Mercury may prove fatal. It is most abundant in rich Beech forests and gravelly woodlands. On good soils it may grow at mountain elevations. However, it is also plentiful in un-inundated riparian forests. Thus it occurs wherever litter is decomposing and good humus produced, and quickly disappears from places with deteriorating humus conditions. It often forms extensive carpets which may hinder the natural regeneration of trees and shrubs.

Yellow Archangel *Lamiastrum galeobdolon* (Labiatae)   ❸
This is a perennial herb, 15—30 cm high with an angular stem bearing alternate, opposite pairs of short-stalked leaves covered with glandular hairs. From April to July, yellow flowers with a typical labiate corolla appear in the leaf axils. The corolla — petals — are joined to form a tube terminating, at the free end, in the upper and the lower labium. The upper labium forms a kind of roof sheltering the reproductive organs, while the lower labium is expanded at the sides to form a platform on which insects can land. Inside the tube there is a slightly curved style and four adjacent stamens of the same shape with anthers hanging on minute stalks from their tips. One pair of stamens is shorter — hence the end of the style (cleft at its end into two stigmas) is located directly in the middle of the stamens. One lobe of the stigma is turned upwards, the other downwards. The insect coming to the flower takes a foothold on the lower labium and inserts its head into the tube, its abdomen sticking vertically upwards. Thus the insect completely fills the space between the two labia and necessarily comes into contact either with the stamen filaments pouring pollen on the upper part of its body, or else presses against the inner arch of the style. This bends downwards and its lower extremity rubs against the insect's body, wiping off the pollen brought from another flower. The Yellow Archangel is a plant of shady forests from lowlands to highlands. It requires an ample amount of nutrients and moist soil.

Lily-of-the-valley *Convallaria majalis* (Liliaceae)   ❹
The rootstock puts forth elliptical, compound leaves which are folded when young. Unilateral racemes with sweet-smelling bell-shaped flowers make their appearance among them in May and subsequently develop into red, globular berries. The whole plant contains poisonous glycosides. It is a typical plant of open deciduous forests and is regarded as an indicator of sites suitable for deciduous trees. Under unfavourable conditions it develops only leaves and no flowers.

112

Deciduous Woods of Lowlands and Hills

Foxglove *Digitalis purpurea* (Scrophulariaceae) ❶

The large lanceolate leaves form a basal rosette from which rises a stem as much as 1 m in height. This bears sessile, ovate-lanceolate leaves giving way to bracts on its upper parts. Showy, solitary, nodding red flowers, darkly spotted inside, start to develop in the bract axils in June. Foxglove prefers places exposed to the sun, mainly clearings, and its leaves and stem are covered with fine hairs to protect the plant from excessive evaporation. The basal leaf rosette is important also: all the rain water flowing down the plant is taken directly to the roots. Foxglove prefers soils rich in nitrogen with favourable humus conditions. The whole plant contains a number of poisonous glycosides used in medicine.

Solomon's Seal *Polygonatum multiflorum* (Liliaceae) ❷

The strong rhizome produces slightly curved, rounded stems up to 1 m in length, overgrown with almost sessile, ovate, entire leaves. 3—5 oblong, tubular, whitish flowers hang from their axils. The flowering period is from May to June, the flowers developing into dark blue berries. It is a plant of shady mixed forests and requires damp soils rich in nutrients. It ranges from lowlands to submontane elevations.

Yellow Balsam, Touch-me-not *Impatiens noli-tangere* (Balsaminaceae) ❸

Yellow Balsam is an annual plant bluish green in colour, covered with a thin layer of wax. Its translucent stem attains a height of as much as 1 m and bears alternate, petiolate, ovoid, serrate leaves. From June to September large, golden-yellow flowers, dotted with red on the inside, may be observed hanging down beneath the leaves. On closer examination the flowers are seen to hang on a stalk growing from the centre of the leaf's midrib. This provides an excellent protection against rain, as the leaf juts out above the flower like a roof. Yellow Balsam has a most interesting fruit — a succulent capsule. After attaining maturity, the capsule carpels burst at the slightest touch and roll backwards; in doing so they strike against the seeds, throwing them a considerable distance. The ejection of the seeds is made possible by the pressure of a sugar solution in the cells. Yellow Balsam occurs from lowlands to mountains on relatively damp soils rich in minerals, and is an indicator of soils suitable for the cultivation of deciduous trees. It is unable to tolerate bright sun and wind.

Pasque Flower *Pulsatilla vulgaris* (Ranunculaceae) ❹

This is a plant of sunny slopes and groves. From March to May its beautiful pale to dark violet flowers, downy on the outside, make their appearance. The most conspicuous part of the flower as regards both size and colour is the calyx, functioning as a lure for insects. In other plants it is usually the corolla (petals) that serves this purpose, while in most cases the calyx is formed by small green sepals situated under the corolla. The petals are here reduced to small, yellow tubes containing nectar and situated inside the calyx. The fruits of the Pasque Flower are also rather extraordinary — they are achenes which have long, hairy tails resembling feathers. The rare Pasque Flower is well adapted to drier localities because its root, as much as 50 cm in length, secures a permanent supply of soil water. Moreover, the entire plant is protected against evaporation by fine hairs. The whole plant is poisonous.

2

4

3

3a

1

Deciduous Woods of Lowlands and Hills

Sessile Oak *Quercus petraea* (Fagaceae) ❶

This is the predominant species of central European oak forests. Its distribution is similar to that of the Pedunculate Oak, but does not extend so far north, neither does it reach the eastern Ukraine where severe winters prevail. The Sessile Oak is an important tree species of hilly and submontane regions, ascending to elevations of 600—700 m. It is a stately tree, 30—35 m in height. Its trunk is straight and long, though not as stout as the Pedunculate Oak. From this it can be distinguished by an attenuate leaf base and a 1—2 cm long petiole. Its acorns, on the contrary, are stalkless and sessile, i. e. closely attached to the twig. In fully stocked stands it starts to bear fruits at about 50 years of age; particularly profuse seed production may be observed at intervals of 3—4 years. The Sessile Oak forms mixed stands mostly with the Hornbeam, and at higher elevations also with birches and pines. Though unable to grow in the shade, this tree species makes no great demands on soil fertility and can even put up with acid soils. Having a deep root system and considerable sprouting capacity, it used to be managed on the coppice system (i. e. stands regenerated from stump sprouts only). It yield wood of first-rare quality with a brown heart; this provides raw material for producing barrels, ships, furniture, and parquet flooring. In the past, the oak was used for an even wider range of purposes. Acorns supplied welcome fodder for swine to feed on in the woods; the bark of young oaks served to obtain tan; oak wood was used to manufacture a wide range of products, and also served as high energy fuel.

Hornbeam *Carpinus betulus* (Corylaceae) ❷

This is the most important tree species accompanying oaks; their life styles complement each other perfectly. The sun-loving oaks occupy the upper canopy, the semitolerant Hornbeam finds the light in the lower canopy sufficient and manages to bloom before the oak flushes. The Hornbeam shades the ground in oak stands, keeping it in good condition thanks to the decomposition of its leaves. Even the root systems of both trees effectively complement each other — the Hornbeam spreads its roots in the upper layers of the soil, while oaks use the lower layers. The Hornbeam is a small tree; the maximum height it attains does not exceed 10—20 m. Its trunk is often crooked and gnarled, and covered with smooth, grey-brown bark until old age. The oblong-ovate leaves are 5—11 cm long and have a serrate margin. They are rounded at the base, light green on the underside, and their stalk is only about 15 mm long. In autumn they turn yellow. The catkins of both male (2a) and female flowers appear at the beginning of May. The fruit is a flat nutlet surrounded by a trilobate bract (2b). The Hornbeam is distributed throughout western, central and southern Europe, extending northwards as far as southern Sweden and Finland. In central Europe it is confined to lowlands and hillsides, ascending to elevations of 600—700 m. It is a shade-tolerant tree making moderate demands on the fertility and humidity of the soil. It has a shallow, flat root system and vigorously spreads from stump sprouts — hence its tolerance of pruning and its use in cultivated hedges. Its hard wood serves as good fuel and is used in model-making and tool production.

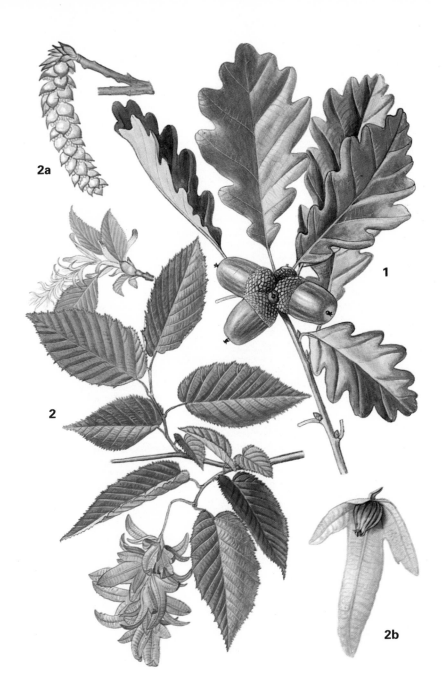

2a

1

2

2b

Deciduous Woods of Lowlands and Hills

Small-leaved Lime   *Tilia cordata*   (Tiliaceae)   ❶

In Europe the Small-leaved Lime inhabits a vast area stretching from England and France across Sweden and Finland as far as the Ural Mountains; southwards it penetrates into the Balkan Peninsula and Asia Minor. In western and southern Europe it occurs in mixed hillside forests, being particularly abundant on screes and rocky slopes. When grown in forest stands it develops a long, smooth trunk with a high set crown, while in the open it has a short, strong trunk with a large, oval crown. As this lime can live for over 1,000 years, there are specimens whose trunks are more than 2 m in diameter. The Small-leaved Lime has cordate leaves 5—9 cm long; their lower surface is greyish-green with rusty hairs in the vein axils. The sweet-smelling flowers are arranged in drooping bunches and open as late as the beginning of July. The fruits are small and round with a leaf-like bract attached to the stalk. Limes are sciophytes making moderate demands on soil fertility and humidity. Their heart-shaped root system penetrates to a great depth, and their capacity to produce suckers is extraordinary. Due to their longevity and large dimensions they were honoured by Slavic nations and planted in sacred groves, in memorable places, at monuments and in avenues. This lime is an important melliferous tree. It yields firm bast fibres used for plaiting various articles, and its soft wood is ideal for woodcarving.

Norway Maple   *Acer platanoides*   (Aceraceae)   ❷

The range of the Norway Maple extends from Norway and France eastwards as far as the river Volga. It forms mixed deciduous stands, occurring most abundantly in valleys alongside brooks and on stony screes. It grows to a height of 25—30 m and develops a straight trunk covered with longitudinally furrowed bark which does not peel in scales as does that of Sycamore. The five-lobed leaves with acuminate lobes are 15—20 cm long, and their stalk exudes a milky sap when broken off. Yellow-green flowers standing in erect umbels appear in April. The fruits are flat, double, and winged, joined at an obtuse angle. Norway Maple is semitolerant of shade and requires relatively fertile, moist soils. Its hard white wood is valued somewhat less than that of the Sycamore.

Field Maple   *Acer campestre*   (Aceraceae)   ❸

This tree is distributed throughout western, central and eastern Europe, especially on lower and warmer hillsides, up to elevations of 500 m. It is commonly found in thermophilic oak forests as well as on dry, warm slopes. It grows to a height of 7—15 m, though on very dry sites often occurs only as a shrub. Such localities are the home of one of its varieties — var. *suberosa* — bearing cork ridges, or lamellae on the twigs. The five-lobed leaves of the Field Maple never exceed 6—9 cm in size, and their lobes are rounded: in autumn they turn golden-yellow. The flowers are arranged in erect umbels and come into bloom in May when the tree has already put forth leaves. In autumn they ripen into double winged seeds, joined in a straight line. The growth rate of the Field Maple is relatively slow, and its trunk is often crooked. Its hard wood is used primarily for working on the lathe.

Twig with an inflorescence (3), twig with fruits — paired winged seeds (3a). *A. campestre* var. *suberosa* — twig with cork lamellae (3b).

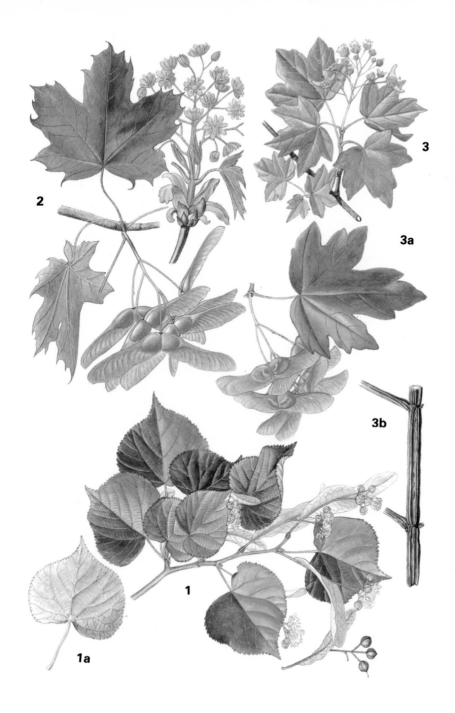

2

3

3a

3b

1

1a

Deciduous Woods of Lowlands and Hills

White Oak   *Quercus pubescens*   (Fagaceae)   ❶

This thermophilic tree is indigenous to southern Europe. It penetrates northwards in warm limestone areas as far as Thuringia, Baden and Bohemia, accompanied by other warmth-loving species — e. g. the Wild Service Tree, the Whitebeam and the Cornelian Cherry. Its height does not exceed 10—15 m and its trunk is usually rather crooked and covered with black, furrowed bark. Its twigs, buds, the underside of leaves and the acorn cup are downy; its leaves and acorns resemble those of the Sessile Oak in shape. The occurrence of this oak species in central Europe is considered a relic of the warmer postglacial period. Its stands are accompanied by a rare thermophilic flora of Mediterranean origin.

Wild Service Tree   *Sorbus torminalis*   (Rosaceae)   ❷

This tree is relatively small, growing to only 10—15 m. It develops an ovoid crown and its trunk is covered with a blackish, scaly bark. Its leaves are 8—12 cm long, each with 5—7 lobes, the last pair of which juts out almost horizontally. Their colour is lustrous dark green above, light green below. The white flowers are borne in broad, erect panicles and open towards the end of May. The fruits are brown, ovoid, berry-like, dotted with yellow and 1—1.5 cm in size. They are edible after exposure to the first frosts. In autumn the leaves turn crimson. The root system of the Wild Service Tree produces far-reaching lateral roots which frequently send out root sprouts. The Wild Service Tree is most abundant on sunny slopes in thermophilic oak forests and prefers calcareous soils. It is distributed throughout southern, western and central Europe, and as far north as Denmark and Pomerania. In hilly regions it grows to an elevation of 600 m and lives for over 100 years. Its wood is one of the hardest: butchers' chopping blocks and various tools used to be made of it.

Cornelian Cherry   *Cornus mas*   (Cornaceae)   ❸

The Cornelian Cherry is a treelike shrub growing to a height of 3—7 m. It has a broom-shaped crown and a trunk covered with yellowish-brown, scaly bark. In winter two kinds of buds may be found on the twigs: lanceolate leaf buds and globular flower buds. The Cornelian Cherry blooms in spring — often as early as March, prior to flushing and is bedecked with clusters of minute yellow flowers. Its leaves are ovate, acuminate, 4—9 cm in length, with an entire margin and four pairs of parallel veins. Cask-like, red, 1.5—2 cm long drupes appear on the shrub in autumn. These are sweet and edible following the first frosts. The Cornelian Cherry is a representative of the Pontic flora and is widespread mainly in southern Europe. In central Europe it has survived in warm limestone areas as a relic of the warm postglacial era. It is a heliophyte tolerant of drought and requires light, humic soil. Its wood is very hard and is used to produce measuring instruments and turned wares.

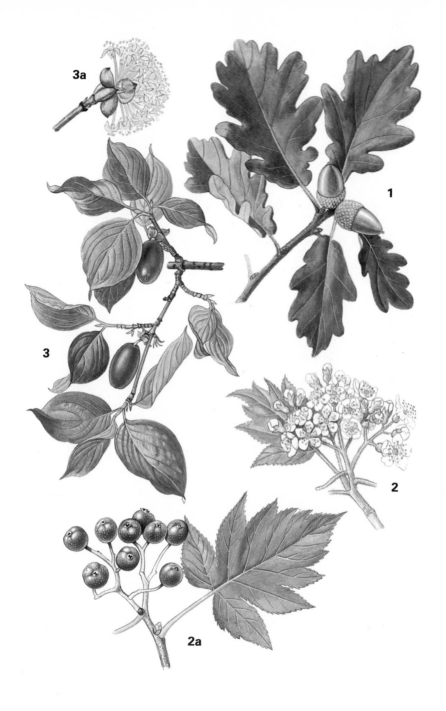

3a

1

3

2

2a

Deciduous Woods of Lowlands and Hills

Aspen *Populus tremula* (Salicaceae)   ❶

The Aspen is distributed all over Europe, penetrating northwards beyond the Arctic Circle and eastwards deep into Siberia. In central and western Europe it grows from lowlands up to elevations over 1,000 m but is most common in the oak forest belt, in stands formerly cultivated on a short rotation where trees were felled at about 40 years of age. The Aspen grows to a height of 20—25 m and develops a thin, high-set crown. The trunk is covered with a smooth greyish-green bark which becomes deeply furrowed and blackish as the tree grows older. The leaves are circular, 3—7 cm long, with a sinuately toothed margin and a long, flattened stalk making them quiver at the slightest breeze. The male and the female flowers are borne separately and appear as early as March, before flushing. The whitish seeds embedded in soft hairs fall from the split capsules as early as the end of May. The Aspen is a heliophyte requiring soils of only average fertility. It is a pioneer tree — its tiny seeds may be carried by the wind for a distance of up to several kilometres, making it possible for them to cover large clear-felled areas. The Aspen has a flat root system spreading up to 10—15 m from the trunk. After clearing the neighbouring area, or after removing the trunk, numerous root sprouts soon appear to fill the cleared space. The Aspen, is a short-lived species, only rarely growing to 100 years. Its wood is light and scissile, hence it is used for producing matches, shingles and cellulose.

Male flowers (1b), female flowers (1a).

Goat Willow, Great Sallow *Salix caprea* (Salicaceae)   ❷

The Goat Willow is the only willow species which not only grows by streams but also commonly occurs in woodland clearings and forest stands. It ranges across the whole of Europe from Norway to the Balkan Peninsula and, in the east, penetrates far into Siberia. It is most abundant in forest glades and clearings which it has occupied as a pioneer species. In western and central Europe it occurs from lowlands to mountain elevations of more than 1,000 m. The Goat Willow tree grows to a height of 5—13 m and develops a large, wiry crown. It lives for only 30—60 years. Its leaves are broadly ovate, 6—10 cm long, with sinuate margins and a grey, downy underside. Its amentaceous flowers — yellow male flowers, greyish-green female ones — bloom in March and are sold as decorative 'pussy willow', the first heralds of spring. Male catkins are shed soon after flowering, female catkins develop into green, ovate capsules. The ripe, downy seeds fall in May and are carried great distances by the wind. The Goat Willow is a light-demanding tree. Its requirements for soil fertility and humidity are not high. It is of significance in forest economy as a tree species which paves the way for the future afforestation of clearings and calamity-stricken areas, where it helps to create adequate conditions for more demanding species. Its flowers provide the first food for bees in spring — hence the virtue in protecting the 'catkins'. In winter, animals like to feed on its twigs and bark.

Male flowers (2b), female flowers (2a), ripe seeds (2c).

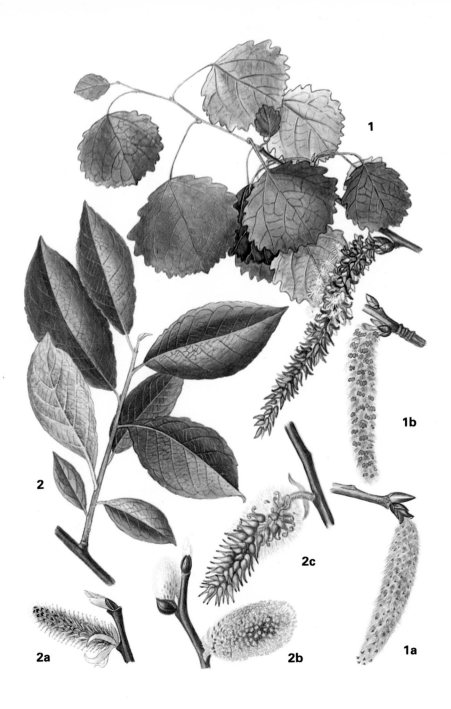

1

1b

2

2c

2a

2b

1a

Deciduous Woods of Lowlands and Hills

Silver Birch, Warty Birch *Betula pendula* (Betulaceae)   ❶

The Silver Birch is distributed over almost the whole of Europe; in the north it reaches beyond the Arctic Circle, in the south it penetrates — at mountain elevations — to Italy and the Balkan Peninsula, and in the east it reaches Siberia. In western and central Europe it grows in both lowlands and mountainous areas up to over 1,500 m. It also occasionally forms pure stands, mostly in northern Europe. It attains a height of 20—25 m and develops a slim trunk bearing a crown with slender, hanging branches. The trunk is covered with an attractive white bark which becomes black and fissured with old age. The Silver Birch has rhombic to triangular leaves, 3—6 cm long, with doubly serrate margins. Flowers are produced in April, simultaneously with the foliage. Minute seeds, or achenes, closely packed in cylindrical cone-like multiple fruits, mature in August and are dispersed great distances by the wind. This fact, together with the modest demands laid by this birch on soil fertility and water content, make it an important pioneer tree, colonizing forest clearings, pastures and fallow ground. It is a light-demanding species, tolerant of both frost and extreme heat. It decorates the forests with its white trunks and fresh green foliage in spring, and with its golden colouration in autumn. Birch sap tapped from holes bored into the trunk is used in cosmetics; young birches provide wickers for brooms; and the hard, flexible wood is highly prized by wheelwrights and joiners.

Male catkin (1a).

Hazel *Corylus avellana* (Betulaceae)   ❷

Hazel occurs over most of Europe, from Spain and Greece northwards as far as Norway and Sweden. In central Europe it grows from the lowlands up to high mountain altitudes, being most plentiful on woodland margins and in clearings, on field margins and in pastures. It particularly favours warm calcareous slopes with plenty of sunshine. The Hazel is a robust, richly-branched shrub, 3—6 m in height. Its leaves are ovate, 7—12 cm long, with a cordate base and a doubly serrate margin. It blooms in early spring — in February or March. The male flowers are carried in pendent catkins, and female flowers have the shape of buds with a number of protruding filiform red stigmas. The pollen of Hazel flowers is one of the first foodstuffs of bees to appear in spring. The fruits are egg-shaped nuts seated within a green bract; they ripen in September and are dispersed by birds and small rodents. Hazel spreads vigorously from suckers and, after the removal of the parent trunk, produces straight and flexible shoots used for making walking sticks. The tasty and nutritious nuts are used in the food industry.

Bud-shaped inflorescences with female flowers (2a), cylindrical male inflorescences — catkins (2b), ripe fruit — nut (2c).

2

2b

2c

1

2a

1

1a

Deciduous Woods of Lowlands and Hills

Dogwood *Cornus sanguinea* (Cornaceae)   ❶

The Dogwood is a shrub widespread throughout Europe, from England across Sweden to the USSR and southwards as far as the Balkan Peninsula. Being shade-tolerant, it forms the shrub layer of riparian and mixed deciduous forests growing in hilly regions. Though it usually favours fresh to moist soils, it may also be found on dry limestone slopes. The Dogwood is a stout, occasionally arborescent shrub, 3−5 m high, with red or green shoots. Its leaves are broadly ovate, 4−8 cm long, with an entire margin and 3−4 pairs of parallel veins. In autumn they become a blood-red colour. White four-petalled flowers arranged in flat-topped cymes appear towards the end of May and mature by the end of September into small, globular, blue-black drupes 6 mm long. The Dogwood possesses an extraordinary capacity to produce shoots from stumps as well as from roots, hence its utility in reinforcing ravines and steep slopes. Its wood is reddish and very hard.

Guelder Rose *Viburnum opulus* (Caprifoliaceae)   ❷

It ranges from England over the whole of Europe eastwards as far as Siberia. In central and western Europe it favours moist localities along brooks and rivers from riparian to submontane forests. Being semishade-tolerant, it also appears in the undergrowth of open deciduous forests. The Guelder Rose is a sparsely branched, 2−4 m high shrub with a yellowish, longitudinally furrowed bark. It has broadly ovate, usually trilobate leaves, 6−9 cm long. Several circular glands are located at the upper end of the petiole. Whitish flowers arranged in broad umbels appear in May and June. Large, sterile flowers are situated along the circumference, while inside the umbel there are smaller flowers which give rise to fruits. These are red, ovoid, 8 mm long drupes containing a flat, pink stone. In the course of ripening, their pulp emits an unpleasant smell. Its full-blooming form is cultivated in parks and gardens. This has globular inflorescences consisting of large, sterile flowers only.

Common Elder *Sambucus nigra* (Caprifoliaceae)   ❸

The Common Elder is widespread over almost all Europe, reaching as far north as Scotland, Norway and Sweden. In western and central Europe it occurs in lowlands and hills up to 600−700 m. It is particularly common in localities rich in humus and is abundant on scrap heaps, in pastures, and in the vicinity of human settlements. Being tolerant of considerable shade, it also appears in the undergrowth of humic forest stands where it is likely to become troublesome. The Common Elder is a large shrub or small tree with a widespreading crown. It may develop a trunk of more than 20 cm in diameter and grow to a height of 10 m. Its odd-pinnate leaves are composed of 5−7 ovate, serrate leaflets. Small white flowers arranged in flat-topped cymes bloom in June and develop by September into black, globular berries 5 mm in size. The berries are eaten by birds and the seeds dispersed in their droppings. Its flowers, fruits and leaves are highly valued as ingredients in herbal medicine.

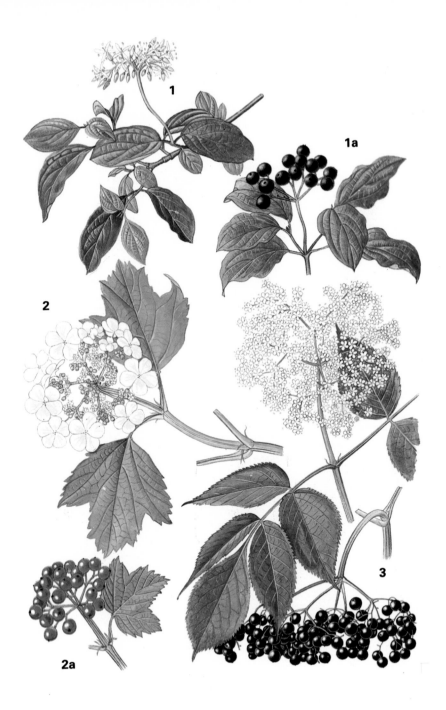

1
1a
2
2a
3

Deciduous Woods of Lowlands and Hills

Blackthorn, Sloe *Prunus spinosa* (Rosaceae) ❶

The range of the Blackthorn includes almost all Europe. Its northern limit coincides with the 68th parallel and in the southeast it reaches to Asia Minor. In central Europe it is most abundant in warm vine-growing regions, forming dense thickets on warm, rocky slopes. It also grows on field and forest margins, as well as on screes. It grows to an elevation of 500−600 m. The Blackthorn is a thickly ramified, thorny shrub attaining a height of 1−5 m. It has oblong-elliptical leaves, 2−5 cm long, with an attenuate base and a serrate margin. The whitish flowers, closely packed on the short and thorny twigs, open in April prior to foliation and remain in bloom for a short time only − the petals are shed very early. The fruits are blackish-blue, pruinose drupes, about 12 mm in size, with an acridly sour taste, but edible when frost-bitten. Because of its densely ramified root system and its capacity to develop root sprouts, the Blackthorn is successfully used for stabilizing stony slopes and afforesting karst areas. Small birds find shelter in its dense, thorny branches. Its flowers, leaves and bark are used in treating various diseases and the fruits to produce wine and liquor.

Privet *Ligustrum vulgare* (Oleaceae) ❷

The Privet is distributed throughout Europe, in the north reaching as far as the shores of the North and the Baltic Seas. It grows from lowlands to elevations of 600−700 m and prefers fertile soils, particularly calcareous ones. It is, however, tolerant of both drier and moister situations. The Privet is a 2−4 m high shrub with drooping branches which take root easily. Its leathery leaves are 3−6 cm long, lanceolate, decussate, with an accuminate apex and an entire margin. Its white tetramerous flowers, densely clustered in upright racemes, appear towards the end of June. The fruits are black, pea-sized berries which ripen in September and remain on the shrub long into winter. Privet stands up well to pruning and is therefore used to form hedgerows of medium height.

Barberry *Berberis vulgaris* (Berberidaceae) ❸

The common Barberry is a warmth-loving shrub indigenous to southern, western and central Europe. It is most commonly found on stony, sunny slopes on forest margins, and on calcareous substrates. It is a light-demanding, drought-resistant shrub. Being a host of a dangerous corn disease, *Puccinia graminis,* it is extremely unwelcome in the vicinity of fields and is eradicated if found there. Barberry is a thorny shrub, 1−2 m high, with upright branches. Its oblong-ovate leaves with serrate, spiny margins, 3−5 cm in size, are piled up in clusters. The yellow flowers open in May and hang down in drooping racemes. The fruits are bright red, oblong berries, 8−13 mm in size and ripen in September. Its wood and roots are lemon yellow.

Deciduous Woods of Lowlands and Hills

Purple Emperor *Apatura iris* (Nymphalidae)

A skilled and nimble flier, the Purple Emperor has a wingspan of 65 mm. It frequents forest footpaths and likes to settle on them after rain, drinking the water. It also has a predilection for the margin of the forest and basks on the bark of the trees in the morning sunshine. It is a very timid butterfly and the slightest disturbance sends it flying up to the top of the tree. The females spend most of their time in the crowns of the trees and come down to the lower layers only to lay their eggs. Only the males have the magnificent blue sheen on the upper surface of their wings. In June, the female lays its olive-green or yellowish eggs on the leaves of Goat Willows. The ochre-brown caterpillars, which are hatched in August, grow slowly and moult only once before the autumn. They hibernate in the branches of the Goat Willow and continue their development in the spring. After their second moult they are green and carry two conspicuous horns on their heads. In their last stage they measure about 6 cm and resemble slugs, both in form and in the slowness of their movements. They pupate in the middle of June, in a pendant chrysalis with a characteristic, sharp dorsal ridge. This butterfly occurs sporadically in Spain and eastwards across the Pyrenees and central Europe. In Great Britain it is found only in the south. It is absent from Scandinavia and southern Europe (Italy, the Balkans). In the Carpathians it is found at altitudes of up to 1,200 metres.

Silver-washed Fritillary *Argynnis paphia* (Nymphalidae)

This butterfly is a typical denizen of the forest and is locally fairly abundant. It is a striking species, with a wingspan of about 60 mm, and flies across glades, footpaths and clearings like lightning. The female lays its eggs in the bark of spruce and pine trunks. The caterpillars are to be found on violets, on whose leaves they feed; they also hibernate there to pupate in the following spring. The Silver-washed Fritillary occurs from western Europe as far as Japan: it is absent in northern England, Crete, Cyprus and the north of Scandinavia.

Mottled Umber *Erannis defoliaria* (Geometridae)

This is one of the commonest moths in lowland woods in the autumn. The male has a wingspan of about 40 mm. Its colouring makes it virtually invisible, especially amongst fallen leaves. The females are wingless and look rather like pale grey, black-spotted spiders. The orange-red eggs are laid in small groups near buds. In the spring, the caterpillars live on the leaves of a variety of deciduous trees, particularly oaks. The chrysalis lies in a loose cocoon in the ground. This moth, which is a serious pest of deciduous trees, is distributed from northern Italy to Scandinavia and also occurs in Transcaucasia.

Lime Hawk *Mimas tiliae* (Sphingidae)

This moderately large moth (wingspan 50—75 mm) has greenish to ochre forewings and yellowish hindwings: the trailing edge of the forewings is crenate. It can be seen during the day from the end of April to the end of June, in the undergrowth or on the bark of trees. From the outset the caterpillars are green with white spots, marked with oblique white stripes and with a bluish spine on their body. They live on the leaves of lime (and occasionally cherry) trees. The caterpillar pupates in the ground, forming a dull, black-brown chrysalis. The moth is distributed over the whole of Europe.

Deciduous Woods of Lowlands and Hills

Buff-tip *Phalera bucephala* (Notodontidae)
The Buff-tip is a moderately large (wingspan up to 60 mm), strikingly marked and very common moth. Its forewings have a silvery-grey sheen, toned to brown along their anterior margin, where they have a characteristic yellow spot in the outer corner. As well as being retiring by nature, the moth is also well concealed by its colouring. It flies from May to August. The female lays her neat hemispherical eggs on the underside of leaves, to which they are attached in groups by their flat, black side, while their bulging part is white, with a black spot. After hatching, the caterpillars remain together until the penultimate stage of their development. They live mainly on lime, willow, poplar, oak, birch and sometimes alder leaves. When resting, the yellow- and black-striped caterpillars, which are covered with fine hairs, raise their stern in the air. They have a black head marked with a spot like an inverted 'Y'. The fully grown caterpillars are about 60—70 mm long and after roaming about for a short time they burrow in the ground, turn into dark brown, shiny chrysalises and hibernate in this form. This moth is distributed over the greater part of Europe, Asia Minor, Siberia and northeastern Africa.

Gypsy Moth *Lymantria dispar* (Lymantriidae)
This species frequents woods and orchards. The females (wingspan up to 70 mm), are creamy white, with dark ripple marks and black spots, including a characteristic L-shaped spot, and are larger than the males (wingspan about 45 mm), which are brown. The males have extremely feathery antennae, a much slimmer body than the females, and are much better fliers. The females hardly fly at all and remain clinging to tree trunks. These moths are active during the daytime, most so at about 2 p.m. At this time the maximum secretion of pheromone occurs, a substance produced by the females, which attracts and guides the males to them. The fertilized females lay hundreds of eggs on the bark of trees, usually near the base of the trunk and cover them with hairs from their abdomen. The caterpillars hatch the following spring. They have a voracious appetite and are polyphagous, that is to say, they can live on a great many (about 500) types of plants. In the forest they mainly attack oaks, limes, willows and poplars. They pupate in a cocoon on the bark of trees and the moths emerge after about 10—14 days. This moth is distributed over the greater part of Europe, Transcaucasia, Asia Minor, the Near and Middle East, Siberia, China, Japan and north Africa. In 1969 it was inadvertently introduced into the USA (Massachusetts), where it has already become a serious forest pest.

Speckled Wood *Pararge aegeria* (Satyridae)
This inconspicuously coloured and shy butterfly is surprisingly common in gloomy woods with little sunlight, where the only undergrowth are the grasses on which the caterpillars live. It is distributed throughout the whole of Europe and produces two generations each year (from April to June and July to September). Quite often, in the foothills of mountains, it is to be found at relatively high altitudes (e. g. 1,200 m). It hibernates in the chrysalis stage, frequently at the foot of a tree.

Oak Gall-wasp, Marble Gall *Andricus kollari* (Cynipidae)
The imago is a small black-brown wasp, 3.5 mm long, which bores holes in thin oak twigs and then lays a single egg in each. The presence of the larva leads to the growth of an excrescence, commonly known as an oak-apple or marble-gall, which matures and turns woody at the end of the summer. The larva pupates in the gall and leaves it the following year as an adult gall-wasp. This insect occurs mainly in Europe.

Deciduous Woods of Lowlands and Hills

Blue Ground Beetle *Carabus intricatus* (Carabidae)

The beetle measures 23—30 mm. Like other members of the genus *Carabus* it is flightless and appears in a variety of forms, as it inhabits relatively restricted areas. It is also — again like the others — a nocturnal beetle and preys on small insects. The larva is likewise predacious. Since it helps to maintain biological balance in nature, it is an important beetle. It occurs primarily in central and northern Europe.

Plagionotus arcuatus (Cerambycidae)

This beetle looks and behaves like a wasp. It is 15—20 mm long, black, marked with curved yellow bands, and its antennae are barely more than half the length of its wing-case. The beetles are usually to be seen from the middle of May to the middle of June. They are fully active in sunny weather, when they fly and run nimbly, with jerky movements, over felled timber. The fertilized females prefer to lay their eggs on oak logs, but are also satisfied with stacked wood and timber lying in the sunshine. The young larvae first of all gnaw their way into the bast and form winding tunnels which often go down into the wood. At the end of the summer they tunnel deeper into the wood forming straight passages about 10—15 cm long, terminating in a curved chamber in which they pupate. The fully grown larva measures about 40 mm. There is one generation a year and the following spring the beetle leaves the chamber through an oval exit. It is a forest pest, not only distributed throughout Europe, but also in the Caucasus, Asia Minor and northern Africa.

Common Cockchafer, Maybug *Melolontha melolontha* (Scarabaeidae)

The ground colour of this moderately large beetle (length 23—31 mm) is black, while its antennae, legs, wing-cases and the last segment of its abdomen are light brown. The beetles emerge at the end of the summer from pupae lying in the ground, hibernate over winter and then swarm in the second half of April and in May. They fly in the evening on the outskirts of deciduous woods and mate while eating. The fertilized females seek out open spaces with only a sparse covering of plants and with warm, sunlit soil. Here they burrow to a depth of 10—40 cm, lay some 10—30 eggs and return to continue their meal. In all, they lay three batches of eggs. At first, the larvae feed on the humus in the soil, but later they gnaw at roots. In central Europe their development takes 4 years, but in southern Europe only 3. There are three stages; the larva moults twice and after a third moult, it pupates. The larvae are fat and white and only their head is brown. The protracted development of Cockchafers means that their numbers peak every 3—4 years. Not only do they eat away the roots of plants, but the imagos strip the trees of their leaves. The Common Cockchafer occurs throughout the whole of Europe, except in its most northerly parts.

Rose Chafer *Potosia cuprea* (Scarabaeidae)

This green or copper-coloured chafer measures 14—23 mm and is of interest because the larvae develop in the nests of the ant *Formica rufa*. The beetles swarm in May and June, when they alight on flowers and on trees with damaged bark. This species is to be found in Europe and Asia.

Deciduous Woods of Lowlands and Hills

Wood Pigeon *Columba palumbus* (Columbidae)

The Wood Pigeon nests in practically every hardwood, conifer and mixed forest in Europe. Its loose, untidy nest is built on a tree or tall bush. As a rule, it has two young, two or three times a year, which the parents both feed for 3—4 weeks inside the nest and then for about a week outside. It lives on seeds, grain and sometimes worms and insects. In flight, the Wood Pigeon can easily be recognized by the white marks at the angle of its wings. It is hunted in most countries in Europe.

Stock Dove *Columba oenas* (Columbidae)

This bird is smaller than the Wood Pigeon, has no white marks on its wings and has quite different habits. It nests solely in holes, such as those in deciduous trees or in large nesting boxes. The two white eggs are incubated by both the parents in turn for about 18 days. At first the chicks are fed on a milky substance produced in the parents' crop, and later on pre-digested seeds and berries. When the young leave the nest, about a month after hatching, the adult birds usually nest again. Like the Wood Pigeon, the Stock Dove is distributed over the whole of Europe: in the warmer parts it is a resident bird, but those breeding in central and northern Europe migrate south-west and to the Mediterranean region in September, usually returning in the early spring. Like the Wood Pigeon the Stock Dove is hunted and in some areas it is already rare because it is unable to find sufficient suitable sites in which to nest.

Turtle Dove *Streptopelia turtur* (Columbidae)

The Turtle Dove occurs over the whole of Europe except northern Scandinavia. In appearance it resembles a small, dainty domestic pigeon. From the end of April, when it returns from its winter haunts in north Africa and the Mediterranean region, it can be seen in any hardwood or mixed forest in lowlands or uplands. Its nest is an untidy tangle of a few twigs and both the parent birds take turns to incubate the 2 white eggs for 14 days. After the young leave the nest, the adult birds breed again. The Turtle Dove lives mainly on seeds, cereals and berries. A few decades ago, the Collared Dove *(S. decaocto)* spread right across Europe from the Balkans. In contrast to the Turtle Dove, this species has a black band across the nape: it also remains in Europe over the winter and lives mainly in parks and large gardens and on the outskirts of small woods.

Common or Ring-necked Pheasant *Phasianus colchicus* (Phasianidae)

Originally a native of inner and eastern Asia, the Common Pheasant was introduced into Europe artificially — first into the south and west, and in the 14th century into central Europe. At first it was kept in preserves, but later became established in the wild. The original dark form was crossed with other imported species and today virtually all wild specimens are hybrids. The male pheasant is very brightly coloured: the female is greyish-brown and spotted. Mating generally takes place in May, when each cock gathers a harem of 3—5 hens. The hens lay 10—15 greyish-brown eggs in a nest on the ground and incubate them for about 25 days. The chicks, which hatch in late May, immediately run hither and thither round the hen; they live on insects and worms, and later on seeds and berries. Pheasants chiefly inhabit the margin of forests, thickets, dense vegetation beside ponds, wooded slopes and copses, where they roost in trees. The Common Pheasant is very useful because it destroys insect pests, while its tasty flesh has made it the most popular gamebird in Europe.

Deciduous Woods of Lowlands and Hills

Green Woodpecker   *Picus viridis*   (Picidae)

If, in a hardwood or mixed forest, you catch sight of a green, red-capped bird about the size of a small pigeon, which flies to the foot of a tree and then quickly climbs up it, it will most certainly be a Green Woodpecker, a bird which inhabits the whole of Europe, except the most northerly parts of Scandinavia, Scotland and Ireland. It is a resident bird, since it can always be sure of finding its main food (insects living behind bark and ants) even in the winter; it actually hunts for ants deep into their anthill. It nests in May in hollows, which both birds excavate in turn, in partly rotting trees. The 5—7 slightly greenish eggs are laid on the floor of the pear-shaped cavity and are incubated for 17 days by both birds in turn. The young leave the nest when 3 weeks old, but still return to sleep there for a few days afterwards.

Middle Spotted Woodpecker   *Dendrocopus medius*   (Picidae)

This bird is a typical inhabitant of hardwood forests in plains and gentle uplands throughout the whole of Europe except northern Scandinavia and England. Since its beak is thinner and weaker than that of other woodpeckers it uses nests abandoned by them, or builds its own in trees already hollow. The 5—6 white eggs are laid at the beginning of May, the young hatch after about 15 days and both parents feed them on the larvae of insects found behind the bark. It is not a migrant, but roams the countryside looking behind bark for hibernating insects and insect eggs. The closely related Lesser Spotted Woodpecker *(D. minor)* inhabits hardwood and mixed forests all over Europe and in Algeria. It often appears in parks, gardens and small copses.

Wryneck   *Jynx torquilla*   (Picidae)

It is hard to believe that this grey-brown, inconspicuous bird only slightly larger than a sparrow belongs to the woodpecker family. It seldom climbs trees, although its feet are adapted for climbing, i.e. two toes point forwards and two backwards. It lives on insects which it catches on the bark and twigs. It never pecks at trees, but often rakes open anthills to catch ants and ant pupae on its long, extensible tongue. These also form the main diet of its young, up to 10 in number. These hatch from white, almost spherical eggs after 14 days and are fed by the parents for almost 4 weeks. Wrynecks also often nest in nestboxes and are not above ejecting the original occupants. They inhabit light deciduous and mixed woods, gardens and parks over the whole of Europe except in the most northerly regions. From September to the middle of April they migrate to the northern half of Africa.

Pied Flycatcher   *Muscicapa hypoleuca*   (Muscicapidae)

In April, a striking black and white bird a little smaller than a sparrow appears in deciduous woods, orchards and parks all over Europe and western Asia. It is the male of the Pied Flycatcher returning from its winter haunts in the northern half of Africa. This bird nests in tree hollows or nestboxes, where the plain brown female lays 6—8 greenish-blue eggs and incubates them unaided for 14 days. Both parents feed the young in the nest for about 14 days and then for a similar period outside it. Pied Flycatchers live on small insects, which they cleverly catch in the air, or on small caterpillars and spiders. They migrate from Europe at the end of September. The Collared Flycatcher *(M. albicollis)* has very similar colouring and habits, but has a white band round its neck.

Deciduous Woods of Lowlands and Hills

Icterine Warbler   *Hippolais icterina*   (Sylviidae)

If, somewhere between the middle of May and the end of August, in a deciduous wood, a luxuriant garden or a park, you see a bird with a yellowish-green back and a yellow belly, singing merrily to itself and imitating the notes of various other birds, you have probably glimpsed an Icterine Warbler. This bird lives throughout central and eastern Europe and in eastern France and Norway to the west, but is absent from England, Sweden and Finland. It nests in a fork of a thick branch of a deciduous tree at a height of about 3 metres, and the deep, cupped nest made of stalks and leaves is masked from the outside by slivers of bark (usually birch). The 5—6 rose-pink, black-spotted eggs are incubated mainly by the female, which sits on them for about 13 days. Both parents feed the young with caterpillars, flies, aphids and other small insects, which also form the main component of the adults' diet. They winter in central and sometimes in southern Africa.

Wood Warbler   *Phylloscopus sibilatrix*   (Sylviidae)

Lowland hardwood forests and upland mixed forests over the whole of Europe except the Iberian Peninsula and northern Scandinavia are the home of this tiny bird with its greyish-green back. It always nests on the ground, in thick grass, where the female builds a relatively large nest of grass blades with a side opening. Up to 7 white eggs, densely covered with brown spots, are laid in May and are incubated for 12—13 days by the female. Both parents feed the young for about 2 weeks on insects (particularly larvae). The Wood Warbler nests only once a year and as early as the end of August leaves for tropical Africa, where it remains until the end of April. The Chiffchaff *(P. collybita)* and the Willow Warbler *(P. trochilus)* are similarly coloured and have similar habits; they are both distributed over the whole of Europe. Bonelli's Warbler *(P. bonelli)* inhabits western and southern Europe, where it occurs chiefly in mountain forests.

Nightingale   *Luscinia megarhynchos*   (Turdidae)

From the middle of April, damp deciduous woods, gardens and thickets in the vicinity of rivers and streams, ring with the melodious song of male Nightingales; they have arrived from tropical Africa and are calling to the females, which return after them. They sing mainly at night, but at mating time can often be heard during the daytime as well. They nest throughout the whole of Europe with the exception of Scandinavia. The nest, woven of grass and dry leaves, is built close to the ground or under dense shrubs. The female incubates 6 brownish green eggs for about 2 weeks. Both parents feed the young for 11—12 days on small insects, larvae, spiders and small caterpillars. The young leave the nest before they are able to fly and the parents continue to feed them outside it. The Nightingale leaves the European lowlands at the end of August, bound for Africa once again.

Short-toed Treecreeper   *Certhia brachydactyla*   (Certhiidae)

Mixed and deciduous woods, gardens and parks in central, western and southern Europe and the northern margin of Africa are inhabited by this small, but very useful bird. It is mostly to be encountered on tree trunks, which it climbs with amazing agility, searching cracks in the bark with its long, slightly curved beak for moths' and butterflies' eggs, larvae and insects. It builds its nest in any convenient hole. The 6—7 white, red-spotted eggs are laid in the second half of April. The young, which hatch after 14 days, are fed by both parents for 15—16 days on various insects. The adult birds nest again in June, but this time have only 3—4 young. The Short-toed Treecreeper is a resident bird.

Deciduous Woods of Lowlands and Hills

Great Tit   *Parus major*   (Paridae)

This is one of the best-known and commonest of the tits. It inhabits the whole of Europe and Asia far to the north. It is a sedentary bird and can be found practically everywhere, from lowlands to uplands (where it is most abundant) and high up in the mountains, in hardwood and mixed forests, and even in spruce monocultures, gardens and parks. In the winter it joins other tits, Nuthatches and treecreepers in small flocks which roam about the countryside. It nests twice a year in tree hollows, walls and nestboxes, where it makes a nest of moss lined with animal hairs. The first clutch usually comprises 8—12 white eggs densely spotted with brown, the second clutch only 4—6. The young, which hatch after 14 days, are fed on insects by both parents. In the nesting season and during the winter, Great Tits consume large quantities of bark insects and their larvae, caterpillars, aphids and spiders. They are regarded as one of the most useful birds.

Blue Tit   *Parus caeruleus*   (Paridae)

In superficial appearance and habits the Blue Tit resembles its larger cousin, the Great Tit. It occurs all over Europe with the exception of northern Scandinavia, and is found in northern Africa and eastwards as far as the Urals. It chiefly inhabits open deciduous and mixed woods and gardens and parks in lowland regions, but is frequently to be seen in the mountains. It likewise nests in hollows and nestboxes. In May it has up to 14 young, but its second brood in June is substantially smaller. The female does not begin to brood until the clutch is almost complete and incubates the eggs for 14 days. Both parents tend the young carefully for 2—3 weeks and feed them on all kinds of caterpillars, spiders, aphids and the larvae of bark insects.

Marsh Tit   *Parus palustris*   (Paridae)

This tiny tit with a characteristic black cap and bib, occurs the whole year round in deciduous and mixed woods all over Europe, from southern Scandinavia to the Mediterranean: it is also common in parks and gardens. It nests once a year in holes in trees and tree stumps and in nestboxes, where the female lays 7—10 white eggs, which have red spots at their blunt end, in a nest made of moss, lichen, rootlets and hair. The young hatch after 14 days and are fed by both parents on various insects for just under 3 weeks, until they leave the nest. In the winter, small flocks of Marsh Tits fly about the contryside, living on whatever seeds they can find.

Long-tailed Tit   *Aegithalos caudatus*   (Aegithalidae)

The Long-tailed Tit inhabits the whole of Europe except the most northerly parts of Scandinavia. With its black and white colouring, long tail and different habits it is hardly like a tit at all. It nests in deciduous woods, parks and gardens, but never in holes. Its ovoid nest, which is up to 20 cm high with an entrance in the side, is built by the female in the branches of a tree, beside the trunk or sometimes in a bush. It is made of moss, lichen, cobwebs and fragments of bark and twigs and is well camouflaged. Up to 12 white, red-spotted eggs are laid at the beginning of April and are incubated by the female for just under 2 weeks. Both parents feed the offspring on small insects for 15—18 days. The adult birds live chiefly on small insects and their larvae, which they also manage to find in the winter.

Deciduous Woods of Lowlands and Hills

Hawfinch *Coccothraustes coccothraustes* (Fringillidae)

In deciduous woods, gardens, parks and cherry orchards we may, on rare occasions, catch a glimpse of a bird about the size of a starling, with a large head and a thick, conical beak. This very retiring bird, the Hawfinch, lives mainly on fruit-stone kernels and other seeds. It nests once a year at the beginning of May, and the 4—6 bluish, grey- and black-spotted eggs are laid in a loosely woven twig nest lined with rootlets and hairs, built at a height of about 10 m from the ground. The white, downy young hatch after about 14 days and for the first few days the parents feed them on insects. The Hawfinch is distributed over large areas of Europe, Asia and northwestern Africa. Birds living in central and eastern Europe migrate westwards in September and their place is taken by birds from more northerly regions.

Yellowhammer *Emberiza citrinella* (Emberizidae)

The Yellowhammer lives in copses and on the outskirts of mixed and deciduous woods, in lowlands and uplands, throughout the whole of Europe except in the most southerly parts bordering the Mediterranean. This common yellowish-green songbird, a little larger than a sparrow, can be seen the whole year round. The nest, which is usually built on the ground, under a clump of grass or a low bush, is made of grass, thin twigs and leaves and is always lined with horsehair and grass blades. By the end of April it contains 3—5 greenish eggs marked with black scribbles. The young, which hatch after 14 days, are fed by both parents on small insects, spiders and worms for about 2 weeks. At the end of June the adult birds nest again, but this time have fewer young. They live mainly on the seeds of various weeds and on cereals.

Starling *Sturnus vulgaris* (Sturnidae)

The Starling is one of the commonest and most familiar birds in the whole of Europe. It inhabits deciduous and mixed woods, where it nests in holes in trees, but it readily accepts nestboxes hung outside houses. Central European Starlings often return from their winter haunts in the Mediterranean region and northern Africa at the end of February and immediately look for a convenient place in which to nest. The nest is made of twigs, rootlets and dry grass and the 4—6 light blue eggs, which are laid in April, are incubated for about 2 weeks by both the parents in turn. The parents feed the young for about 3 weeks inside the nest and then for a few days more outside it. Starlings usually nest a second time in June. The adult birds live partly on insects, larvae and worms, especially in the nesting season, and later on berries and seeds. They may do considerable damage in cherry orchards and vineyards. They migrate southwards in September.

Jackdaw *Corvus monedula* (Corvidae)

Church towers and ruined castles are the favourite haunts of Jackdaws, which nest there in colonies, although they also often nest in deciduous trees and rock crevices. The tall nest, which is built in April, is made of interwoven twigs and lined with straw, hay, hairs and feathers. The 4—6 greenish, grey-spotted eggs are laid in May and the female usually incubates them unaided for just under 3 weeks. Together with the male, she feeds the chicks for a whole month on insects, worms and sometimes frogs. In addition to insects and small vertebrates, the adults live on seeds, grain and various berries. Occasionally they attack the young of small birds or steal their eggs. The Jackdaw is a resident bird, except for its most northerly populations, which migrate to central and western Europe in the winter.

Deciduous Woods of Lowlands and Hills

Common Shrew *Sorex araneus* (Soricidae)

The Common Shrew occurs all over Europe and Asia, at all altitudes, beside water and in meadows, having a predilection for damp spots in deciduous and mixed woods. It is a useful animal, since it lives mainly on insects, slugs, snails and spiders. It can be distinguished from the mice by its tapering snout and short legs. Its many natural enemies include owls, birds of prey and small mammalian predators. The Common Shrew generally settles in mouse holes, where it makes a warm nest lined with moss, grass and leaves. Its 5—8 young are blind for almost 3 weeks and do not eat flesh until their eyes open. This useful animal deserves every protection.

Water Shrew *Neomys fodiens* (Soricidae)

This animal lives near water in deciduous and mixed woods throughout the whole of Europe and northern Asia. In contrast to the brown Common Shrew it has a black coat; it is also larger (it measures up to 10 cm) and has different habits, living solely beside streams, small rivers and stagnant water. Much of its food comes from the water, since it lives on aquatic insects, newts, worms and small fish, as well as young birds and small mammals. In fact, it will eat anything and no aquatic animal is safe from it. It lives in burrows dug in the soft earth at the water's edge. Its 5—8 young are born blind and do not open their eyes until about 3 weeks old. When they leave the nest they immediately take to the water; they are proficient swimmers and divers and when chasing prey can remain submerged for a considerable time.

Muskrat *Ondatra zibethicus* (Microtidae)

The Muskrats distributed today over practically the whole of Europe and northern Asia, are the offspring of a few pairs released in central Bohemia in 1905 and of further animals introduced elsewhere at later dates. The Muskrat lives beside stagnant and flowing water thickly bordered by rushes and other aquatic plants, whose roots and stems form its staple diet. It also builds tall rush nests in the water, in which it lives mostly during the winter. In summer it prefers tunnels, several metres long, which it digs beside ponds and where, in a nest chamber, it rears 5—10 young up to four times each year. The Muskrat multiplies relatively quickly, and remains quite common despite the price of its very valuable coat (musquash). Although a pest — it damages the dams and embankments of small reservoirs and destroys the nests of aquatic birds (when it occasionally breaks its vegetarian diet) — it deserves to be protected, at least during the breeding season.

Otter *Lutra lutra* (Mustelidae)

Few people can boast of having seen an Otter — one of the largest mustelid beasts of prey in Europe — near a stream or small river with overgrown banks. Two factors contribute to this: first, Otters are very cautious and timid and second, in many places they are already very rare. Fishermen persecute them because of their mainly fish diet, although they also eat frogs, small mammals and birds. The lair, or holt, excavated in the river bank, opens below the surface of the water. The 2—4 young do not open their eyes for 4—5 weeks and only after 2 years are they fully grown. The Otter is a skilled swimmer and perfect diver. Since it mostly catches weak and sick fish, and is in danger of dying out in Europe, Asia and North America, it ought to be afforded every protection.

Deciduous Woods of Lowlands and Hills

European Hedgehog   *Erinaceus europaeus*   (Erinaceidae)

The Hedgehog is to be found almost anywhere in Europe, except high up in the mountains and in the northern parts of Scandinavia. Its favourite haunts are thick vegetation on the outskirts of deciduous woods, parks, gardens and bushy hillsides, where it builds a nest lined with moss and dry grass in the shelter of a dense bush or in a pile of old leaves. In June, after a 5−6 week pregnancy, the female usually gives birth to 5−10 young. The young are blind and at first have fine white spines, but these soon turn brown. The Hedgehog is omnivorous and hunts for worms, insects, larvae and even mice, lizards and snakes: occasionally it manages to catch an Adder. Its destruction of insects makes it very useful, but in pheasant preserves it can do considerable damage among the eggs and chicks. At the end of October it retires to its den, its body temperature drops markedly, and it spends the winter hibernating, without eating. Apart from in pheasant preserves it should be protected everywhere.

Brown Hare   *Lepus europaeus*   (Leporidae)

The Brown Hare, which is an important game animal in Europe and weighs 3.5−4 kg, is distributed over the whole of the continent from southern Scandinavia to western Siberia. Its largest populations occur in fertile lowlands and its numbers diminish at increasing altitudes. It occurs mainly in fields and at the margins of forests, and lives on grass, clover, Lucerne and (in forests) on the buds and shoots of bushes and trees, especially Aspen, Goat Willow and acacias. Since it has many predators, it does not come out to graze until after dusk or at night. Even where Hares occur in large numbers, the damage they do in the fields and woods is negligible. They breed the whole year round, except in October and November. Since the female produces 2−5 young three or four times a year (the gestation period is 6 weeks), they are common from March to September. The young, which lie in a nest on the open ground, are able to see at birth. In the winter, when they cannot scratch in the hard, frozen ground, foresters and hunters have to feed them, as otherwise they would eat the bark of deciduous trees and severely damage them.

Red Squirrel   *Sciurus vulgaris*   (Sciuridae)

This squirrel's habits confine it to woods and large parks, since it spends the greater part of its life in the trees, looking for food such as tree (especially spruce) seeds, buds, insects and young birds. After a 5 week pregnancy, the female gives birth to an average of 4−5 young, once to three times a year. For 4 weeks the young are blind and for the whole of that time the female suckles them. The nest is made of branches and is built in the crown of a tree, sometimes in an old nest abandoned by jays or by birds of prey. The Red Squirrel is distributed over the whole of Europe and northern Asia, from the lowlands to high up in the mountains. Its colour varies from a rusty yellowish-red to almost black: those living further east are lighter and greyish in colour.

Edible Dormouse   *Glis glis*   (Gliridae)

The Edible Dormouse is fairly abundant in deciduous woods and large parks and gardens in the uplands of southern and central Europe. It is a nocturnal animal and lives on various fruits, birds' eggs and insects, and in the spring on buds and shoots. In August it gives birth to an average of 4 young. The nest is built in a hole in a tree or on the branches, and here it hibernates, without eating, in a snug bed of leaves and moss.

Deciduous Woods of Lowlands and Hills

Common Dormouse   *Muscardinus avellanarius*   (Gliridae)
This relatively abundant, light yellowish-brown dormouse, is about the size of a House Mouse and inhabits the whole of Europe except the most northerly and southerly parts. It is a nocturnal animal and begins to look for its food — which comprises seeds (particularly acorns and beechnuts), wild strawberries, bilberries and other forest fruits — in the evening. It hibernates in a nest under dry leaves. For its young it sometimes builds a nest in a bush, just above the ground. Twice a year (in June and August) the female gives birth, usually to four young, which do not open their eyes for over 2 weeks. The Common Dormouse lives in the brushwood layer of deciduous and mixed forests at all altitudes; it is also a common inhabitant of large gardens and parks.

Yellow-necked Field Mouse   *Apodemus flavicollis*   (Muridae)
This mouse occurs in every large, shady hardwood and mixed forest, over the whole of Europe and Asia. It likes dense undergrowth, where it builds a nest between the roots of trees, in holes, in piles of stones and sometimes high up in the foliage. It breeds several times each year, often starting early in the spring, and has 4—8 young in each litter. Tree seeds (acorns, beechnuts and conifer seeds) and, on the outskirts of the forest, cereals, form the bulk of its diet. It is therefore a nuisance and in years when it is numerous causes considerable seed losses. It can be distinguished from the House Mouse by its greater size, its tail (which is the same length as its body) and its large black eyes. Despite its many predators, it is abundant in forests everywhere, since it reproduces relatively quickly and is always able to find enough food.

Bank Vole   *Clethrionomys glareolus*   (Cricetidae)
The Bank Vole is to be found at all altitudes, but is commonest in deciduous upland forests, where there is the biggest supply of the many seeds and insects on which it lives. In the winter it often gnaws the branches of young trees. It builds its nests in a hole just below the surface of the ground and, each year, produces up to five litters of 4—6 young. The young are blind for about 14 days, but after 3 weeks, become independent and leave the nest. The Bank Vole is easily distinguished from other voles by its rusty coat and longer tail. It also differs in habits from the Common Vole, which occurs mainly in fields and eats cereals and the seeds of weeds. All voles are important pests, both in agriculture and in forestry.

Large Mouse-eared Bat   *Myotis myotis*   (Vespertilionidae)
If we glimpse a silent shadow flitting swiftly across the evening sky in an almost straight line, in all probability it will be a Large Mouse-eared Bat, one of the commonest members of the bat family, whose approximately 270 species are distributed all over the world. Bats are a specialized group of mammals, as a thin, wing-like membrane stretched between their body and limbs enables them to fly. They live on insects, which they hunt at night and catch only on the wing. During the day they sleep in caves, towers and attics, and sometimes in cellars and holes in trees. They also hibernate in these places, hanging head down, suspended by their hind claws. Whole colonies numbering hundreds of bats often hibernate together in a cave or a barn. This species inhabits the whole of central and eastern Europe, where it is commoner than in western Europe. It is a very useful animal, as it destroys many insect pests.

Submontane mixed forests

This type of forest community is to be found on uplands and the lower slopes of mountains, i. e. at altitudes of about 550 to 700 metres, in places with an average annual rainfall of up to 900 mm. The characteristic trees of these regions are mainly the Beech *(Fagus sylvatica)*, followed by firs and, at high altitudes, spruces.

The Beech was the last tree to spread to central Europe during the postglacial period and it began to assert itself immediately, ousting all other trees except the firs. Although beechwoods are the characteristic submontane forest, they are distributed over a wide range of altitudes. In the Mediterranean region they occur only at high altitudes, whereas in southern Scandinavia — their most northerly occurrence — they also descend to the plains. In general, beechwoods need a damp climate with a seasonally distributed rainfall, but a comparatively dry, rich soil. Of all European forest communities, seasonal changes are most striking in beech forests. In the spring, before the trees start to bud, the soil is easily reached by the sun's rays, and since it is covered with dry leaves its surface soon warms and the ground vegetation grows. Consequently, beechwoods usually have a striking array of spring plants, such as the Primrose *(Primula vulgaris)*, the wild violets (*Viola* spp.) and Jack-by-the-hedge *(Aliriaria petiolata)*. After the trees have flushed, the crowns form a solid roof below which a subdued twilight prevails. This naturally alters the composition of the undergrowth and a large number of plants which grow almost solely in beechwoods now appear. In general, grasses preponderate in the undergrowth of low altitude beechwoods on dry slopes, while short herbaceous plants, such as Woodruff *(Asperula odorata)*, predominate on northern slopes at low altitudes, and ferns and tall herbaceous plants such as Beech Fern *(Thelypteris phegopteris)* and Ragwort *(Senecio jacobaea)* are most common at high altitudes. On poor soils there are even beechwoods without any kind of undergrowth, or only with Bilberries *(Vaccinium myrtillus)*.

The copious harvest of dead leaves produced by beech trees usually keeps the soil in good condition. Beech avoids both wet and excessively dry soils, which are colonized by oaks. It is more common for Beech to grow in company with firs, Sycamore *(Acer pseudoplatanus)*, larches and spruces. The firs have always accompanied Beech, since the two have the same ecological requirements. It was Man, in the interests of higher wood production, who was responsible for ousting the Beech in favour of firs. Present day fir stands can therefore be regarded as the remnants of former beechwoods. A similar situation arose in high altitude Beech stands, where they came into contact with spruce woods. On stony and gravelly ground Beech may be accompaniend by Sycamore.

The middle tree layer of these submontane forests does not usually contain many species of trees. If it exists at all, it is generally composed of young trees belonging to the upper layer and of a few shrubs, such as the Red-berried Elder *(Sambucus racemosa)* and honeysuckle *(Lonicera)*, which grow at the margin of the wood, while the Yew *(Taxus baccata)* and Mezereon *(Daphne mezereum)*, and in western Europe the Holly *(Ilex aquifolium)*, are to be found in the shrub layer.

Submontane forests usually have a very diverse fauna comprising species typical of both deciduous woods and montane spruce forests. The commonest moths whose caterpillars damage deciduous trees are the Goat Moth *(Cossus cossus)*, the December Moth *(Poecilocampa populi)* and various geometrid moths, while beetle pests include longicorn beetles and leaf beetles. Conifers are attacked by the same pests as in the mountain belt — the spruces by bark beetles, the Black Arches *(Lymantria monacha)*, and aphids, for example, and the firs by various scale insects. A large variety of birds and mammals can be seen in these forests; mostly species also found in oakwoods or spruce forests. The most common are certain birds of prey, owls, finches, Robins *(Erithacus rubecula)*, leaf warblers, the Nuthatch and the majority of the tits. Likewise many game animals find an adequate food supply in these forests, chiefly the Wild Boar *(Sus scrofa)*, though the Roe Deer *(Capreolus capreolus)* also visits the margin of the woods and in central Europe the Mouflon *(Ovis musimon)* has been introduced into them.

Submontane Mixed Forests

Wood Horsetail   *Equisetum sylvaticum*   (Equisetaceae)   ❶

In spring, its underground rhizomes send forth unbranched, white, reproductive stems bearing sporiferous spikelets at their apices (1 a). After attaining maturity and shedding all their spores, these spikelets fall off, though the stems turn green and do not wither as do those of the Common Horsetail *(E. arvense)*. At the same time they put forth feathery branches. The lateral branches are tetragonal or pentagonal, and bend downwards in an arch-like curve. The stem has rough ribs (1 b). The Wood Horsetail is semitolerant to tolerant of shade, and is incapable of enduring direct exposure to sunlight. In suitable localities, its attractive stems cover quite extensive areas. It is characteristic of moist and humic localities and though it can put up with temporary flooding, it cannot survive in stagnant waters. It is not exclusively warmth-loving and ranges from lowlands up to the mountains; neither does it particularly depend on any specific forest community. The sporiferous spikelet consists of hexagonal scutella bearing swollen sporangia on their undersides. Spores are released from these after they attain maturity. The spore surface is provided with a membrane bearing four minute strips coiled in a spiral. These uncurl when dry and shrink when wet. Such movements enable the strips to bind a number of spores, thereby increasing the probability of fertilization of the female cell. The spores of horsetails germinate to give rise to the so-called protonemata — some of which are male, others female. The protonemata are green, leaf-shaped, with a lobate margin. The smaller the distance between differently sexed protonemata, the higher is the probability of the transfer of male sexual cells (spermatozoa) to a female sexual cell (oosphere). As is the case in the majority of sporiferous plants, the spermatozoa swim to the oosphere through the water film. The sporiferous plant develops from fertilized female cells.

Cladonia fimbriata   (Cladoniaceae)   ❷

The bottom part of the thallus is composed of minute, rounded, tough, greyish-green squamules bearing 1.5—3 cm high, mealy cups. The cup margin is often notched and dotted with brown. This lichen grows in forest clearings, on rocks and boulders, and is very often found on stumps and old wood, having a marked preference for dry localities. The range of this rather common lichen extends throughout Europe, from lowlands up to the mountains.

Phegopteris polypodioides   (Polypodiaceae)   ❸

This relatively small fern is 15—30 cm in height; its simply pinnate fronds have an elongated triangular outline. An important distinguishing characteristic is that the last pair of pinnae turn distinctly backwards. The frond blade is a bright yellow-green. The spore-bearing sporangia are located along the lateral veins. It is a species peculiar to moist soils moderately rich in nutrients and is an indicator of favourable conditions of humus decomposition. Though semitolerant, it becomes a heliophyte when growing in areas rich in springs where it is commonly found. Being intolerant of acid substrates, its occurrence in moist localities necessarily requires porous soils rich in oxygen. It is widespread mainly in the submontane and montane forests of the Beech zone.

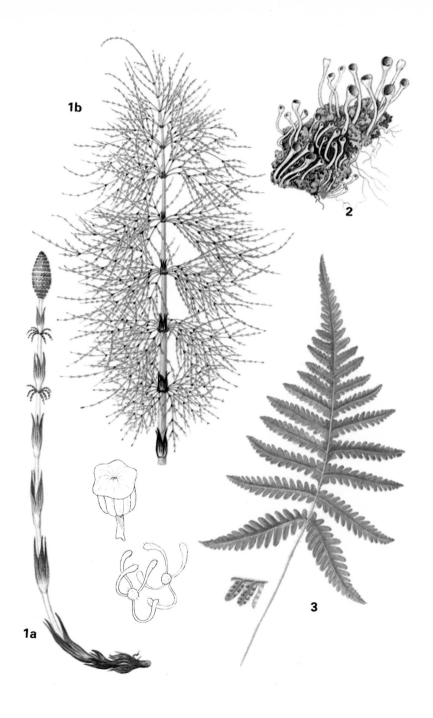

1b

2

1a

3

Submontane Mixed Forests

Trametes versicolor   (Polyporaceae)   ❶

This is one of the extensive family of pore fungi which are of such great importance in forestry and forest economics. This is due to the fact that 75 % of the fungi which attack and destroy trees are pore fungi (polypores). In central Europe alone there are about 260 species. For the most part they grow on dead wood which they gradually decompose and thus destroy. There are, however, many species which attack live trees and cause a serious disease which often results in the death of the tree. The nutrients required by wood-destroying fungi are obtained from the wood by special proteins called enzymes which break the wood down into simple, easily absorbed substances. This chemical process also makes the rotting wood change in colour. In principle, there are two main types of rot: brown rot caused by fungi depriving the wood exclusively of cellulose, and white rot, which decomposes other constituents of wood also. As the progressive decomposition of wood reduces its structural strength, trees attacked by fungi are liable to snap. The semi-circular fruiting bodies of *Trametes versicolor* form roof-like tufts. Their surface has a silken sheen and is marked with black, olive and yellow concentric stripes, the tubes are white to yellowish. This polypore is one of the most common pests of deciduous trees, subjecting their wood to very intensive decomposition by white rot. In many places it also attacks live trees.

Polyporus betulinus   (Polyporaceae)   ❷

This fungus has a soft, semi-circular or kidney-shaped, ochre- or grey-coloured fruiting body. The tubes are white below, arranged in lamellae, and are suggestive of gills at first sight. It lives either as a parasite on the trunks of live deciduous trees, or as a saprophyte on their dead, decaying wood. It often occurs in great numbers on the trunk, resulting in rapid death of the tree. The trees most commonly attacked are birches — but also oaks and Beech. It causes white rot and the decomposed wood is conspicuous for its black stripes giving the impression of having been drawn on with Indian ink.

Fomes fomentarius   (Polyporaceae)   ❸

Its large, console-shaped, stratified fruiting bodies are striking. They are pale grey on the outside, brown inside. The tubes are ochre-coloured initially, their orifices becoming rusty in the course of time. This polypore causes serious damage to Beech but also attacks other deciduous trees — both living and dead. It causes white rot, the first symptoms of this being black lines on the trunk. In the final stage of decay the wood is friable and white. The infection is transferred to live trees through injuries such as cuts in the bark.

Fomes marginatus   (Polyporaceae)   ❹

The fruiting bodies of this species are highly variable in colour. They are bright orange to reddish-brown on the surface, black in the older middle part. The margin is pale ochre-brown with a narrow, white stripe. Profusely shed drops of water are typical of the fresh fruiting body. This is perhaps the most harmful of the pore fungi since it attacks nearly all forest trees, including fruit trees, both live and dead. Mountain forests are its favourite habitat. The invaded wood turns brown and disintegrates into cubiform pieces, and plates of white mycelium can then be seen in the fissures. This polypore is a frequent cause of the untimely death not only of spruces but also of other trees. The action of the fungus reduces the strength of the wood — consequently in a strong wind or after a heavy snowfall, the trunk is very likely to snap in the area of the fungus attack.

Cowslip *Primula veris* (Primulaceae) ❶

The Cowslip is a perennial plant whose rootstock sends out a basal rosette of oblong, wrinkled leaves and a 10—20 cm high stem bearing fragrant, golden-yellow flowers in simple umbels. The flowers appear in April and the ensuing fruits are like capsules. The Cowslip grows from lowlands to highlands on humic, moist soils relatively rich in minerals. In some Cowslip flowers the stigma is situated above the stamens, approximately where the corolla becomes tubular in structure, the stamens being located about the middle of this tube. In other flowers the stigma is out of sight being in the middle of the tube, while the stamens are above it. Hence, the position of stamens in one type of flower corresponds to the position of the stigma in the second. This interesting phenomenon was observed originally by Charles Darwin who discovered that the optimum development of seeds is secured if pollen from high stamens reaches a high stigma, and vice versa. This arrangement serves as a protection against self-pollination.

Creeping Buttercup *Ranunculus repens* (Ranunculaceae) ❷

Its creeping stems bearing glossy, ternate leaves are about 50 cm in length. From May to September it produces bright golden-yellow flowers. It has no strict requirements for soil fertility and temperature, and grows from lowlands up to alpine altitudes. Although it mostly appears on fresh humic substrates, it may be found even on the downtrodden ground of woodland paths. Its extraordinary tenacity enables it to bear trampling and mechanical damage; this makes it an extremely troublesome weed, particularly in forest nurseries. It multiplies vigorously by means of runners, which root into the soil producing new plants.

Honesty *Lunaria rediviva* (Cruciferae) ❸

This is a conspicuous perennial herb whose thick creeping rootstock produces a stem as much as 140 cm in height, bearing large cordate leaves. Its pale violet flowers appear from May to July, yet even after these fade it continues to attract attention by its large, flat, elliptical seed pods which are up to 5 cm long. After reaching maturity both lids of the pod fall off, leaving only an elliptical frame with a silvery-white central partition on which the long-stalked seeds are seated. These dry remains are used in winter for decorative purposes. Honesty is widespread predominantly throughout the Beech forest belt, favouring humic soils rich in minerals. Its occurrence at lower elevations is confined to shady northward-facing slopes. The plant requires good humus and disappears with deteriorating quality of soil. As it grows in dense carpets, it creates unfavourable conditions for the natural regeneration of the forest. It multiplies both by seeds and by rhizomes.

Garlic Mustard *Alliaria petiolata* (Cruciferae) ❹

This stately herb, up to 1 m in height, has an unbranched stem bearing reniform, petiolate, coarsely toothed leaves, and opens its brightly white flowers from April to June. It is characterized by giving off a smell of garlic when rubbed. Its fruit is an angular silique which splits open by two lids; these subsequently fall off, and no more than a membranous partition with a narrow frame, to which the hanging seeds are attached, remains on the stalk. If this partition is exposed to gusts of wind, the seeds fall off. Garlic Mustard grows in shady deciduous or mixed forests from lowlands to mountain elevations. Since it requires soils well provided with nutrients, it is an indicator of substrates adequate for cultivating demanding deciduous trees, such as Ash, maples and elms.

4

2

1

3

Submontane Mixed Forests

Herb Robert   *Geranium robertianum*   (Geraniaceae)   ❶

This annual herb is 20–40 cm high, with leaves composed of three to five pinnately lobed leaflets. The whole plant is covered with glandular hairs, hence its unpleasant smell. Its reddish-purple flowers appear from May to October, and are borne in pairs at the end of long branchlets. Herb Robert – just like all the other geraniaceous plants – has typical rostrate fruits which, when ripe, split into five single-seeded locules. Each of the five seeds is equipped with flexible awns which, by turning about, gradually separate the seed from the central column. After reaching the ground, the awns burrow the seed into the earth by the action of winding motions produced by the changing pressures of intracellular water vapour. Herb Robert grows from lowlands to montane elevations, mainly in shady woodlands on moderately rich to wet substrates. Its presence indicates favourable decomposition of litter and soils suitable for cultivating valuable deciduous trees. It does not tolerate direct sun.

Red Campion   *Melandrium rubrum*   (Caryophyllaceae)   ❷

The stem of this attractive perennial attains a height of about 60 cm. Branches in the leaf axils in its upper part end in beautiful red flowers which bloom from May to August. Characteristic of the Red Campion, as well as of all the other plants of this family, is the inflated calyx bearing the corolla. This protects the plant against insects who try to steal nectar without aiding pollination. Many insect species endeavour to reach the nectar from the outside, by biting through the bottom part of the corolla. The Red Campion's inflated calyx, sheltering the tube of the corolla, makes this impossible. The insect is thus compelled to reach the nectar in the usual way, and so helps in pollination. The fruit is a capsule. Red Campion grows from lowlands to the mountains. It requires humic, relatively rich and damp soils. Though shade-tolerant at lower elevations, it becomes a heliophyte at higher altitudes.

Wood Sorrel   *Oxalis acetosella*   (Oxalidaceae)   ❸

Its long-stalked leaves composed of three cordate leaflets spring directly from a long, thin, scaly rhizome. White flowers marked with red veins bloom from April to May. Its clover-like leaves contain a large amount of calcium oxalate which gives them a pleasant, sourish taste. As a rule, the first flowers of the Wood Sorrel are not pollinated; it is only in the summer flowers that self-pollination takes place, as is the case in the violets. The fruit is a seed-ejecting capsule. The Wood Sorrel occurs from lowlands to the mountains on soils with balanced humidity and rich nutrient supplies. Thus it is absent from poor soils and sunny localities since it cannot bear direct sunlight. Although it frequently forms continuous carpets, it does not hinder the natural regeneration of the forest.

❹

Rose-bay Willow-herb, Fireweed   *Chamaenerion angustifolium*   (Onagraceae)

This perennial has a stately, purple-coloured stem up to 120 cm tall, overgrown with lanceolate, oblong-apiculate leaves. From July to August, the stem terminates in a loose raceme of purplish-violet flowers which develop into elongate, quadrilateral, cylindrical capsules enclosing many downy seeds, which are distributed by the wind. The seeds germinate rapidly when exposed to light; in shade, however, they may stay in the earth for several years without losing their viability. The Rose-bay Willow-herb grows from lowlands to mountain elevations as a typical species of woodland clearings. It grows wherever there is an abundance of light and a rapid decomposition of organic matter.

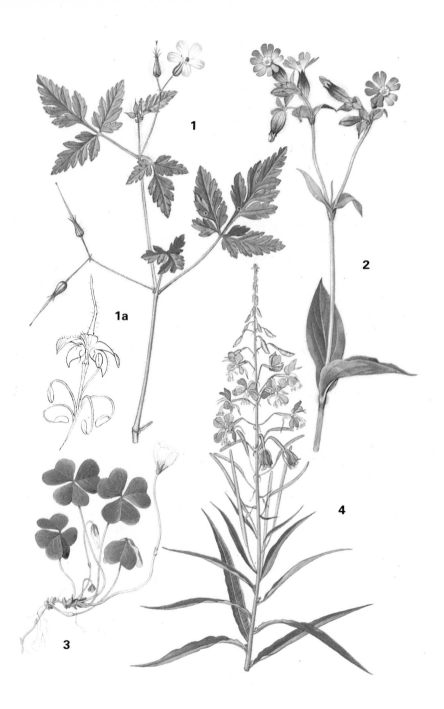

1

1a

2

3

4

Submontane Mixed Forests

European Silver Fir   *Abies alba*   (Pinaceae)   ❶

The European Silver Fir is a tree indigenous to central and southern Europe, the western limit of its range being France and the Pyrenees. Since it is sensitive to severe winter frosts, it is absent from the Scandinavian countries to the north as well as from the USSR to the east. In central Europe it ascends from the hills to the mountain forests — from 300 to 1,200 m. In Germany it is most common in the Vosges, the Frankenwald and the Schwarzwald. It attains a height of more than 50 m and is the tallest European tree. In virgin forests it lives for 500—600 years and grows up to 2 m in diameter. The trunk is covered with a smooth greyish-white bark, and the crown is cylindrical, reaching down to the ground. The needles are flat, 2—3 cm long, with an emarginate apex and two whitish bands on the underside; they are bilaterally arranged on the twig. The leaf scars marking the place of their attachment are circular. Fir flowers, grouped in conical structures, appear towards the end of May — the yellowish male ones clustered on the underside of last year's shoots, the greenish female ones situated in the upper parts of the crown. By autumn the latter develop into 10—20 cm long cylindrical cones, standing, in contrast to spruce cones, in an erect position. The cones disintegrate towards the end of October and the winged seeds fall to the ground. This fir starts to reproduce relatively late: solitary trees when about 40 years old, trees in the undergrowth at about 50 years. When young, the European Silver Fir tolerates rather deep shade, but its demands on aerial and soil humidity are relatively high. It is now disappearing from regions with rainfall below 600 mm or with noticeable air pollution. It thrives best in moist submontane areas on heavy, fresh soils. Having a deep root system, it is not easily uprooted by the wind. Its soft, light wood is used in water constructions and for producing beams and cellulose.

Male flowers (1a), female flowers (1b).

European Larch   *Larix decidua*   (Pinaceae)   ❷

The European Larch is a deciduous conifer common in the mountains and hills of central Europe, especially in the Alpine and Carpathian regions. It is also widely cultivated outside the range of its natural distribution. It is 30—40 m high and straight-trunked, with a high-set crown. Its soft needles grow singly on last year's shoots, whereas on older twigs they form clusters of 25—40. It blooms in early spring, at the beginning of April: red and green female flowers and yellow male ones make their appearance on the twigs together with the sprouting needles. By autumn they develop into ovoid cones, 1—3 cm in size, and stay on the tree for several years. This larch begins to reproduce on reaching 15 years of age. It is a light-demanding, rapidly growing tree requiring airy situations and full exposure to sunlight. It is resistant both to frost and heat, and its cordate root system anchors it firmly in the ground. It is an attractive tree thanks to its fresh green colour in spring and its golden-yellow foliage in autumn. It yields very good resin and first-rate wood with a reddish-brown heart used in boat building, for wall-panelling, wooden staircases and light furniture.

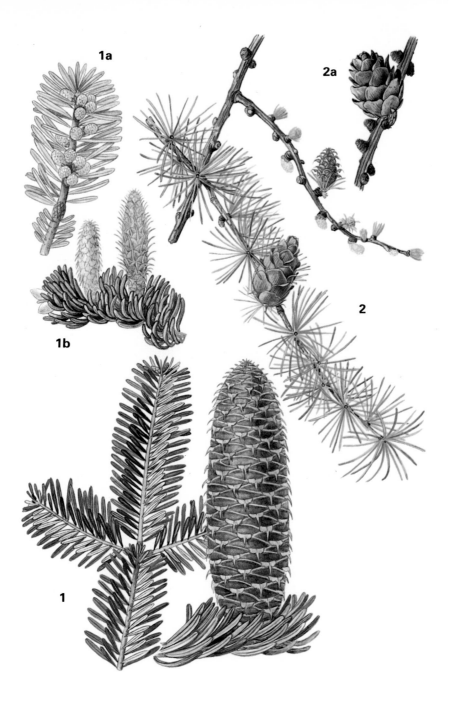

1a

2a

1b

2

1

Submontane Mixed Forests

Beech *Fagus sylvatica* (Fagaceae)   ❶

The Beech is distributed throughout western, central and southern Europe, but is absent from the Scandinavian countries and eastern Europe where relatively harsh winters prevail. It is a shade-tolerant, expansive tree often forming pure, unmixed stands. It sometimes grows in mixed stands with both coniferous and deciduous trees. At lower elevations (400—600 m) it is often accompanied by oaks, firs and Hornbeam, at higher elevations (700—1,200 m) by firs and spruces. It avoids wet and frosty situations, preferring lighter soils and, in particular, calcareous ones. It foliage, when shed, promotes good soil conditions, and since it is rarely attacked by pests it is highly valued in forestry. The Beech grows to a height of 30—35 m and develops a tall, smooth trunk with a silvery-grey bark and a high-set crown. Its alternate leaves are ovate, 5—10 cm long, with an entire margin. Beech forests are a lovely sight in spring after sprouting their fresh green leaves, and again in autumn thanks to their golden-brown colouring. Male and female flowers appear in May and the fruits mature in October. The three-sided reddish-brown, oily beechnuts are borne within a spiny cupule and forest animals like to gather them after they fall to the ground. In Beech, years of increased seed production are rather rare — they occur at intervals of 5—8 years. Beech stands do not start reproducing before 50 years of age. When young, Beech is a slow-growing tree tolerant of shade. It efficiently multiplies from seeds germinating under the parent growth. It yields hard wood used for producing furniture, parquet flooring, sleepers and cellulose.

Wych Elm   *Ulmus scabra*   (Ulmaceae)   ❷

The Wych Elm has an extensive distribution: from Spain it stretches northward to the 65th parallel, and eastwards as far as the Urals. It ascends from hilly regions to high mountain elevations, being most plentiful in stream valleys, moist ravines and screes with fertile soil. It is a semitolerant tree species capable of abundant natural regeneration. The Wych Elm is a robust tree with a cylindrical, long trunk covered with a furrowed bark. Its leaves are broadly ovate, 8—12 cm long, usually with a three-pointed tip and a slightly asymmetrical base. Globular flower buds are already clearly visible in winter, and the rather inconspicuous flowers open at the beginning of April. The fruits ripen and fall towards the end of May and are located in the centre of a membranous wing, about 2 cm long. At lower elevations, up to 600 m, the Wych Elm is attacked by a fungus disease, graphiosis, causing the tree to desiccate from the top and die off in a few years. At mountain elevations it has, for the time being, succeeded in avoiding this disease. It yields medium-heavy wood with a brownish heart which is used to produce furniture, vehicles and rifle butts.

Flowers (2a), fruits (2b).

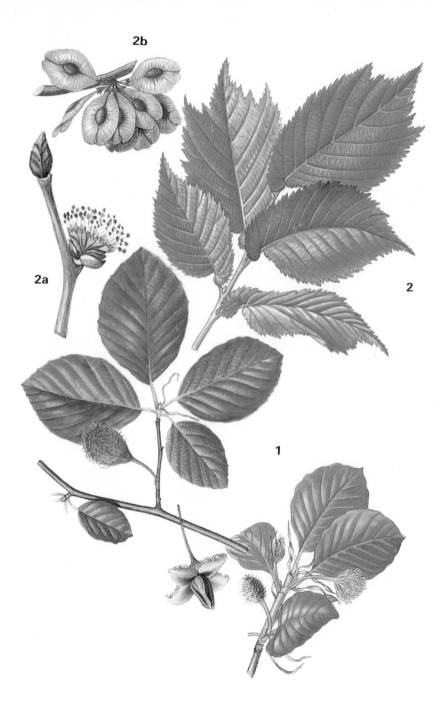

2b

2a

2

1

Submontane Mixed Forests

Yew *Taxus baccata* (Taxaceae) ❶

The Yew is a tree favouring maritime climates distributed in western, central and southern Europe, from England to Poland and Greece. In central Europe it inhabits hills and submontane regions, growing at the lower levels of mixed forests. It never forms pure stands since it occurs only solitarily or in small groups, particularly on rocky slopes and calcareous substrates. In the course of recent centuries, the occurrence of the Yew in Europe has been substantially reduced due to intensive exploitation and clean-cutting. In the majority of countries, this tree is now protected by law. Its estimated numbers are approximately 30,000 in GDR and FRG, 10,000 in Austria, 200,000 in Czechoslovakia, and 50,000 in Hungary. The Yew attains a height of 10—15 m, but frequently develops only as a shrub. Its trunk is covered with a thin, reddish-brown bark which peels off in large scales. It may live as long as 1,000 years. The flat, apiculate needles are 2—3 cm long, lustrous dark green above, light green below, and located on the twig in two rows. The dioecious flowers appear in March. Cask-shaped, 7 mm long seeds surrounded with a red, fleshy aril ripen on the female trees in autumn. They are much-favoured and distributed by birds. Both the needles and the twigs of the Yew are poisonous. In the past, its heavy, reddish-brown wood was used to make bows and quality furniture.

Twig with male flowers (1a), twig with seeds within a cup-shaped berry (1b).

Grey Alder *Alnus incana* (Betulaceae) ❷

The Grey Alder is a tree indigenous to northern Europe: in central and southern Europe it appears in higher mountains only. It grows to be 10—20 m high and its trunk is covered with a smooth grey bark. Unlike the Common Alder it has ovate and apiculate leaves, 4—9 cm long, which are greyish-green on the undersurface. It flowers in early spring, a fortnight before the Common Alder, and its seeds, borne in cones, are light brown. It has a great capacity to produce stump suckers. Its root system is flat and commonly produces root shoots. The Grey Alder is a pioneer tree on alluvial deposits along mountain brooks and rivulets, at elevations of 600—1,400 m. It is widely planted as a nurse crop in barren areas to raise their nitrogen content and prepare for future afforestation. Its pale wood is not highly prized and is mostly used as fuel.

Female inflorescence and cone (2a), male inflorescence or catkin (2b).

Red-berried Elder *Sambucus racemosa* (Caprifoliaceae) ❸

The Red-berried Elder is widespread in western, central and southern Europe, growing from hilly regions to high mountain altitudes up to 1,500 m. It favours similar conditions to the Common Elder, especially liking humic soils with a high nitrogen content. It is an important pioneer species wherever trees have been uprooted or destroyed by fire or gales. The Red-berried Elder is a 1—4 m high shrub with strong shoots containing a broad, rusty-brown pith. Its odd-pinnate leaves are composed of 5—7 ovoid, lanceolate leaflets, about 10 cm long. Yellowish flowers, densely clustered in ovoid panicles, make their appearance in April and May. By the end of summer the shrub is adorned with red berries, each about 4 mm long.

1

1a

2a

2b

1b

2

1

1b

2

3

Submontane Mixed Forests

Mezereon   *Daphne mezereum*   (Thymelaeaceae)   ❶

Mezereon ranges almost all over Europe, populating the floor of forests (especially Beech forests). It requires moist, humic soil, and in such localities it can be found from hilly regions up to the mixed mountain forests. It is a sparsely branched, 50—150 cm high shrub with a greyish-brown, smooth bark. Its lanceolate leaves, about 6 cm long, have an entire margin and are clustered at the twig ends. The flowers appear very early, in March, prior to foliation, and attract the first spring butterflies with their intoxicating scent. Small, globular red drupes, about 8 mm across, ripen by the end of July. They contain a single, blackish-brown, ovately globular pip. Both the fruits and the bark of Mezereon are poisonous. Because of its ornamental, sweet-smelling flowers, Mezereon used to be dug up and carried home to private gardens; this resulted in its rather rare occurrence in the woods. Today it is protected by law in a number of countries where its destruction and misappropriation are liable to punishment.

Holly   *Ilex aquifolium*   (Aquifoliaceae)   ❷

This is a slender evergreen tree attaining, in old age, a height of 12—18 m. It is naturally distributed throughout western Europe in regions with a maritime climate, penetrating northwards as far as Sweden. It tolerates relatively deep shade and grows on the floor of mixed stands; in the mountains it ascends to altitudes above 1,000 m. It makes no special demands on the soil, requiring only sufficient water, but is sensitive to severe winter frosts. This is why it is absent from the eastern parts of central Europe. Holly has attractive leathery leaves, ovate in form, 3—8 cm long, dark green and lustrous on the upper side, with sinuous and prickly margins. Whitish four-petalled flowers appear in the leaf axils in May and develop by autumn into red berries which are greatly favoured by birds. Holly twigs are used to decorate houses at Christmas time, and it has become a popular shrub in gardens.

Fly Honeysuckle   *Lonicera xylosteum*   (Caprifoliaceae)   ❸

Fly Honeysuckle is a shrub widespread over almost all Europe, penetrating far into eastern Siberia. In central and western Europe it occurs on hills and on mountains up to 1,000 m. It grows not only in woodland margins and on shrubby slopes, but, being able to endure shady habitats, also in forest undergrowths. Fresh, fertile soils rich in lime are particularly suitable for its successful development. Fly Honeysuckle is a richly branched shrub, 1—2 m high, with buds sticking out at right angles to the twigs, which are hollow inside. The leaves are broadly elliptical, 3—6 cm long, and entire. The paired flowers come into bloom in May. In autumn the shrub is adorned with blood-red berries, 7 mm long, also arranged in pairs, each pair sharing a stalk. Fly Honeysuckle is frequently used for hedgerows in parks and gardens.

3a

3

1a

2

1

Submontane Mixed Forests

Goat Moth   *Cossus cossus*   (Cossidae)

The Goat Moth is a robust, thick-bodied, ungainly moth with rounded wings with a span of 65—90 mm. It is greyish-brown, with fine dark ripple markings. It is common throughout the whole of Europe, except in the more northerly parts, and occurs chiefly in hardwood forests, where it attacks various deciduous trees. The caterpillars, however, develop in apple, pear, plum and other fruit trees. The moths fly clumsily in June and July and are active in the evening and at night. Their fecundity is considerable; the females lay up to 800 eggs, in groups of 15—30, in cracks in the bark of a tree. When the caterpillars hatch, a week later, they immediately burrow behind the bark. By the autumn they measure 2—3 cm; they hibernate together in a common passage and the following spring they separate and tunnel their own passages, leaving one for expulsion of their excreta. In their second year the caterpillars are extremely voracious and grow very fast. After a further hibernation they travel down the wood of the trunk to the bottom of the tree, where they make a hole (which they fill up with wood débris) and pupate. The chrysalis stage takes from 2 to 10 weeks. Before the imago emerges, the chrysalis actively pushes itself out through the hole by means of spines on its abdominal segments. The Goat Moth is a dangerous pest of various deciduous trees, since it only attacks trees with healthy wood, thereby weakening them and making it easier for other, secondary pests (e. g. fungi, moulds) to attack later on.

Brimstone   *Gonepteryx rhamni*   (Pieridae)

This is one of the best-known European butterflies. The imago hibernates, but at the first sign of spring it takes to the wing again. It mates in the spring and the female lays its eggs on different types of buckthorn. The caterpillars live on the young leaves, which are just starting to flush when they hatch. The caterpillars develop over 3—7 weeks, throughout which time they are green and thinly covered with hairs. The pendant chrysalis has a girdle. The butterflies, which emerge after a short pupation period, are sexually dimorphic; the male is sulphur-yellow, while the female is much paler and resembles a Cabbage White *(Pieris brassica)* (wingspan about 60 mm). This species has modest environmental requirements and is to be found in forests at all altitudes: in the Alps and the Carpathians it occurs up to 2,000 metres.

Brown Hairstreak   *Zephyrus betulae*   (Lycaenidae)

This butterfly occurs mainly in northern and central Europe and is absent from the more southerly parts. Nowhere is it abundant, however, and it tends to occur sporadically. It is the largest European member of this genus and has a wingspan of up to 45 mm. The upper surface of its wings is brown (with the addition of orange spots in the female). The adults fly from the end of the summer to the early autumn. The green, black-headed caterpillars live on blackthorns, birches, Hazel and other deciduous trees. The ochre-brown chrysalis lies on the ground among fallen leaves.

Red Admiral   *Vanessa atalanta*   (Nymphalidae)

The Red Admiral is a migratory butterfly and the density of its population, especially in the more northerly parts of Europe, depends upon the extent of its migration. It occurs in North America as well as in Europe but in Asia is replaced by the similar *V. indica*. The butterfly appears in May (usually having flown from further south) and remains until the autumn. Very often it sucks ripe fruit and the sap of damaged trees. The caterpillars are black, with a light stripe down their sides and live among nettles, which they join together with a silky thread. The chrysalis is brown.

Submontane Mixed Forests

Poplar Moth, December Moth   *Poecilocampa populi*   (Lasiocampidae)

This moth does not fly until the late autumn, i. e. in October and November, and even tolerates slight frosts. Very often it is attracted by light. It is reddish-brown and its forewings are marked with two whitish bands, its hindwings with one. The finely haired caterpillar is grey with a reddish-yellow spot behind its grey-brown head and dark brown spots on its underside. From the spring until July it lives on oaks, birches, limes, Aspen, Hawthorn and Sloe bushes and fruit trees. Before pupating the caterpillar spins a strong, ash-grey cocoon, in which it turns into a fat, tubby, black-brown chrysalis.

Larch Looper   *Poecilopsis isabellae*   (Geometridae)

Until quite recently, this moth was considered to be rare, but intensive research has shown it to be much commoner than was once supposed. It appears in the early spring and while occurring in submontane forests, where it is confined to larch growths, it is by no means rare in low-lying country. One is most likely to encounter the imago at the end of February or in March. Individuals of both sexes, often already paired, cling to the trunks of old larches, from the foot of the tree to a height of 2 metres. The females, which have only vestigial stumps instead of wings, are extremely hairy and are covered with orange-red scales. The males, which have feathery antennae, are less easy to detect, because of the cryptic colouring of their scaly wings. The moths become active after dusk. The caterpillars live on larches from May to July, though are sometimes to be found on spruces and, in northern Europe, even on birches. The reddish brown chrysalis lies in the ground. The male moth has a wingspan of about 30 mm; the female's body is up to 20 mm long.

Archiearis parthenias   (Geometridae)

This is the commonest species of the genus *Archiearis*. Two more similar species are known and all three belong to the true spring moths, so-called because they emerge very early and are usually to be seen in the middle of March. *A. parthenias* is associated with birch growths and sometimes requires no more than a few solitary birches. The moths are most active at midday, when they are very hard to catch because of their tireless, zigzag, darting flight. Very often they will settle on animal corpses or manure heaps. Both sexes have striking orange-red hindwings. The females lay their greenish eggs on birches, on whose leaves the striped green caterpillars feed. At the end of the summer the caterpillars wrap themselves in a leafy cocoon, pupate and hibernate. The moths have a wingspan of 35—40 mm. The similar species *A. notha* mainly frequents poplars and aspens. *A. puella* is the third member of the genus; it occurs chiefly in southern European lowlands and in the warmer parts of central Europe.

Mottled Beauty   *Alcis repandata*   (Geometridae)

This moth occurs in mixed forests throughout the whole of Europe and Asia. The imagos like to cling to the trunks of conifers, especially in the darker parts of the forest. They are easily startled and fly away from intruders to a safe distance. They are further protected by their cryptic colouring, which blends perfectly with their surroundings. The caterpillars live on plants in the undergrowth and on the leaves of birches, willows, Aspen, Sloe and on conifer needles. They hibernate in the caterpillar stage.

Submontane Mixed Forests

Elephant Hawk   *Deilephila elpenor*   (Sphingidae)

This moth occurs in Europe and in parts of Asia, largely frequenting steppe country, the margins of forests and sunny clearings. It is most common in lowlands, but can also be seen in the foothills of the highest mountains of Europe. The moth, which has a wingspan of about 70 mm, generally emerges in May and June, but occasionally in August also. Like other hawk moths, it is a good flier and becomes active in the evening: during the daytime it remains hidden away in the undergrowth. The females lay their eggs singly, mainly on narrow-leaved willows and various types of bedstraw, and in the south on vines. The caterpillars can be found from June to September, never far from the ground. Their basic colour is brown, though occasionally they may be green. The fully grown caterpillar is about 8 cm long and has an inconspicuous spine on its body. It wraps itself in a loose cocoon just above or below the ground, and turns into an ochre-brown chrysalis.

Plumed Prominent   *Ptilophora plumigera*   (Notodontidae)

This is one of the latest European moths, since it flies from October until December. It has extremely feathery antennae. Its colouring is very variable: the ground colour is generally ochre-brown, although blackish specimens are also known. Its wings have a span of about 35 mm. Although it appears so late in the autumn, the moth likes warmth and frequents deciduous and mixed woods on sunny slopes facing south. It is one of the rarer species of puss moth. The caterpillars, which hatch in the spring, live on maple and Sycamore leaves. They pupate in lined holes in the ground, in which they turn into dark brown, black-spotted chrysalises.

Garden Tiger Moth   *Arctia caja*   (Arctiidae)

This is a common and familiar tiger moth. Its wings, which have a span of 55–65 mm, are differently coloured, the forewings being brown, with white zigzags, and the hindwings red, with black spots with a bluish lustre. This moth is nocturnal and flies in July. The female lays up to 2,000 eggs on a wide variety of plants. The caterpillars, which are hatched the same year, grow very slowly and hibernate. In their last stage they are black and covered with long black hairs and short rusty-red hairs. They pupate in a brown cocoon among leaves on the ground.

Black Arches   *Lymantria monacha*   (Lymantriidae)

This is one of the most important forest pests. It has white forewings with black zigzag markings, though dark forms are also known and in some populations they preponderate. The moth can be seen from the middle of July to the middle of August. With their long ovipositors, the females lay groups of eggs in cracks in the bark of trees, where they remain during the winter. When the caterpillars hatch out in the spring, they climb up into the crowns of both conifers and deciduous trees and in years of high density, strip the trees completely bare. They are particularly dangerous to conifers, which die if all their needles are eaten. The fully grown caterpillars are grey and have blue tubercles on their backs. They pupate in very loose cocoons in clefts in the bark. The brown chrysalises, which have tufts of hairs on each of their segments, gleam with a metallic sheen. The Black Arches is distributed throughout the whole of Europe, except in arctic regions and the south of Spain and Italy. When this species becomes too numerous, it has to be combated by chemical and biological means.

Submontane Mixed Forests

Adelocera murina (Elateridae)

This beetle has an oval body, 11—17 mm long and is blackish-brown in colour. It is covered with short brown, russet, whitish and grey hairs. The slightly flattened larvae, familiar under the name of 'wire-worms', measure up to 27 mm. It is a serious forest pest, since it attacks the underground parts of all cultivated plants. It is especially feared in tree nurseries, where it eats the roots of seedlings. The imagos are to be seen in the forest practically the whole year round, from early spring to the autumn. In years when it becomes over-abundant, the adult beetle can likewise do damage, since it bites the buds of deciduous trees (mainly oaks and Beech). It is also hated by farmers for the damage it does to grain crops and fruit trees. It is distributed over the whole of Europe, extending to the Caucasus and Siberia, and is likewise abundant in North America.

Strangalia maculata (Cerambycidae)

The imago, which measures 14—20 mm, is a slender beetle with a tapering abdomen. Its head and thorax are black and its yellow wing-cases are decorated with brown bands which sometimes break up into small spots. The beetle can frequently be observed on flowers, feasting in the sunshine together with two-winged flies (Diptera). The larvae develop in the rotting wood of deciduous trees and occasionally in spruces. Although very common, this species is harmless.

Rosalia alpina (Cerambycidae)

The shape of this beetle's body clearly shows that it belongs to the longicorn beetles (Cerambycidae). It measures 15—38 mm, has a slim body and its antennae, which are 1 1/2 times to twice the length of the body in the male, are substantially shorter in the female. Its ground colour is bluish-grey, which takes on a deeper hue on the legs and the antennae. Each third of the wing-case is marked with black, light-bordered spots, the middle ones merging to form a band. These markings are, however, very variable. These beetles are especially active on sunny days, when they fly busily about and mate. The larvae live in old Beeches and possibly in Hornbeams as well. Although belonging to the mountain fauna, these beetles like warm slopes facing south; they can also often be seen around the trunks of felled trees or near piles of timber. They swarm from June to September. In Europe this species is distributed as far as the south of Sweden, but is most abundant in central and southern Europe: it also extends to the Crimea, the Caucasus, Turkmenistan and Syria. It is the only European species of the genus *Rosalia,* of which only six species are known altogether.

Melasoma populi (Chrysomelidae)

This beetle, which measures 10—12 mm, has a regularly domed body and brick-red (sometimes yellowish-brown), finely spotted wing-cases. The very similar species, *M. tremulae,* has the same colouring, but the curve of its wing-cases is highest towards the rear of its body and its scutum is also a different shape. The two species are much alike in their habits. The adults hibernate in the soil, under fallen leaves, and reappear in April. The females generally lay their eggs on the undersides of young poplar, Aspen and willow leaves, which afterwards provide food for the larvae. The adult beetles also damage these trees. They are distributed throughout Europe and Russia.

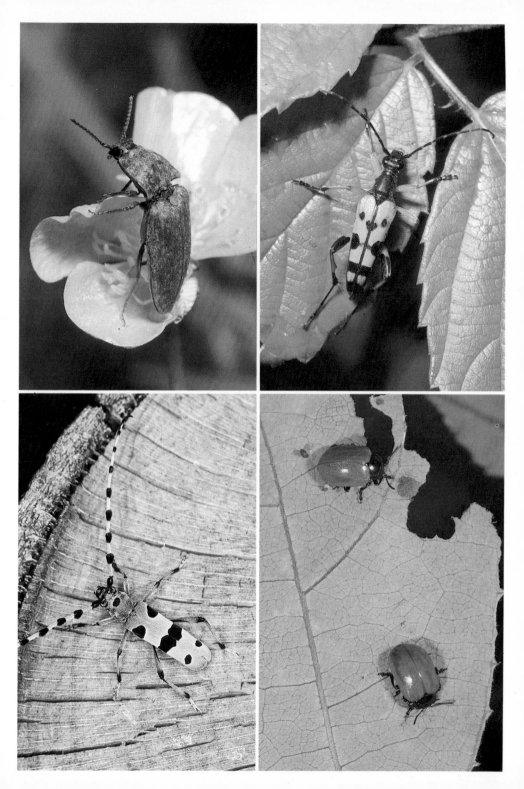

Submontane Mixed Forests

Cardinal Beetle *Pyrochroa coccinea* (Pyrochroidae)
This beetle, which is 14—15 mm long, is fiery-red to yellowish red and swarms in May and June. The predacious larvae pursue other insects behind the bark of dry trees and tree stumps. Here is a typical example of warning colouration, which in this case is particularly effective, since insectivorous vertebrates leave the beetle alone. It is distributed throughout Europe and extends as far as Syria.

Spring Dor Beetle *Geotrupes vernalis* (Scarabaeidae)
Although thickset and ungainly, this dor beetle, which measures 12—20 mm, may fly rapidly on sunny days. It has a short, wide semicircular, comparatively flat body, black in colour, but often brightened by a green, blue, violet or mixed metallic lustre. It is a very common beetle and occurs mainly in forests. Like most dung beetles it constructs underground galleries for the development of its brood. The larvae live mainly on the excreta of herbivorous animals, so the passages are dug either below or near a pile of dung. The main shaft, which is funnel-shaped, divides at the bottom into side tunnels used as food stores. Both sexes take turns in the work of digging the passages and filling them with dung. When the passages are full, the beetles mate. Afterwards they crush the dung and prepare the chambers for the future larvae. The females lay eggs singly, one in each chamber, and place a supply of food by each. The beetles breed in August and September, the larvae pupate the following year and the imagos emerge in June. This species is distributed over the whole of Europe and as far east as Asia Minor and Iran.

Calosoma sycophanta (Carabidae)
This carabid is metallic-green with fiery-red edges to the wing-cases. Its body is 24—30 mm long and has a heart-shaped scutum and relatively wide wing-cases. The larvae are white at first, becoming dark later; when fully grown they measure 40 mm and have a black back. Both the beetles and the larvae travel nimbly over the bark of trees and on the ground, looking for insects, and caterpillars in particular. The beetles also climb into the crowns of trees and destroy vast numbers of Nun and Gypsy Moth caterpillars. The larvae pupate in the ground in June. The beetles emerge the same year, in September, but spend the winter hibernating in the ground and do not leave their shelter until the following May. In July and August they again go underground and hibernate a second time. They may live for up to three years. The Carabidae, or ground beetles include some of the species most important for maintaining biological balance in the forest. During its active life, every individual destroys some 400 caterpillars of large species of moth each summer. This species is distributed throughout Europe and Asia. *C. inquisitor* is a similar, but smaller, species (length 16—22 mm).

Carabus auronitens (Carabidae)
This beetle, which measures 18—26 mm, has a golden sheen and three longitudinal ribs on each of its wing-cases. Both the beetle and the larva are predacious. Both are active at night, when they come out of their shelters below stones, behind bark or in tree stumps to hunt their prey. They live on slugs, earthworms and all kinds of insects. The beetles can run very swiftly, but are unable to fly. They pre-digest their food by injecting their prey with a liquid which quickly decomposes the musculature and thus makes work easier for the insect's jaws. They hibernate in mouldering wood behind the bark of fallen trees and in tree stumps. This, and a number of similar species are distributed throughout the whole of Europe.

Submontane Mixed Forests

Sacchiphantes abietis (Adelgidae)

This is one of the commonest and most troublesome spruce aphids. In its complicated life-cycle, which takes several years, generations of winged and wingless females alternate with each other, and the host trees and the sites at which the larvae attack them also change. The sucking activity of the females which found a generation, gives rise on young spruce shoots, in the spring, to green cone-like galls which are subsequently occupied by the larvae hatched from eggs laid by the female at the base of the buds. The galls contain large numbers of cells and are about 30 cm long. When the larvae mature (July, August), the galls dry up and numerous openings appear in them. Winged females fly out of these openings and make their way to further spruces, where they complete their development the following year. Spruces are also infested by the similar aphid *S. viridis*, whose winged females use the larch as an intermediate host.

Yellow-legged Snake-fly *Raphidia flavipes* (Raphididae)

This is a common species in conifer and hardwood forests from May to August. The fly has a wingspan of 24—27 mm. Both the flies and their larvae are very agile, hunting small insects on and behind bark and are thus useful species.

Urocerus gigas (Siricidae)

This wood wasp is one of the largest European members of the order Hymenoptera. The fat-bodied female measures up to 44 mm, the more slender-bodied male only 32 mm. In addition to morphological differences (the more robust females have an ovipositor), the sexes are differently coloured. Both are black, with yellow legs, antennae and cheeks; however, the middle of the female's abdomen is black, and the first and last segment are yellow, whereas the male has a reddish abdomen and the first and last segment are black. The two pairs of membranous wings are completely transparent and have a smoky hue. The imagos fly from the end of May to August and are to be found chiefly near freshly felled, unbarked timber. The females attack conifers (mainly spruces) and with a single thrust of their ovipositor lay 4—8 eggs at a depth of 5—10 mm. In all, each female lays 50—350 eggs. At first, the six-legged, whitish larvae gnaw the soft sapwood, but later they penetrate towards the centre of the trunk. After a time they make their way back to the surface of the tree and form a chamber in which they pupate. The pupa is naked and unattached, while the passages are crammed full of fine wood débris. The insect's development takes 2—3 years and the imago leaves the trunk through a circular hole. Wood wasps are serious forest pests because of the damage they do to the timber.

Pine Wood Wasp *Paururus juvencus* (Siricidae)

This resembles the preceding species, but the female's ovipositor is black, with a bluish-violet lustre. Unlike the female, the middle of the male's abdomen is reddish-yellow. They are 25—30 mm in length. These wood wasps attack unbarked coniferous timber, laying 2 eggs with each thrust of their ovipositor. They fly from June to August. Not only are they very common, but also very destructive, since in laying their eggs they simultaneously infect the host trees with the spores of fungi which attack wood and thus hasten the death of weakened or otherwise damaged trees.

Submontane Mixed Forests

Honey Buzzard   *Pernis apivorus*   (Accipitridae)
The Honey Buzzard is similar in size (about 55 cm), and appearance to the Common Buzzard, but in contrast, lives chiefly on insects, in particular wasps and their larvae. Its feet are also better adapted for raking open wasps' nests than for gripping prey and it attacks young birds, mice, voles and lizards only when there is a shortage of insects. It nests in European forests everywhere except in the most southerly and northerly regions. It builds a nest in a tall tree or makes use of old nests abandoned by Crows and other birds of prey. The parents take turns to sit on the 2 reddish-brown, marbled eggs, which are incubated for about 5 weeks; the young are fed on insects for about 40 days. In August and September Honey Buzzards migrate to central Africa and often do not return until May. They are very useful and deserve to be protected in every way.

Sparrowhawk   *Accipiter nisus*   (Accipitridae)
This skilled flier nests practically everywhere in Europe (except the northern tundra), northern Africa and Siberia. The male (up to 30 cm) is always smaller than the female (up to 40 cm). It mainly inhabits regions with mixed and conifer forests, but catches its food — small birds up to the size of a Jay — in fields and villages and on the outskirts of towns. It builds its nest high up in the branches of conifers, where the female incubates the 4–6 white, brown-spotted eggs for about 5 weeks. The male brings prey and the female feeds the young, which fledge after about a month, though they continue to spend the night in the nest long after they are independent. Since sparrows form more than half of its diet, they ought to be protected, at least while breeding. The Sparrowhawk is a resident bird and only northern populations migrate to central and western Europe for the winter.

Goshawk   *Accipiter gentilis*   (Accipitridae)
The Goshawk looks and hunts like the Sparrowhawk, but is larger. The male has a wingspan of up to 100 cm and the female up to 140 cm, with a body length of up to 60 cm. The Goshawk lives in every type of forest and near villages and towns, but is very seldom seen, as it is a wary bird. It lives mainly on pigeon-sized birds, partridges and small mammals and will even take owls and the smaller birds of prey. In game preserves it attacks small game, especially pheasants. The 3–4 greenish eggs are laid in a nest made of interwoven twigs, high up in a tree, and the female usually incubates them alone. The male brings food and when the young are hatched the female tears it up into small pieces for them. The young leave the nest after about 8 weeks. The Goshawk inhabits the whole of Europe, North America and Asia. It is mainly a resident bird and only the north European populations fly south and west in the winter.

Hobby   *Falco subbuteo*   (Falconidae)
This small bird of prey, which is about the size of a pigeon, is one of the fastest fliers. It catches small birds — buntings, swallows and swifts — on the wing, but also frequently eats insects. It usually has 3 young, which hatch after 4 weeks from light brown, spotted eggs. The parents feed the young for 4–5 weeks, until they fledge and leave the nest. Hobbies nest on tall trees in deserted nests abandoned by other birds, especially Crows and birds of prey. They like thickets in fields, and the margins of upland and foothill forests, and are to be found all over Europe, Asia and northern Africa. In September and October they migrate to southern Africa, returning at the end of April or in May. In some parts of Europe the Hobby is already quite rare.

Submontane Mixed Forests

Tawny Owl *Strix aluco* (Strigidae)

The Tawny Owl (wingspan about 90 cm) nests mainly in deciduous and mixed woods, parks and large gardens all over Europe, except the northern parts of Scandinavia. It does not build a nest of its own and the female lays her 3—5 eggs, usually in April, in a hole in a tree, in a crack in a rock, or on rafters in a tower, barn or attic. A nestbox may also be used provided the entrance is large enough. The young hatch out in succession and the female feeds them on food supplied by the male. They fledge after 4—5 weeks, but still sit about round the nest, where the parents continue to feed them. The Tawny Owl's diet consists chiefly of mice and voles, with an occasional small bird, and perhaps the young of small game. Tawny Owls hunt only by night and spend the daytime roosting against the trunk of a tree to escape detection by predators such as birds of prey. They are useful birds and merit every protection.

Pygmy Owl *Glaucidium passerinum* (Strigidae)

This owl — the smallest in Europe — is about the size of a Starling. It is commonest in eastern and northern Europe, but also occurs in large upland conifer forests in other areas. It nests at the beginning of May, in deserted tree hollows or Starlings' nestboxes. The eggs (usually 6) are white and the young hatch the following month. The parents feed them mainly on mice, shrews and small birds and their young. Occasionally the Pygmy Owl will hunt during the day, keeping lookout from a branch, and quite often it stores up food reserves in the hole it has its nest in.

Long-eared Owl *Asio otus* (Strigidae)

The Long-eared Owl inhabits small mixed, hardwood and conifer forests throughout the whole of Europe, Siberia and northern Africa, where it uses old nests built by other birds. Its 4—6 eggs are laid in April; the young hatch 28 days later and leave the nest after 3 weeks. Long-eared Owls live chiefly on mice and voles and seldom eat other birds. Like the two preceding species they swallow their food whole and regurgitate undigested components in the form of pellets. An analysis of these pellets provides a clear picture of the birds' diet. The Long-eared Owl is very useful and ought to be strictly protected.

Common Cuckoo *Cuculus canorus* (Cuculidae)

The Common Cuckoo is a fairly numerous inhabitant of mixed woods with abundant undergrowth in most parts of Europe and Asia. At the end of April it returns from its winter haunts in the southern half of Africa. The first to arrive is the male, whose familiar call can be heard immediately afterwards; the female follows a few days later. The Cuckoo is a nest parasite, that is to say, it does not build a nest of its own, but lays its eggs in other birds' nests, carefully imitating the colouring of the host bird's eggs. In all, the female lays an average of 20 eggs, each in a different nest. The young hatch after 12 days and when only a few hours old, throw the host bird's eggs or newly hatched young out of the nest. The 'step-parents' feed the young Cuckoo on insects for 3 weeks in the nest and for a further 2—3 weeks outside it; after that the Cuckoo begins to fend for itself, living chiefly on hairy caterpillars, beetles, butterflies and spiders. Cuckoos, which migrate singly, fly southwards in August and at the beginning of September.

Submontane Mixed Forests

Chaffinch *Fringilla coelebs* (Fringillidae)

In Europe, the Chaffinch occurs in open hardwood forests in lowlands and uplands, in mixed woods and conifer forests in mountainous country and in large gardens and parks in towns and cities. It nests twice a year − at the end of April and again in May or June. The nest, which is built by the female, is usually situated fairly high up beside the trunk of the tree or on a forked branch. It is a neatly woven, strong structure made of moss, lichen and fine grass and is lined with feathers and hairs. The female incubates the 5 grey, brown-spotted eggs for about 2 weeks. The parents both feed the young for about 14 days in the nest and then for a few days more outside it. The young are fed mainly on small insects and spiders, while the adult birds live on seeds and berries. In the autumn, most Chaffinches migrate to the Mediterranean region, but in central and western Europe some remain behind.

Siskin *Carduelis spinus* (Fringillidae)

The favourite nesting sites of the tiny yellow-green Siskin are conifer and mixed forests with plenty of spruces in submontane regions all over Europe. Here the Siskin remains until August, when it migrates, in small flocks, to the lowlands, where it lives on alder and birch seeds. At the same time it moves steadily southward, sometimes as far as the Mediterranean. The female lays 4−5 whitish, faintly spotted eggs (of which there are usually two clutches a year) in a neatly woven nest made of thin twigs, bark and lichen, often situated as much as 20 metres above the ground, and incubates them unaided for 2 weeks. The young are fed for about 14 days by both parents on small insects, after which they progress to an adult diet of different kinds of seeds.

Kingfisher *Alcedo atthis* (Alcedinidae)

The Kingfisher makes its home beside small rivers and streams with overgrown banks, flowing through upland and mountain forests. It occurs throughout the whole of Europe and Asia except in the north. Since it is a very timid and wary bird one is fortunate to glimpse its bright greenish-blue plumage as it skims the water like a streak of lightning. It is most likely to be seen sitting motionless on a branch on the lookout for small fish, which form the bulk of its diet. The young, however, are fed at first on larvae and insects. The nest is built by both parents in a steep bank. Using their beaks, they burrow a passage about a metre long, which ends in a chamber in which the 7−8 eggs are laid. The young hatch after 3 weeks and are fed by the parents for about the same length of time. The Kingfisher always frequents the same hunting grounds, even in the winter.

Hoopoe *Upupa epops* (Upupidae)

The Hoopoe was once a common bird everywhere in Europe (except Scandinavia) and Asia and Africa (except for desert regions), but intensive felling of the trees in which it nested severely reduced its populations, since convenient holes became hard to find. The Hoopoe likes to live on the margins of mixed woods with adjacent pasture, where it probes animal dung with its long beak in search of insects. The female lays an average of 6 eggs and sits on them for 15−16 days. The young, which hatch out in succession, are fed on larvae and insects by both parents. Hoopoes winter in equatorial Africa and return to Europe in the first half of April.

Submontane Mixed Forests

Robin *Erithacus rubecula* (Turdidae)
This relatively common bird about the size of a sparrow, familiar to all as 'Robin Redbreast', inhabits mixed and deciduous woods over the whole of Europe apart from Scandinavia. It is a partial migrant, some birds wintering in southern Europe and northern Africa. In a pile of brushwood or a hole in the ground, the female makes a neat nest out of rootlets and grass and lines it with fur and feathers. She incubates the 5—6 yellowish, finely red-spotted eggs for about 2 weeks. The parents take turns to feed the young, which for 13—14 days consume huge quantities of small insects and spiders. When the young leave, the adult birds nest again, this time producing a somewhat smaller family. Robins which do not migrate live on berries and other forest produce during the winter.

Willow Warbler *Phylloscopus trochilus* (Sylviidae)
The Willow Warbler inhabits the whole of Europe except the south, and all of Siberia to the Far East. It is relatively abundant in mixed and deciduous woods, where it flies about among the tops of the trees and in the undergrowth, looking for small insects and their larvae. At the end of May the female builds a nest on the ground for the 5—7 white, red-spotted eggs. The nest, which has an entrance in the side, looks like a rough bundle of leaves, grass and moss. The eggs are incubated for 2 weeks and the young leave the nest at about 14 days of age. Like all *Phylloscopus* species, the Willow Warbler is a migrant and spends the winter in central and southern Africa.

Redstart *Phoenicurus phoenicurus* (Turdidae)
The Redstart inhabits mixed and hardwood forests throughout the whole of Europe and western Siberia. It has grown used to Man and often settles in holes or nestboxes near human dwellings. Here the female weaves a nest out of rootlets, grass blades and moss, lays 5—7 blue eggs in May and incubates them for 2 weeks. Both parents share in the task of feeding the young, which are given insects, butterflies, caterpillars, beetles, grubs and spiders. Nesting Redstarts destroy vast quantities of insects and are thus extremely useful. They generally nest again in July, but this time have fewer young. The Redstart migrates to northern Africa at the end of September or the beginning of October and returns at the beginning of April. It can be identified by its typical 'curtseying' and its quivering tail, as well as by its black throat and russet breast.

Wren *Troglodytes troglodytes* (Troglodytidae)
The Wren, one of the smallest European birds (it measures only 9 cm and weighs 8—9 gms), frequents forest undergrowth, parks and gardens all the year round. In addition, it occurs all over inner Asia, in parts of northern Africa and in North America. It is relatively frequent in places where there are dense shrubs, in which the male, early in the spring, begins to build several nests made of dry leaves and moss. The females then chooses one of these and lines it with fur and feathers. The 6—7 tiny, white, finely spotted eggs are incubated for about 2 weeks, mostly by the female. The young, which are fed by both the parents, consume large quantities of insects. The Wren is mainly a resident bird and only its northern populations migrate southwards to warmer climes in the winter.

Submontane Mixed Forests

Coal Tit *Parus ater* (Paridae)

This tiny black-headed tit with two black stripes on its throat bears a fleeting resemblance to the Great Tit *(P. major)*. It is resident in conifer and mixed woods, from lowlands up into the mountains, all over Europe, north Africa and Asia as far as Japan. The Coal Tit begins to nest at the end of April, in a hole in a tree, a hollow tree stump or an underground burrow; it is particularly fond of nestboxes in conifer stands. Up to 11 red-spotted eggs are laid in a mossy, hair-lined nest. The young hatch after 14—16 days and are fed on insects by both parents for about 16 days. The Coal Tit nests again in June, but the second clutch is smaller than the first. Although the Coal Tit eats insects and is thus very useful, its diet consists largely of conifer seeds, especially in the winter.

Crested Tit *Parus cristatus* (Paridae)

The Crested Tit abounds in conifer forests (and in western Europe in mixed and hardwood forests also) over the whole of Europe as far as the Urals, with the exception of northern Scandinavia and Italy. Its black crest distinguishes it from all other tits, although it has otherwise much the same habits. It nests at the end of April, in various types of holes and in nestboxes. The first clutch comprises up to 10 white, red-spotted eggs, which are incubated for an average of 15 days. At 21 days of age the young leave the nest and in June the adult birds nest again, but this time fewer eggs are laid. Nesting Crested Tits consume large quantities of small insects, especially bark beetles and weevils. In the winter, when they roam the countryside with other tits, they live mainly on various types of seeds.

Willow Tit *Parus montanus* (Paridae)

The Willow Tit is very common in the conifer and mixed forest belt of North America, Europe and Asia. In colouring and size it closely resembles the Marsh Tit, but its black cap is dull instead of glossy and extends further down its back. It prefers to nest in holes excavated by the female in rotting stumps or the trunks of old coniferous and deciduous trees. The 7—9 round, white, red-spotted eggs are laid in May and the female incubates them for about 2 weeks. Both parents feed the young for over a month, including the first 2 weeks after they leave the nest. Small beetles — in particular bark beetles and weevils and their larvae — form more than half the Willow Tit's diet; forest (mainly conifer) seeds comprise the rest.

Nuthatch *Sitta europaea* (Sittidae)

A frequent inhabitant of woods, parks and gardens all over Europe and Asia, except in the northern parts of Scandinavia, the Nuthatch is a sedentary bird and only in severe winters does it roam the countryside in the company of tits, approaching human settlements and visiting feeding tables. At the beginning of May the female lays 6—9 white, red-spotted eggs in a hole in a tree or a nestbox. The nest is always lined with small fragments of bark (usually pine). The female — and sometimes the male as well — walls up the entrance to the hole with a mixture of clay and saliva, until only they themselves can slip inside. Nuthatches nest once a year. Both parents feed the young for up to 28 days. As soon as they are fledged, the young fly straight to the nearest tree and immediately begin running up and down the trunk in search of insects and spiders hidden in cracks in the bark. In the winter the Nuthatch lives mostly on seeds.

Submontane Mixed Forests

Carrion Crow   *Corvus corone*   (Corvidae)

Carrion Crows are to be encountered almost anywhere, in small woods, in fields and in parks. Southern, western and part of central Europe are inhabited by the black form, while further east we find a grey form (the Hooded Crow). Both belong to the same species, however, and hybrids occur where their ranges overlap. The Carrion Crow is disliked by hunters, since it devours the young of game animals and steals birds' eggs. It also destroys mice and voles, however, and eats carrion, insects, berries and seeds. It is a solitary nester and usually adds to its nest every year. The female alone incubates the 5—6 blue-green eggs for about 3 weeks. On leaving the nest at the end of May, the young form flocks which roam the countryside in search of food. Carrion Crows are resident birds and only those inhabiting northern and eastern Europe migrate south and west in the autumn.

Rook   *Corvus frugilegus*   (Corvidae)

Rooks are most often encountered in the winter, in large flocks composed mostly of birds which have migrated from the north to spend the winter in central and western Europe. They keep company with Carrion Crows, from which they can be distinguished by the grey, bare skin at the base of their beak and the blue-black lustre of their plumage. They nest in colonies in the lowlands over the whole of Europe and Asia, except the more southerly parts. The colony often comprises several hundred nests, which are made of twigs and are situated in the tops of tall trees. At the end of March or in April the female lays 3—5 greenish, grey-spotted eggs. The young hatch after about 17—18 days and the parents feed them on a very varied diet, which includes cereals, seeds, insects, larvae and caterpillars, with an occasional vole or mouse.

Jay   *Garrulus glandarius*   (Corvidae)

This fairly common, brightly coloured bird is about the size of a pigeon and inhabits the whole of Europe, inner Asia and northern Africa, being absent only in the far north. It is to be found in even the smallest woods at practically all altitudes, but has a distinct preference for mixed forests containing oaks and Beech. Acorns, beechnuts and other forest tree fruits are its favourite food in the autumn, while in the nesting season it subsists chiefly on birds' eggs and young voles, mice and lizards. It nests on the outskirts of forests, high above the ground, and the nest, which is made of dry twigs, is lined with a layer of dry plants and moss. Its 5—7 grey-green eggs are laid in April and are incubated by both parents for about 17 days. Three weeks later the young fledge, leave the nest and roam the countryside in small flocks until the spring comes round again. Jays are always on the alert and their raucous voice gives warning of the approach of every intruder.

Magpie   *Pica pica*   (Corvidae)

The black and white, black-tailed Magpie is a little larger than a pigeon. It frequents small copses in fields, overgrown hillsides and the banks of lowland and upland streams over the whole of Europe and northern Asia and in part of North America. The nest is always built high above the ground and is made of thorny twigs, lined with turf and soil and finally with a surface layer of leaves and grass blades, and usually has a brushwood 'roof'. The 3—8 greenish, brown-streaked eggs are incubated for just under 3 weeks and the young are fed for 3—4 weeks on nestlings, voles, lizards and even young hares, partridges and pheasants, although they are also often given insects, cereals, fruit and berries. Its destruction of birds' nests and young game at nesting time makes the Magpie a particular nuisance in game preserves and its population has to be limited by regulated shooting. It is a resident bird.

Submontane Mixed Forests

Pine Marten *Martes martes* (Mustelidae)

The Pine Marten occurs in wooded regions over the whole of Europe and northern Asia, where it is relatively abundant. It is a nuisance in game preserves for the losses it causes among the young of small game animals, but it is also useful, since its diet consists mainly of rats, mice and squirrels. It mates in July and August, but does not produce a litter until the following May, when the young are born in a hollow tree or the abandoned nest of a crow or a bird of prey. The cause of this long gestation period is that the embryo does not begin to develop until 6 months after the ovum has been fertilized. The 3—6 young are blind for about 5 weeks; the female suckles them for about 2 months and tends them with the greatest care. The closely related Beech Marten *(M. foina)* inhabits the same regions as the Pine Marten. It is somewhat smaller and has a white bib stretching down to its forelegs (the Pine Marten has a yellow bib); it is not a forest-dweller, but lives in the vicinity of Man, e.g. in attics and barns, and its diet consists chiefly of rats and mice.

Weasel *Mustela nivalis* (Mustelidae)

The relatively small, slim Weasel, which is only some 20 cm long, is distributed over the whole of Europe, northern Africa and northern Asia. Its back is reddish-brown and its underside whitish, although some weasels living in more northerly regions turn white in the winter. It lives mainly on mice and voles and often goes after them into their holes. If there is a dearth of rodents it will eat the young of small game and birds. In the summer it lives mostly in the fields and on the outskirts of woods, but in the winter it withdraws into the woods themselves, where food is more plentiful. Its 3—4 young are born under a pile of stones, under a tree stump or in a hole in the ground; in years in which there is an overabundance of voles the litters are usually much larger. The gestation period is 5 weeks and it is usual for the Weasel to have several litters a year, so that young may be found from the spring until well into the autumn. The Weasel does more good than harm and ought therefore to be better protected.

Stoat, Ermine *Mustela erminea* (Mustelidae)

The Stoat closely resembles the Weasel, but is about one third larger, and in the winter, hen the rest of its coat turns white, the tip of its tail remains black. It is common all over Europe (except in the most southerly parts) and in northern Asia and North America. It is to be found mostly in copses, on the outskirts of forests and on bushy hillsides, where it catches the mice and voles which form the bulk of its diet. It also feeds on small mammals and birds, however, and has a special liking for their young. Its litter of 3—4 young are born in April or May. Stoats pair in July, however, and the embryos do not begin to develop for several months (pregnancy is delayed). The young open their eyes after 5 weeks and are suckled for about 2 months.

Polecat *Putorius putorius* (Mustelidae)

The Polecat is distributed over the whole of Europe and northern Asia, where it occurs in fields, on the outskirts of forests, on overgrown hillsides and near rivers and ponds. In the winter it frequents human habitations and causes considerable losses among poultry. During the summer it lives chiefly on small mammals, rats, Muskrats, frogs and fish, but also eats Rabbits, hares and pheasants, so that gamekeepers regard it as a nuisance. It usually lives under a loose pile of stones, in a hollow tree or an abandoned burrow. Here, after a 40 days' pregnancy, the female gives birth to 4—8 young, which are blind for about 5 weeks and are adult at 8 months. The lighter coloured Steppe Polecat, *P. eversmanni,* which occurs in eastern Europe and some of the warmer parts of central Europe, is a much more useful animal, since it is a field-dweller and lives chiefly on shrews, mice and voles.

Submontane Mixed Forests

Roe Deer   *Capreolus capreolus*   (Cervidae)

The Roe Deer — one of the best known and commonest large European mammals — inhabits forests all over Europe except in northern Scandinavia. It prefers small woods interspersed with fields, and the outskirts of forests, but also frequents riparian woods and occurs high up in the mountains, as far as the upper limit of the tree belt. In the winter it generally withdraws deep into the woods, but in some regions may live in the open the whole year round. The Roe Deer has adapted itself well to the 'civilization' of the countryside and tolerates both the large numbers of people who visit the woods, and the mechanization of work in field and forest. In summer, the Roe Deer is russet (the young have white spots until August), while in October it grows a long, brownish-grey coat with a white rump. The antlers are shed every year in November, and new, larger and stronger ones grow during the winter. At first, they are covered with fine hair known as velvet, which the deer removes in April by rubbing its antlers on the trunks of small trees. Rutting (mating) occurs in July and August: the gestation period is 40 weeks, and the embryo does not start to develop until the winter. The white-spotted calves (of which there are usually two) are born in May or at the beginning of June and a few days later are already able to accompany the female when she goes grazing, although she often suckles them well into the autumn. In the winter Roe Deer form small groups numbering 5—10 animals, which tend to spend more time in the woods and frequent feeding troughs there. Their diet comprises herbaceous plants, grasses, young tree shoots and field crops. If they are looked after properly, and especially if they have a regular supply of extra food during the winter, the damage they do in field and forest is negligible. The Roe Deer is an important game animal; it can weigh up to 15—25 kg and has excellent flesh.

White-tailed Deer   *Odocoileus virginianus*   (Cervidae)

The North American White-tailed Deer is closely related to the Roe Deer and in some parts of Europe, the descendants of specimens which escaped from parks and preserves, etc. have taken to living in the wild. The White-tailed Deer is larger than the Roe Deer. Its tail measures up to 30 cm and when the animal runs it is raised to show the white underside. The antlers likewise have a typical shape and curve forwards and outwards in the form of a basket. Like the Roe Deer, it visits fields and lives on grass, foliage and shoots, but does not strip the bark from trees. In November, at rutting time, the males do not roar like the Red Deer, but utter hissing sounds. The young, of which there are usually two, are born in May. These deer usually live in small groups, although the males are frequently solitary.

Wild Boar   *Sus scrofa*   (Suidae)

Once distributed over the whole of Europe, Asia and northern Africa, the Wild Boar was heavily hunted throughout northern and central Europe until it was only to be found in game preserves. Since World War II its numbers have increased, however, and it is now quite plentiful everywhere, except Britain, where it does not occur. It is omnivorous and lives on forest and field produce, insects, worms, rats and mice, young birds and mammals and even carrion. In the forest it makes itself useful by rooting up larvae from the soil, but in the fields it does considerable damage for the same reason. Its favourite haunts are small woods with Beech and oaks not far from fields and meadows with patches of mud. Mating takes place in the winter. The gestation period is 16 weeks and 4—10 young are born some time between March and May. The striped piglets accompany the female — which keeps a very watchful eye on them — until the autumn. Wild Boar live in small groups during the winter. They shun all contact with Man, and are dangerous only if wounded or when defending their young. They are highly valued as game: an adult boar can weigh as much as 150—200 kg and a sow a third less.

Submontane Mixed Forests

Mouflon   *Ovis musimon*   (Bovidae)

This is the only European wild sheep to have been successfully introduced from its original home, in the rocky wilds of Sardinia and Corsica, to central, southern and western Europe. At first it was kept in enclosures, but later was set free to fend for itself. Mouflons are most widespread in central Europe, and particularly in Czechoslovakia, which was the first country to breed them. In the summer Mouflons are a rusty brown: in the winter their coat is thicker and darker and the rams have white saddle markings. The rams' horns curve backwards and outwards: they are not shed, but grow steadily longer every year until by 8—10 years they may measure as much as 100 cm. They are greatly coveted hunting trophies. Mouflons chiefly inhabit small woods, bushy slopes and the outskirts of forests where the soil is dry and hard, and seldom venture into the fields. They live in large herds, which are usually led by an old female; only old rams live solitarily. Their requirements are modest and they subsist on forest undergrowth, grass, bilberries, Heather, moss and lichen. If these are in short supply, they will nibble leaves and young tree shoots. At rutting time, which lasts from October until the end of November, the rams engage in stubborn fights for the favour of a few females. In March or April, after a 5 month pregnancy, the female gives birth to one or two young. After 3 weeks the young begin to feed themselves, but the female still suckles them for several months more. The Mouflon ewe is adult at 2 years, the ram at 3. Their average age is 15 years. A good sized ram may weigh up to 50 kg and a ewe 20—30 kg. The forests of central Europe seem to suit Mouflons better than their ancestral Mediterranean islands, as evidenced by the greater weight, better developed horns and greater fecundity of central European animals.

Sika Deer   *Cervus nippon*   (Cervidae)

This small deer, which can be found in nature reserves all over Europe and can occasionally be seen roaming the woods, bears some resemblance to the Fallow Deer. It also has white spots, but is generally darker and in the winter the spots disappear. It has similar antlers to the Red Deer, although they are much smaller and narrower. The Sika was imported to Europe in the last century from its natural home in Manchuria, Japan and Korea, whose two varieties are to be found — a Manchurian variety (also known as Dybowsky's Deer) and a Japanese variety, which is smaller and weighs about 60 kg. In the rutting season, which is in October, the males do not roar, but utter prolonged whistles. The young are born in May, usually one per hind. Like other members of this genus, Sika occasionally strip the bark from conifers. As game it is not an important animal, but it is undoubtedly a valuable addition to the European fauna.

Fallow Deer   *Dama dama*   (Cervidae)

The Fallow Deer, which originally came from the Mediterranean region and Asia Minor, has been kept in game reserves since the Middle Ages. At the beginning of the present century it was also turned loose into the wild and became thoroughly acclimatized to European conditions. It mainly frequents well-lit copses and small woods with clearings and glades. The Fallow Deer has a fawn-coloured coat, with rows of white spots running the length of its body. The male's palmated antlers are not shed until May and growth of the new ones is completed by September. Rutting occurs during October and November and the young are born in June. The female suckles the fawns — usually two in number — until the end of November, at which time Fallow Deer gather into herds, the males separate from the females and young. They live on the usual herbage, but do not nibble trees or peel off the bark. The Fallow Deer's antlers are a much coveted hunting trophy and its flesh has an excellent flavour. The male weighs 40—80 kg, the female not more than 50 kg.

Montane spruce forests

Spruce forests are naturally confined to high altitudes with abundant rainfall and it was not until the nineteenth century that commercial forest practice spread spruces further west, making them the commonest trees in uplands and lowlands, far below their normal altitudinal range. As extremely valuable timber, spruces have been — and still are — given priority over all other trees, often without taking their natural habitat requirements into account. Of all forest communities the natural mountain spruce forests have suffered least from Man's meddling, since spruce stands have always been almost pure monocultures.

Throughout their entire area of distribution spruces behave like mountain trees, and it is only in the north that they also find suitable conditions in the lowlands. They are adapted to a harsh, damp continental climate and have modest soil requirements — though they are more exacting than the pines. They must, however, have sufficient moisture and if this is not available will not prosper at low altitudes. They are consequently absent from sandy soil.

Natural spruce forests have a rich moss layer and their commonest herbaceous plant is the Bilberry *(Vaccinium myrtillus)*. At higher altitudes we find various grasses, such as reed-grasses and the like. At the upper limits of the forest, where the trees thin out, ferns often preponderate. Spruces are most frequently accompanied by the Rowan *(Sorbus aucuparia)* (whose seeds are spread by birds) and occasionally by birches, firs and larches. Spruces with 'prop' roots are a familiar sight in spruce woods. The seeds from which these trees grew landed on a fallen tree or a stump and the seedling pushed its roots through the wood until it reached the soil. In the meantime the fallen trunk or tree stump rotted and disappeared and the tree was left standing on rooty stilts.

Spruce forests usually mark the upper limit of the tree-line. After them comes the crooked timber or kneewood belt, which acts to protect the soil and the water supply and to prevent avalanches. When we speak of the upper limit of the tree-line we mean that line joining the highest points of continuous natural forest. In places where Man has not interfered with the forest, this is the climatic limit at which trees still find the conditions necessary for development and is determined by the interaction of two factors — the temperature and the water supply.

Large spruce forests in mountainous regions are inhabited by various typical insects and other animals. In natural growths we are sure to find, behind the bark of every ailing spruce, several species of bark beetles, the commonest being *Ips typographus*, whose larvae are attacked by various ants and also provide food for woodpeckers, especially the Black Woodpecker *(Dryocopus martius)*, the Great Spotted Woodpecker *(Dendrocopus major)* and the Green Woodpecker *(Picus viridis)*. The seeds of spruces feed large flocks of Crossbills, which spend the winter in the forest, and Nutcrackers *(Nucifraga caryocatactes)*, which inhabit certain mountainous regions as well as the far north. The Capercaillie *(Tetrao urogallus)* is a typical bird in the undergrowth, while at the margin of clearings and mountain meadows we find the Black Grouse *(Lyrurus tetrix)*. High up on the rocky mountainside, the last few pairs of Golden Eagle *(Aquila chrysaetos)* have their eyries. Montane forests are also inhabited by Red Deer *(Cervus elaphus)* and by their greatest natural predator, the Lynx *(Lynx lynx)*. Other large, and now rare, animals, like the Bear *(Ursus arctos)*, the Wild Cat *(Felis sylvestris)* and the Wolf *(Canis lupus)*, can still find refuge there from the march of civilization. The highest slopes, above the natural forest limit, are the home of Marmots *(Marmota marmota)*, Ibexes *(Capra ibex)* and Chamois *(Rupicapra rupicapra)*, which never come down further than the periphery of the forest, even in the hardest winter.

Montane Spruce Forests

Marchantia polymorpha (Marchantiaceae) **❶**

It has a creeping, broadly cut thallus with a midrib along which, on the underside, there are conspicuous black stripes. It is a sun-loving to semishade-tolerant liverwort abundant on damp and fresh soils; it is particularly plentiful on old fire sites, and is also found on old woodland trails and in ditches soaked with water. In more shadowy woods, this liverwort gradually becomes less common. Decorative sessile patellae can often be observed on its thallus. These produce small, green, lenticular corpuscles, which are dispersed by water. In a suitable place they give rise to new thalli. Besides this vegetative (asexual) reproduction, liverworts also multiply sexually. The sexual organs are borne by peculiar stalked discs resembling small palms which are, in fact, the most noticeable feature of the whole plant. Each disc is either male or female. The male discs are lower (1a), and irregularly lobed. The still more conspicuous female discs have the shape of a multiradiate star seated on a rather longer stalk. Fertilization is effected by raindrops striking against the flat male discs, severing the spermatozoids and transferring them to the female discs. The fertilized female cell gives rise to a globular capsule enclosing numerous spores which, after attaining maturity, develop into new plants.

Polytrichum commune (Polytrichaceae) **❷**

This is the largest central European moss whose simple erect stem may attain a height of as much as 50 cm. The stem is densely covered with linear, apiculate leaflets whose margins are sharply serrate. The midrib of the leaflet is strongly developed and passes into a brown, serrate awn. When dry, the leaflets are appressed to the stem, while when wet they stick out. The capsule stem is strong, red, and up to 15 cm long; the capsule itself is covered with a brown calyptra. It is a typical moss of moist to wet, strongly humic to peaty localities, and is light-demanding, tolerating slight shade only. Being calcifugous, it cannot stand lime-rich soils. Though most common in forest clearings, it is also relatively abundant in open peat bogs, in hollows, caused by uprooted trees, and in ditches containing stagnant water. Only rarely does it share its habitat with other mosses, and if so, this indicates the desiccation of the soil. On the other hand, if it is found in company with peat mosses, it indicates rising soil humidity. It is a typical species of montane elevations.

Capsule (2a above), leaf (2a below).

Polytrichum attenuatum (Polytrichaceae) **❸**

This moss closely resembles the preceding species with which it is frequently confused, but it occurs in greater abundance. The stem or caulicle is usually shorter, not exceeding 10 cm. The leaflets jut out from the caulicle even when dry, in the wet they are deflexed. The subulate leaflets are sharply serrate all along the margin. The 4—8 cm long capsule stem is red near the base, while near the top its colour turns to yellow. The capsule is oblong, yellowish-green, covered completely with a reddish-brown calyptra. This moss forms extensive continuous growths in coniferous forests and is considered an indicator of moderate to favourable conditions. It is a species tolerant of shade or semishade. As it cannot survive on thick layers of raw humus, it never accompanies the Bilberry. It tolerates even swampy substrates but is absent from forest clearings, being unable to stand direct exposure to sunlight.

Capsule (3a on the left), leaf (3a on the right).

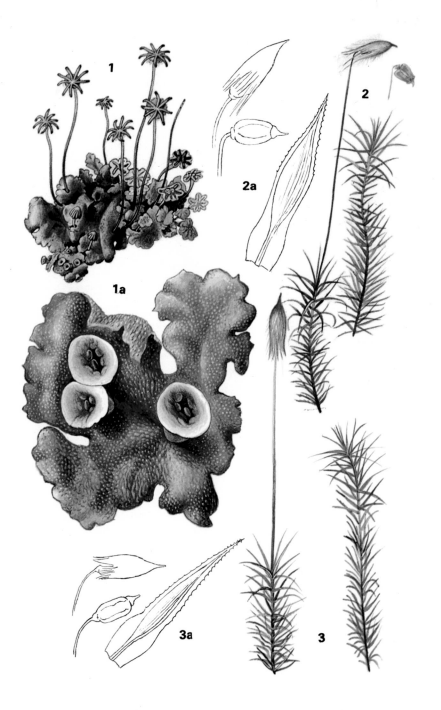

1

1a

2

2a

3

3a

Montane Spruce Forests

Sphagnum palustre   (Sphagnaceae)   ❶

Peat mosses (Sphagnaceae) are aquatic or marsh plants often forming extensive growths. The structure of their caulicle is specially adapted for storing water. Besides normal cells serving the purposes of photosynthesis the leaf blade contains a great number of vacant cells connected by pores where water is accumulated in the wet to function as a supply during dry weather. The whole caulicle is strewn with twig clusters which are amassed at its tip to form a little head. Peat mosses have two kinds of leaves which differ in shape: caulicle leaves and branched leaves. A short bristle bears a rounded, brown, lustrous capsule capped with a calyptra from the earliest stage of development. This, however, soon falls off. All peat mosses are calcifugous. They always form large carpets and constitute the most significant floral component of peat bogs. In moist woods they are usually confined to less extensive areas. Their caulicles exhibit an annual growth of about 3 cm, while their bottom part dies off at the same rate. *Sphagnum palustre* is the largest of all peat mosses and requires full exposure to sunlight, hence its occurrence on open peat-bogs. Its caulicles are 10−40 cm high, and usually unbranched. It forms continuous soft carpets, whitish or bluish-green in colour. It is very fertile and its capsules are larger than those of all the other peat mosses.

Sphagnum girgensohnii   (Sphagnaceae)   ❷

Its upright caulicles, tapering to a long, thin point, form pale green to white cushions, about 20 cm in height. It is a species tolerant of shade or semishade. Peat mosses usually absorb water accumulated on an impermeable substrate after rain. This peat moss moreover requires high air humidity.This is why it usually appears in the bottom parts of cavities and hollows made by windfallen trees, while the upper parts of these are populated by other species. It forms continuous, thick cushions of raw humus, several metres deep, thus greatly hindering natural forest regeneration.

Funaria hygrometrica   (Funariaceae)   ❸

It has unbranched caulicles, about 3 cm high, bearing shortly apiculate, entire leaflets with a discernible rib terminating at the leaflet tip. The capsule bristle is 2−5 cm high, yellow to red, and twisted into a curved shape. The pear-shaped capsule is furrowed and covered with a pointed calyptra. *Funaria* grows on bare ground, forming pale green cushions. It is a moss characteristic of places devastated by fire, but may also be found on swampy soils, sands, walls and roofs. Its range extends from lowlands to the mountains. It is a heliophyte and reproduces all the year round.

Dicranum scoparium   (Dicranaceae)   ❹

This moss forms pale green, lustrous, discontinuous cushions. Its erect, slender caulicles, up to 10 cm high, are covered with rust-coloured or whitish down. The dense leaflets are lanceolate, apiculate, and finely toothed towards the tip. The thin rib terminates at the tip of the leaflet. The capsule bristle is strong and red, and grows 2−4 cm high. The slightly curved capsule is equipped with a red lid and totally enclosed in the calyptra. This sun-loving to semishade-tolerant moss grows on infertile soils and rocks. It is capable of surviving in very dry localities and avoids moist soils. It thrives best in sparsely populated coniferous forests where it forms continuous cushions of variable size, tolerating relatively poor localities with unfavourable humus decomposition. It will even survive on extremely acid soils. The cushions of this moss are of little significance in storing water for the forest: like *Leucobryum glaucum,* they supply the soil with little water and seriously hinder the forest's natural regeneration.

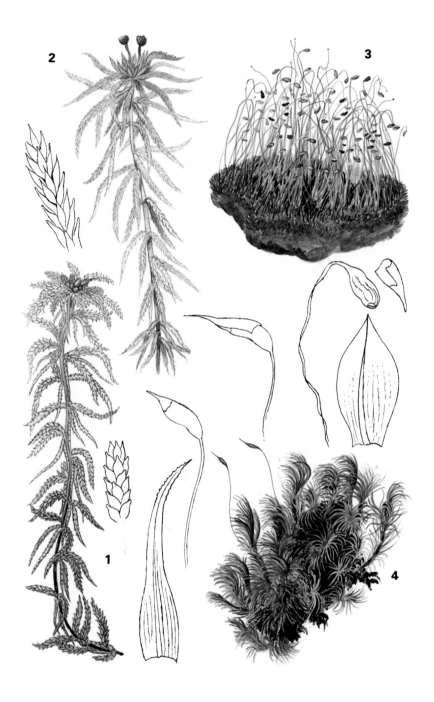

Montane Spruce Forests

Hard-fern *Blechnum spicant* (Polypodiaceae) **❶**

From its protruding rhizome, this fern sends out fronds of two kinds. Infertile, short-stalked fronds with a simply pinnatilobate blade and obtuse lobes, grow from the outer parts of the frond rosette — these dark green, leathery fronds survive over winter. Inside the rosette are the fertile fronds, longer than the former (about 45 cm), whose blades bear narrow linear leaflets. On the underside of these, along the medial vein, sporangia develop, which later grow to cover the leaflets' entire lower surface. This attractive fern, a companion of montane spruce forests, tolerates both shade and semishade, and is confined to areas with a relatively harsh climate — in particular where rainfall is high — and to acid soils. Hence it is an indicator of substrates relatively poor in minerals and containing acid raw humus.

Stag's-horn Moss *Lycopodium clavatum* (Lycopodiaceae) **❷**

Lycopodium species have a creeping stem bearing small, sessile leaves. Their sporangia are usually arranged into a spikelet. They require shade, a constantly humid atmosphere, and an ample supply of humus. The Stag's-horn Moss is the most common *Lycopodium* of montane forests. Its long, creeping stem may attain a length of as much as 1 m. From this, other erect, forked stems arise, whose lower parts are densely overgrown with finely notched leaflets. These erect stems bear a thin stalk sparsely covered with yellowish, entire leaves each of which usually carries two sporiferous spikelets. It is widespread in open coniferous forests on humic, acid substrates but can also be found on drier heaths. It very often accompanies the Bilberry. Under favourable conditions it is capable of intensive vegetative reproduction with the aid of its creeping stems.

Interrupted Clubmoss *Lycopodium annotinum* (Lycopodiaceae) **❸**

Its creeping stem, similar to that of the preceding species, sends out short, erect caulicles. The linearly lanceolate, decurved leaves with sharply indented margins are more sparsely distributed over the stems. The spore-bearing spikelets have no stalk but are attached to the erect caulicles. It is most abundant in montane spruce forests on moist, mossy soils. In view of the fact that it occurs in moister localities than the Stag's-horn Moss, it indicates a decelerating decomposition of litter and the beginning of raw humus formation. Being shade-loving, it disappears from woodlands with a decreased tree population. It never forms continuous growths but occurs only in small groups.

Lady Fern *Athyrium filix-femina* (Polypodiaceae) **❹**

This is a stately fern with bipinnately arranged leaves whose blade is oblong-lanceolate and tapering at both ends. It may grow to a height of 1 m. The petiole is shorter than the blade and is brown underneath. The sporangia, situated alongside the lateral veins, are covered with sickle-shaped indusia (membranous covers). Though it can also be found at lower elevations, it is most abundant in mountain forests which provide it with sufficient moisture. When growing on shady, fresh forest soils rich in decomposed humus, it gives rise to extensive fern growths. Dry substrates, and also those abounding in raw humus, are avoided. It is the most attractive fern of European forests.

3

2

1

4

Montane Spruce Forests

Edible Boletus   *Boletus edulis*   (Boletaceae)   ❶
The average size of the cap of this species is 6—25 cm. In most cases it is convex when young and more open later on, and light to dark chestnut brown in colour. The pores are yellow, with round orifices, minute when young, broader and greenish-coloured later on. The stipe is ventriculous, swollen at the bottom, and bears a fine whitish reticulum on a white to rusty-brown background. The flesh is also whitish and has a pleasant smell. Its range extends throughout Europe. Between July and November it grows from lowlands to submontane elevations, mostly in spruce stands, for it lives in symbiotic relationship with the roots of spruces. It also associates with oaks. The fruiting bodies of the Edible Boletus have an excellent taste. In this connection the reader might wonder about the nutritive value of mushrooms. They contain 85—90 % water, 3—9 % protein, 1—6 % carbohydrate, and 0.2—0.5 % fat. The protein content compares well with meat, yet humans are incapable of absorbing more than approximately one half of the proteins involved: the gastric juices cannot fully dissolve mushroom cells which, in contrast to plants, are permeated with chitin, the same substance insect bodies are composed of. We can, however, absorb all the carbohydrates contained in mushrooms. Mushroom fats are also digestible. Moreover, mushrooms contain a number of vitamins, especially B and D, and promote digestive processes by means of their indigestible cellular membranes and radical aromatic substances.

Yellow Chanterelle   *Cantharellus cibarius*   (Cantharellaceae)   ❷
The cap is 2—7 cm wide, with an inrolled margin. The whole mushroom is yolk-yellow, the flesh is tough and white inside. The gills are thick and lamelliform, mostly running down the stipe. The stipe is tough, of the same colour as the cap, and tapers towards the base. The Yellow Chanterelle is at home in coniferous forests throughout the northern hemisphere, both in lowlands and in the mountains, and appears particularly in August and September. The caps of specimens occurring in various tree stands differ somewhat in colour, being usually paler in deciduous forests. It is a very aromatic and popular mushroom, yet less digestible than other species, and consequently must be cooked for a longer time. It is only exceptionally attacked by worms, this being one of its major advantages. It has a high vitamin B content.

Fly Agaric   *Amanita muscaria*   (Amanitaceae)   ❸
Its brilliant red cap scattered with white warts makes this species an attractive feature of European woods. The stipe is white, robust, and swollen at the base. Both the flesh and the gills are bright white. This toadstool is poisonous, for it contains the alkaloid muscarine which attacks the nervous system. The symptoms of poisoning include a decrease in cardiac activity, an increased secretion of bile, saliva and sweat, and a simultaneous intoxication, i. e. the same as in alcoholic poisoning. At the initial stage, the fruiting bodies of the toadstools are enveloped in two membranes: the so-called universal veil *(velum generale)* enveloping the entire fruiting body, and the partial veil *(velum partiale)* covering the cap only. As the fruiting body pushes up, these membranes split and only their remnants may be observed on the adult specimen. All that remains of the universal veil is a cup-like structure around the base of the stipe *(volva)*, and wart-shaped fragments on the cap. The ring encircling the stipe below the cap is a remnant of the partial veil.

Calocera viscosa   (Dacrymycetaceae)   ❹
This is an attractive little mushroom accompanying predominantly spruce forests. It has a gristly, golden-yellow fruiting body branched like antlers and suggestive of *Clavaria*. It can easily be distinguished from this, however, by the elasticity of its fruiting body, while that of *Clavaria* is brittle. It is abundant on dead wood, especially on stumps. Though not poisonous, it does not make good eating.

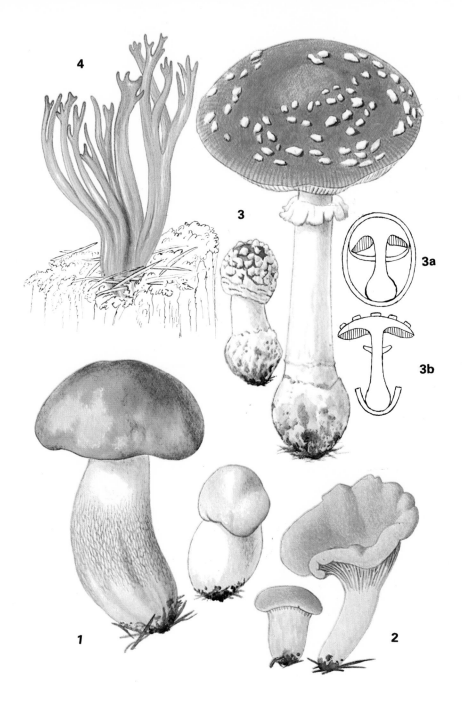

4

3

3a

3b

1

2

Montane Spruce Forests

Clavaria aurea   (Clavariaceae)   ❶
The richly branched fruiting body is golden-yellow in colour with an orange hue. The terminal branchlets have obtuse and finely notched tips. They are fragile and do not change colour when pressed. The flesh is pure white, aromatic and palatable. It appears in mixed forests on heavier soils as early as the beginning of summer, and continues to grow in the same spot for a relatively long time.

Fomes annosus   (Polyporaceae)   ❷
This polypore is a particular pest of spruces, but also attacks other trees. It is found mainly in spruce stands cultivated outside their natural distributional range and catastrophic damage has been recorded in first-generation stands planted on agricultural soils. The brown to dark fruiting bodies have an irregular shape, and the pores are white. Very often the fruiting bodies are resupinate, i. e. attached to the host by the entire upper surface, so that it is only the white pores that are visible. It grows at the base of the trunk and on the lower surface of the main roots of live trees. It is the most serious and insidious spruce pest, for its fruiting bodies appear relatively rarely, and always long after the trunk has been attacked. The action of the fungus makes the heartwood turn brown, until in the final stage the interior of the trunk is completely hollowed out. Such trunks are sometimes characterized by a bottle-like swelling at the base. The afflicted tree usually lives to be very old, without betraying any manifestation of the disease. In fact the trunk can be said to be putrescent inside while gaining in girth on the outside. This of course destroys the most valuable part of the trunk. The infection reaches the tree through the roots.

Honey Fungus   *Armillaria mellea*   (Tricholomataceae)   ❸
In autumn its fruiting bodies appear in large clusters on stumps. The cap is pale brown at first but becomes darker later on and is scattered with small scales, which are almost absent in old age. The stipe is brownish and bears the remnant of the partial veil in the form of a ring. The gills are white, with a reddish hue later on. The Honey Fungus can live on dead wood, but is also a dangerous pest of living coniferous and deciduous trees. The infection usually spreads by the mycelium penetrating the roots through various wounds, but healthy roots may also be attacked. The mycelium spreads between the bark and the wood where it forms white, branched strands. An abundant flow of resin is typical of attacked trees. The rotten wood, especially the roots, can often be seen phosphorescing at night. Spruces are the most susceptible to infection, particularly if they are cultivated outside their normal range.

Sulphur Tuft   *Hypholoma fasciculare*   (Strophariaceae)   ❹
This common mushroom covers stumps with its dense clusters of sulphury yellow fruiting bodies. The cap is orange-brown and smooth in the centre, and the gills are densely arranged, at first sulphury yellow, then green to dark. The stipe is cylindrical, yellow and hollow. The flesh is sulphury yellow. It is saprophytic on partly decomposed wood.

Montane Spruce Forests

Chickweed Wintergreen *Trientalis europaea* (Primulaceae) ❶

Chickweed Wintergreen is a small perennial plant, about 20 cm in height, with a simple stem bearing in its upper third a rosette of several oblong-ovate leaves. From May to July a solitary, long-stalked white flower with seven crown petals grows from their axil. The fruits are globular capsules with a greyish powdery covering. Because it requires considerable soil humidity, it usually grows at higher elevations with abundant rainfall. Being tolerant of strongly acid soils, it is also an indicator of localities where peat formation is under way, i. e. where an acid, wet humus is accumulating. It makes no particular demands on soil nutrients and does well in deep shade as well as in full sunlight.

Yellow Bird's-nest *Monotropa hypopitys* (Monotropaceae) ❷

The Yellow Bird's-nest is a non-green saprophytic plant, i. e. it derives its nourishment from dead organic matter. There are only about 160 saprophyte species among the world's seed plants (Spermophyta). Their common characteristic is the absence of chlorophyll and the consequent transformation of their leaves — which are of practically no use — into scales. Root hairs are also lacking: instead, the roots are covered by the mycelium of a mycorrhizal fungus which lives with the plant in a symbiotic relationship. The Yellow Bird's-nest is a typical saprophytic herb. In the wood it offers an attractive sight: fleshy, waxy yellow stems, about 20 cm high, sparsely scaled, grow directly from the ground. The stem ends in a short raceme of yellow flowers bent hookwise when young but erect later on. The flowers are not shed after wilting but only desiccate and envelop the fruit — the capsule. It ranges from lowlands up to mountain altitudes and may be found in both deciduous and coniferous woodlands. However, a thicker layer of humus is a precondition for its occurrence in any locality.

May Lily *Maianthemum bifolium* (Liliaceae) ❸

A thin rhizome sends out a stem growing to a height of 25 cm, half-way up which are two alternate, petiolate, entire, cordate leaves. In April, a raceme with clusters of small, white, sweet-smelling flowers appears. These develop into red, globular, glossy berries. May Lily occurs in great abundance from lowland to montane elevations, primarily on acid soils and is an indicator of deteriorating soil conditions.

Red Hare's Lettuce *Prenanthes purpurea* (Compositae) ❹

This is a perennial herb with a stately stem up to 1.5 m in height, bearing greyish-green leaves varying in shape from the base of the stem to its middle. It is only in the top parts of the stem that they acquire a stable shape: here they are lanceolate, stalkless, and clasp about the stem. Sparse panicles of purple-coloured flowers appear in the leaf axils from July to September. It is a typical plant of mountain forests requiring wet soils in which humus is actively decomposing.

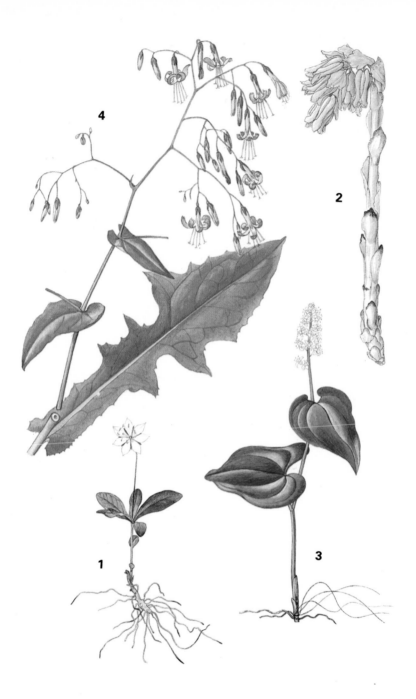

Whorled Solomon's Seal   *Polygonatum verticillatum*   (Liliaceae)   ❶
The Whorled Solomon's Seal is a perennial herb whose underground rhizome sends forth a 30—100 cm high stem bearing whorls of 3—7 narrowly lanceolate leaves. From May to June, small, tubular, greenish flowers may be seen hanging from the leaf axils, usually in pairs on one split stalk. It is a plant of higher elevations, particularly of montane spruce forests, and requires moist soils with a good rate of humus decomposition. The entire plant is poisonous.

Senecio nemorensis   (Compositae)   ❷
Its stem, exceeding 1 m in height, bears lanceolate-ovoid, almost sessile leaves with hairy undersides. The stem terminates in a panicle of yellow racemose inflorescences. Its flowers appear from July to September, the small ripe seeds bearing a parachute of fine hairs. These are carried great distances by the wind. It is most common in woodland clearings and glades from submontane to montane elevations. It requires an ample supply of nutrients, and is particularly demanding as concerns nitrogen and soil moisture. In clearings it usually forms dense, continuous growths which hinder the development of tree and shrub seedling. Like the Rose-bay Willow-herb *(Chamaenerion angustifolium),* it is also a typical plant of forest clearings and glades. Both have one characteristic in common: they produce a huge mass of hairy seeds which are dispersed by the wind, enabling them to inundate the neighbouring area. This is why, under favourable conditions, these plants appear in vast multitudes. What constitutes 'favourable conditions' for these forest clearing species? Each species makes certain demands on the environment; that is, under natural conditions it grows in the places it finds most suitable. In some plants these demands are relatively specific, and they are consequently confined to certain places only. Just such a specific flora can be found in woodland clearings. The deforestation of an area brings substantial changes for the plants that remain. Numerous plant species formerly growing under the protection of the tree crowns disappear, giving way to new species which find the climate of open spaces satisfactory. The Rose-bay Willow-herb and *Senecio nemorensis* are the very first pioneers colonizing a clearing in any number. Their growth is favoured by the abundance of humus accumulated under the trees. Both disappear from forest clearings and glades after having exhausted the nitrogenous substances contained in the soil, or when the crowns of the new stand cut off the sunlight.

Wood Cudweed   *Gnaphalium sylvaticum*   (Compositae)   ❸
This perennial has a simple, erect stem up to 60 cm high, covered with a silky white down and bearing narrow lanceolate leaves. The stem passes into a raceme of small heads composed of yellowish-white florets. The Wood Cudweed blooms from July to September. It occurs from lowlands to montane altitudes in woodland clearings and alongside roads. It is satisfied with dry to slightly moist soils moderately rich in nutrients and with a favourable decomposition of humus: it avoids limey soils.

Alpine Coltsfoot   *Homogyne alpina*   (Compositae)   ❹
This is a perennial herb with reniform, lustrous, indented, long-stalked leaves; 30 cm tall stem grows out from among them. This violet stem is covered with scales, and terminates in a single head of violet flowers which open from May to June. It grows in montane spruce stands and penetrates up to the mountain pine belt. It is considered an important species of spruce forests in their original distribution range. It requires damp soil, rich in minerals, and containing an acid humus.
   One flower from the head or capitulum (4a).

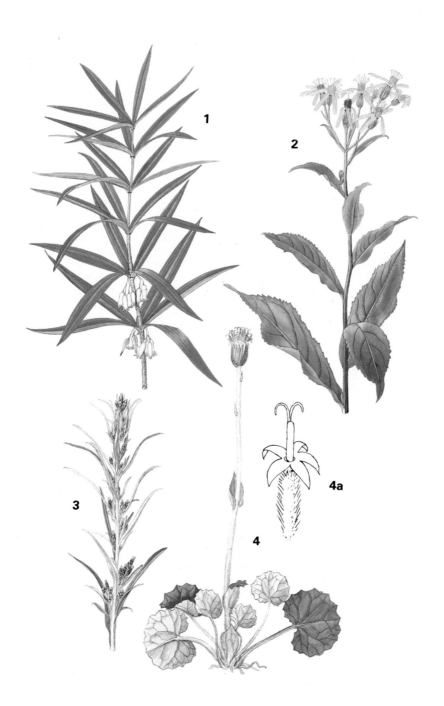

1

2

3

4

4a

Harebell   *Campanula rotundifolia*   (Campanulaceae)   ❶

This perennial attains a height of 30 cm and has two types of leaves: those on infertile shoots are oval-reniform and serrate, while those on the flower-bearing stems are lanceolate to linear. Dark blue pendent flowers appear from June to September. The pollination process in the Harebell is most interesting. Within the undeveloped flower there is a short, hirsute style tightly encircled by stamens with nectar-producing glands at their bases. As the flower unfolds, the anthers adhering to the style start to open and the pollen they shed sticks to the hairs of the style. At the same time the growing style wipes off the pollen from the bursting anthers. After releasing all their pollen, the stamens wither. Meanwhile the style grows longer and the flower opens fully. Thus the style provides a support within the flower along which an insect can climb to the nectaries. In doing so, the insect rubs against the style and either wipes off the pollen, or leaves the pollen brought from another flower on its hairs. It is only after all the pollen has been wiped off the style hairs by insects that the style splits, exposing spiral stigmas. The next insect entering the flower must rub against these since the stigmas partly close the flower entrance. Only at this moment does pollination take place. These complicated preparations generally secure pollination. If, however, bad weather prevents insects from visiting the flower, the stigmas open still further, bending backwards so as to touch their own style with the grains of pollen brought by insects from other flowers. The fruit of the Harebell is a capsule. The Harebell occurs on poor to moderately rich acid soils, from lowland to mountain elevations. Being a heliophyte, it does not flower when growing in shade.

Marsh Rosemary   *Andromeda polifolia*   (Ericaceae)   ❷

Marsh Rosemary is a decumbent shrub with a 40 cm long stem bearing narrow, lanceolate leaves with ash-grey undersides. From May to June it produces umbels of drooping, long-stalked flowers with a rosy calyx and a pink bell-shaped crown. These mature into five-sided capsules. It is found on peat bogs on hills and mountains. It is poisonous.

Cranberry   *Vaccinium oxycoccus*   (Ericaceae)   ❸

This small decumbent shrub with its thin, creeping, slightly woody stem growing to a length of 80 cm is a typical plant of montane peat bogs. It is sparsely overgrown with small, perennial, ovate, leathery leaflets with short petioles and ash-grey undersides. Its beautiful flowers hang on long, thin stalks from May to July. They have a red calyx and a rosy crown deeply cleft into four lobes. They ripen into large, red, edible berries.

Crowberry   *Empetrum hermaphroditum*   (Empetraceae)   ❹

This is a small decumbent shrub, 5—20 cm in height, resembling Heather. Its stem is overgrown with linear, evergreen leaves, arranged in whorls. Small dioecious flowers bloom from May to July. Male flowers have a rosy crown consisting of three petals, while the crown of the female flowers is purple. They develop into red, sourish drupes. This plant inhabits montane peat bogs all over the northern hemisphere.

Montane Spruce Forests

Bog Whortleberry, Bog Huckleberry *Vaccinium uliginosum* (Ericaceae) ❶

The Bog Whortleberry is a shrub resembling a large Bilberry. Its leaves are also deciduous but are greyish green with an entire margin. Its flowers appear from May to June. Their pink corolla is ovally urceolate and develops into a dark blue, sour-tasting berry. Though not poisonous, it leads to vomiting if consumed in large amounts. It is most abundant in mountain areas and requires considerable soil moisture and raw humus.

Cotton-grass *Eriophorum vaginatum* (Cyperaceae) ❷

Cotton-grass forms conspicuous mound-shaped tufts, its greyish-green stems standing up to 70 cm high. The stems, which stand erect even after flowering, terminate in a single spike, covered with numerous perianth bristles. In the course of development, these bristles grow in length and flutter from the spikelets like silver wool. Cotton-grass flowers from March to June. It is a plant of montane peat bogs, meadows and swamps and promotes peat formation.

White False Helleborine *Veratrum album* (Liliaceae) ❸

The White False Helleborine is a robust herb reaching as much as 150 cm in height. A strong rootstock produces a rosette of large, elliptical, longitudinally plicated, entire leaves. The strong stem bears rather narrow lanceolate leaves and, from June to August, terminates in a raceme of green star-shaped flowers which later develop into seed capsules. It inhabits damp mountain meadows. The entire plant is deadly poisonous.

Common Sundew *Drosera rotundifolia* (Droseraceae) ❹

The Common Sundew is a perennial herb, 10—20 cm high, with a basal rosette of rounded leaves, each covered with about 200 red tentacles. These exude drops of sticky fluid which glitter like dew-drops. A thin, spring-like stem grows from the centre of the leaf rosette and from June to August bears several white florets in a monochasial cyme. The Common Sundew is an interesting and typical plant of peat bogs. It is an insectivorous plant. Only 400 of the 150,000 species of flowering plants obtain nourishment in this peculiar way. While most plants are able to obtain all the necessary nutrients from the soil, insectivorous plants have adapted to grow on peaty soils, poor in nutrients, particularly nitrogen. They are able to secure their supply of nitrogenous substances in other ways. Sundew can, in fact, grow without 'meat' but such plants have been shown to be much smaller and infertile. The glittering drops on the leaves lure insects to the plant. As soon as one settles on the leaf the tentacles start bending towards it from all sides, and trap it with their sticky secretion. The coiling of the tentacles takes a relatively short time; the first reaction of the plant follows about 10 seconds after the insect lands. On a sunny day the insect is fully enclosed in about one hour, whereas in cloudy weather this may take as long as five hours. The tentacles squeeze ever harder on the insect, jamming it against the leaf blade which simultaneously bends into a dish shape. The glands on the leaf blade start to exude a digestive secretion and the dished form prevents this fluid from running off the leaf. One leaf is capable of repeating the digestive process about four times, after which it withers. After the insect has been digested, the tentacles straighten again and the undigested remains of the insect are blown away by the wind.

218

1

2

3

4

Montane Spruce Forests

Norway Spruce *Picea abies* (Pinaceae)   ❶

The Norway Spruce is a typical tree of the north European taiga and of central European mountain forests, and is absent from western Europe with its maritime climate. In central Europe it forms pure stands high in the mountains near the timberline, while at lower elevations it grows in mixed stands with Beech and firs. It particularly thrives in cool regions with abundant precipitation and inhabits the lower hills only along cool, damp stream valleys. Norway Spruce is a stately tree growing to a height of 40—50 m. It develops a dense, pointed, conical crown reaching down to the ground in the case of solitary trees. Its reddish-brown bark changes with age into a scaly, flaky brown bark. The needles, rhombic in cross-section, 10—26 mm long, are attached to padlike projections which give a warty appearance to the bare twigs after the needles have been shed. The flowers appear in May — male ones in yellow catkins, the small red female cones standing erect at the end of the twigs. After pollination these turn downward and develop into cylindrical, 8—16 cm long cones. They open in spring to release dark brown, winged seeds, 4—5 mm in size. When growing in stands, this spruce starts reproducing at the age of 50 years. Because of its shallow, flat root system, surpassing the circumference of the crown, it is easily uprooted by the wind. It is semitolerant of shade, resistant to severe frosts, and requires considerable humidity and fresh soil. Its soft, flexible wood has a wide range of uses, especially in the building industry. It has regular, narrow annual rings and is a resonant wood suitable for the production of musical instruments. Spruce bark is used to make tannin. Because it is widely used as timber and profitable to grow, it is now cultivated in pure stands at lower elevations, outside its native distribution.

Male flowers (1a), female flowers (1b).

Cembran Pine *Pinus cembra* (Pinaceae)   ❷

This pine is a tree of high mountains growing near the tree line in the Alps and the Carpathians at altitudes of 1,500—2,400 m. It never forms pure stands but occurs either solitarily or in small groups with larches, Mountain Pine and spruces. It grows to a height of 20 m and, in the harsh alpine environment, its knotty trunk and thick, ovoid crown make an impressive sight. Its needles are grouped in clusters of five on the rust-coloured, downy shoots. The broadly ovate cones, 5—8 cm long, take 2 years to ripen. After attaining maturity, they disintegrate liberating wingless seeds, 1 cm long. These sweet, oily seeds are a favourite food of birds and small rodents. Cembran Pine is a slow-growing species. It is semitolerant of shade and well able to withstand frost, stroms and deep snow. Its wood is light and strong, and was used in the past for making furniture and for woodcarving. Nowadays it is strictly protected by law, a very rare tree lending beauty to high mountains.

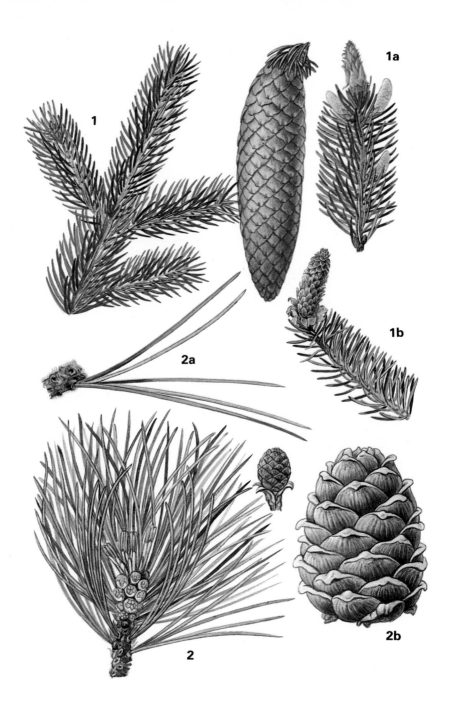

Montane Spruce Forests

Sycamore *Acer pseudoplatanus* (Aceraceae) ❶

The Sycamore is native to western, central and southern Europe; in the north it does not penetrate beyond the Baltic Sea, neither does it occur in eastern regions with a continental climate. It never forms pure stands, being only a secondary species, usually scattered throughout Beech and spruce forests. It is most abundant on rocky screes and along mountain valleys in fertile, moist localities. In the mountains it ascends to altitudes of 1,500—1,800 m. It is a tree semitolerant of shade, reproducing successfully under the forest canopy. The Sycamore is a robust tree attaining a height of 30—35 m. When young, its trunk is covered with a smooth bark which becomes scaly and easily flakes off with growing age. Its 5—7 lobed leaves are 10—16 cm across, with a coarsely serrate margin and a bluish underside, and are borne on a 15 cm long stalk. Greenish flowers appear in hanging racemes at the beginning of May; fruits ripen towards the end of September. The latter are paired, with a globular achene and wings forming almost a right angle. The Sycamore has a powerful, cordate root system which anchors it firmly in the ground. Its pale, hard wood is used in the production of furniture, musical instruments and other objects. During the blockade of Europe in the Napoleonic Wars, attempts were made to use its sap for producing sugar.

Mountain Ash, Rowan *Sorbus aucuparia* (Rosaceae) ❷

The Mountain Ash is distributed almost all over Europe; in the north it extends beyond the Arctic Circle, in central and western Europe it is mostly confined to mountain elevations. It is a useful pioneer species in clear-felled and disaster areas from submontane and montane elevations up to the Mountain Pine belt above the timberline. It resists severe frost, lays small claims on soil fertility, and thrives even on limestone substrates. It is more shade-tolerant when young, becoming a heliophyte in old age. The Mountain Ash is a medium-sized tree, growing to a height of 12—20 m. Its life is relatively short: 80—100 years. The trunk is covered with a smooth, greyish-brown bark until old age. Its odd-pinnate leaves, 12—17 cm in size, are composed of 9—15 oblong, elliptical leaflets with sharply serrate margins. White flowers in dense panicles first appear in May and develop by autumn into bright red, pea-sized berries. Birds have a special liking for these — in fact the Latin designation *aucuparia (avis capere)* indicates that fruits of the Mountain Ash were used by fowlers for catching birds. Cultivated Mountain Ash varieties have been developed and are grown in rougher regions as fruit trees. Their sweet fruits are used in preparing compotes, jams and liquors. The wood of the Mountain Ash is not very durable and is mostly used as fuel. Because of its attractive red fruits and its unpretentiousness, it is often planted along urban roads.

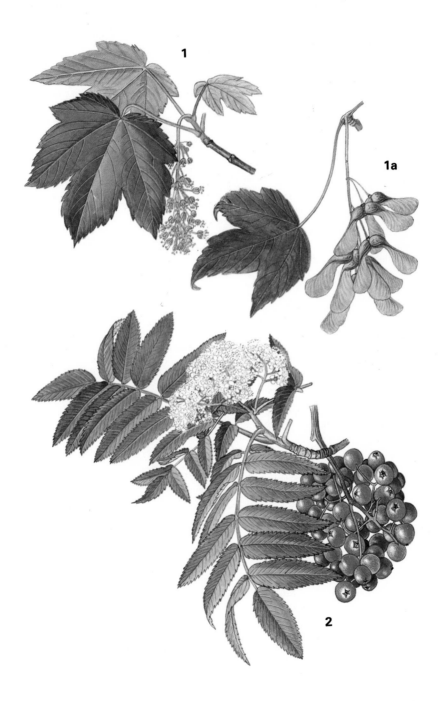

1

1a

2

Montane Spruce Forests

Black Honeysuckle   *Lonicera nigra*   (Caprifoliaceae)   ❶

This is a shrub of central European submontane and montane forests and is common, though not overabundant, in the Alps, Sudetes and Carpathians at elevations of 600—1,500 m. It grows on rocky slopes and on humus deposits alongside brooks, and is a shade-tolerant species resistant to frost. This honeysuckle is an erect, sparsely branched shrub, 1—2 m high. Its leaves are entire, oblong-elliptical, 4—6 cm long, and greenish-blue on the undersurface. The flowers are a dull pink, and arranged in pairs on one stalk. They appear towards the end of May. Its fruits — blackish berries, 8 mm in size, again borne in pairs — mature in August. In the Alps it is often accompanied by the Blue Honeysuckle *(Lonicera coerulea)* which has paired yellow flowers and large, blackish-blue berries.

Alpine Currant   *Ribes alpinum*   (Grossulariaceae)   ❷

The range of the Alpine Currant extends throughout central and southern Europe, where it grows from hills to mountain elevations of about 1,000 m. It particularly favours damp and stony localities on the margins of forests, but also grows in forest undergrowth, being tolerant of relatively deep shade. The Alpine Currant is an erect shrub, 1—2.5 m high, with an easily peeled, yellowish-grey bark. It has 3—5 lobed, small leaves, 3—4 cm in size, with apiculate lobes and serrate margins, usually flat or broadly cuneiform at the base. The inconspicuous yellowish-green flowers are dioecious, and are borne in erect racemose inflorescences. Red, globular, insipid berries, 5 mm across, ripen on the female shrubs in July. Since the Alpine Currant stands up well to pruning, it is used in gardens to form medium-sized hedgerows.

Rock Redcurrant   *Ribes petraeum*   (Grossulariaceae)   ❸

The Rock Redcurrant is confined to alpine localities in central and southern Europe. It is relatively common in the Alps, Sudetes and Carpathians where it ascends up to the Mountain Pine belt, i. e. to an altitude exceeding 1,800 m, where it grows in sufficiently moist rocky localities. The Rock Redcurrant is a thornless, erect shrub growing to a height of 1.5—2 m. Its branches are covered with a reddish-brown, easily peeled bark, its leaves are 3—5-lobed, 5—9 cm long, hirsute on the underside, and heart-shaped at the base. Reddish flowers in pendent racemes open in June and develop by August into red, sourish berries, 6 mm in diameter. The Rock Redcurrant was the species from which several cultivated varieties, now grown in gardens to yield palatable fruits, were developed.

1
1a
2
3

Montane Spruce Forests

Mountain Pine *Pinus mugo* (Pinaceae) ❶

The Mountain Pine, although well able to endure long, severe winters and heavy falls of snow, does not grow in northern Europe, but occurs only in central and southern Europe. It occupies two distinct habitats: high mountains at altitudes between 1,400—2,500 m, where on rich mineral soils it forms continuous stands near or above the timberline, and on both montane and submontane peat bogs. In each case it adopts a different growth habit. In the first case it develops as a tree, attaining a height of 10—20 m, and in the second as a decumbent shrub, 1—3 m high. The arboreal habit is found near the timberline in the Pyrenees, Vosges, and western Alps, as well as on some peat bogs; the shrubby form grows in the Sudeten Mountains, in the Carpathians, on the Balkan Peninsula, and in most peat bogs. The needles of the Mountain Pine are paired, 3—7 cm long, and densely clustered on the twig. The arboreal form develops asymmetrical cones with reddish-brown scales bearing hook-like projections (1a); the shrubby form has symmetrical, widely opening cones with flat, reddish-brown scales. The cones take 2 years to mature and the seeds are released in the spring of the third year. The seed is varicoloured, winged, and 4 mm long. The Mountain Pine is a light-demanding species which makes small claims on soil fertility and depth but requires lots of moisture. It is important in binding loose soils, thus preventing avalanches and soil erosion. The decumbent form is highly valued as an ornamental woody plant.

Mountain Alder, Wavyleaf Alder *Alnus viridis* (Betulaceae) ❷

The Mountain Alder is an alpine species widespread mainly in the Alps and in the Carpathian Mountains, where it forms continuous shrub growths above the timberline, at elevations of 1,300—2,200 m. As it is able to grow in greater shade than the Mountain Pine, it is most commonly found on the moister northward-facing slopes. Along streams and gullies it occasionally penetrates to lower elevations where it invades barren land. It readily produces stump-shoots, and spreads rapidly using root suckers. It binds loose mountain soils and prevents snow and stone avalanches. The Mountain Alder is a shrub which branches at ground level and grows to a height of 1—3 m. Often several small, slightly crooked trunks shoot up from the ground. The shoots are greenish-brown, and the stalkless buds alternately arranged. It has ovate leaves with serrate margins, 3—5 cm long, green both above and below, and rounded at the base. Amentaceous flowers appear simultaneously with the leaves in April and May. Female flowers develop by autumn into cone-shaped multiple fruits, 1 cm long, pale brown and less woody than those of other alder species. The small, yellowish-brown, winged seeds are similar to those of birches.

Male pendent and female erect flowers (2a), cone-shaped fruits (2b).

1

1a

2

2a

2b

Montane Spruce Forests

Hairy Alpenrose   *Rhododendron hirsutum*   (Ericaceae)   ❶
It occurs mainly in the eastern parts of the Alps, and does not reach further west than Switzerland. It is abundant at altitudes of 1,200—2,500 m, primarily on limestones, and in the Dolomites, in the undergrowth of open forests, and in the Mountain Pine belt. The western parts of the Alps and the Pyrenees are the home of its close relative, the Alpenrose, *R. ferrugineum*. This occurs in the Mountain Pine belt and above the timberline. In contrast to the above species, it is calcifugous and grows mostly on acidic rocks such as on granite, gneiss and biotite. *Rhododendron hirsutum* attains a height of 50—100 cm. It has evergreen, oblong-elliptical leaves, 1—3 cm in length, which are hairy on the undersides. Its flowers are bright red, campanulate, and five-lobed, arranged in groups of 3—10 in racemous panicles. Its fruits are brown, pentaloculate capsules which mature towards the end of September. At this time they split along their five septa to shed a great number of small seeds, each 1 mm in size. In *R. ferrugineum*, the leaves are covered with rusty red hairs on the lower surface, and the flowers are a darker red. Both these *Rhododendron* species are semitolerant of shade and prefer rather damp, humic soils. They have become popular in garden rockeries.

False Medlar   *Sorbus chamaemespilus*   (Rosaceae)   ❷
This is a shrub inhabiting the sub-alpine belt of high mountains in central and southern Europe: the Alps, Sudetes, Black Forest and Carpathians. There it thrives on soils rich in lime, on sunny, rocky slopes among Mountain Pine, Mountain Alder and rhododendrons. It is a low, tree-like shrub growing to a height of 1—2 m. Its rather leathery leaves are oblong-ovate, 3—7 cm long, with glossy green uppersides and pale green, hairless undersides. Salmon coloured flowers arranged in sparse corymbs appear towards the end of May. Its elliptic red berries, 8—10 mm across, ripen by the end of September. At present *Sorbus chamaemespilus* is protected by law in a number of countries.

Dwarf Juniper   *Juniperus nana*   (Cupressaceae)   ❸
The Dwarf Juniper is widespread in the far north, beyond the Arctic Circle, and in the high mountains of central and southern Europe, especially in the Alps and Carpathians, where it grows at elevations of 1,300—2,200 m. It particularly favours mossy and peaty localities or stony slopes. The Dwarf Juniper is a prostrate shrub, about 50 cm tall. Its thick, prickleless needles, 5—10 mm long, are borne in densely clustered whorls. It is dioecious, its flowers opening towards the end of June. In autumn of the following year, the female flowers develop into small, blackish, berry-like, pruinose cones resembling the berries of the Common Juniper.

3a

3

1

2

Montane Spruce Forests

Map-winged Swift *Hepialus fusconebulosa* (Hepialidae)

Ghost moths (Hepialidae) are a family of relatively primitive moths whose fore- and hindwings have practically the same markings. This species, which has a wingspan of 38—48 mm, is inconspicuous both in its habits and its colouring. It is basically brown with light spots on its forewings. The lighter borders round the spots and the pronounced spots on the margins of the wings are typical features. The males are rather more brightly coloured than the females, which are larger and a more greyish-brown. The caterpillars are likewise inconspicuous in their habits, living in the ground where they feed on the rhizomes of ferns. The insect's development is very protracted and the caterpillars, which hatch late in the summer, hibernate twice before pupating in their second spring. The moth, which is not very common, is a typical inhabitant of submontane and montane forests, also venturing out into damp meadows and gardens nearby. It flies in June and July. In Europe it occurs at high altitudes in the Pyrenees, Alps and Carpathians and is also to be found as far afield as the Urals.

Apollo *Parnassius apollo* (Papilionidae)

The Apollo has become rare in most of Europe and is now protected by law. It is striking in appearance and by no means shy. Its forewings, which have a span of 70—90 mm, have four black spots on their anterior margin and one on their posterior margin. The outer margin of the wings is free from scales and is therefore transparent. The hindwings are marked with two red, black-bordered ocelli. The wings are also dusted, to varying degrees, with black scales, especially near the roots. This species is primarily bound to mountain massifs, although in the Carpathians it is also known in many lowland localities at altitudes of not more than 300 m. Isolation of the various populations has given rise to many geographical races differing, among other things, in their markings and the caterpillars' host plants. It was precisely the variability of this species that made it so interesting to collectors and eventually led to its disappearance in many of its original haunts. It flies in July and August, when the female lays its eggs on Wall-pepper and Houseleek plants. The larvae, which hatch in the following spring, are black with red spots when fully grown and pupate on the ground in June. This butterfly is distributed throughout the mountains of western Europe and southern Scandinavia; in central Europe it is disappearing and it was never present in Great Britain. In the east it occurs in the Carpathians and extends into inner Asia.

Dark-green Fritillary *Mesoacidalia aglaja* (Nymphalidae)

This butterfly, which flies with great agility and has a wingspan of 50—60 mm, is still abundant in some places. It frequents clearings, forest footpaths and the outskirts of forests, and is distributed over the whole of Europe and Morocco and into Asia as far as China and Japan. It occurs in mountains as well as in uplands and even ascends to the limit of the forest belt. It may easily be identified by the pattern on the underside of its hindwings. The caterpillar lives from August to May on violets and other plants, such as Bistort.

Lesser Marbled Fritillary *Brenthis ino* (Nymphalidae)

This fritillary now occurs only sporadically and is already rare. It frequents marshy meadows and mountain peat bogs, and in such places is still abundant, especially near brooks and mountain streams, where it sucks nectar from thistles, Bramble and other flowers. The caterpillar hibernates and pupates in May: its host plants are the Bramble and Spiraea bush. It is to be found in central and northern Europe, the Pyrenees and the Alps.

Montane Spruce Forests

Marbled White *Melanargia galathea* (Satyridae)
This butterfly is one of the 'light' species of the genus *Melanargia*. In central and western Europe (from Germany to the coast and in southern England) it is common from the lowlands up to altitudes of 1,500—1,700 metres. It occurs in forest glades and clearings and also in damp meadows, wherever Timothy Grass and Couch Grass grow. It is absent from Scandinavia and Denmark. The butterfly is basically creamy-white to yellowish, the females being lighter than the males. The chequered markings are a deep black-brown in the males and brownish in the females. The males have a wingspan of 46—52 mm, the females of about 56 mm. The markings are very variable, and several distinct geographical races occur in Europe. The chrysalis is yellowish-grey, with spots on the sides of the head segment; it lies unprotected on the ground.

Sudeten Ringlet *Erebia sudetica* (Satyridae)
This butterfly (wingspan 34—36 mm) occurs in only a few small areas in Europe. It is confined to certain mountain ranges, such as Jeseníky, the Carpathians and a few localities in the French and Swiss Alps. It has a predilection for Bistort and Knotgrass flowers. The caterpillar probably lives on different types of meadow-grass of the genus *Poa*.

Peppered Moth *Biston betularia* (Geometridae)
This moth is one of the largest of the European geometrids, though with its thick body it is not typical of the family. It has a wingspan of 50—60 mm. Apart from the basic light (pepper-and-salt) form, dark to black forms also occur. The latter type was first discovered in England near Manchester. This phenomenon is today described as industrial melanism and is known in various species of butterflies and moths. Much intensive research was required to show that this is a protective colouring in a changed environment. The original light form is difficult to detect on the trunks of trees overgrown with lichen, but in an environment polluted by industrial smoke this colouring affords no protection at all; on dark trunks without any lichen the light-coloured moths are very conspicuous and easily seen by insectivorous birds, which prey on them selectively, thus allowing the dark form to become relatively more abundant. It is now hard to find examples of the light form, while the dark form *('carbonaria')* occurs even in the mountains, where there is no pollution. This moth is fairly abundant and occurs in lowlands, foothills and mountains. In warm regions it produces two summer generations, but in the mountains only one. The caterpillars vary greatly in colour and may be yellowish-green, grey or brown. Their host plants — apart from birches — are oaks, willows, Goat Willow, poplars, Ash, Sloe and various other trees and shrubs. They pupate in the ground in the autumn, and the moths emerge at the end of the following April or May.

Rheumaptera hastata (Geometridae)
This is a very beautiful, vividly marked geometrid. The intricate black pattern on a creamy white ground is very variable and tends to be darker in mountainous regions. The wings have a span of 35 mm. From May to July the moth abounds on marshy meadows where birches grow. The caterpillars depend on birches for their sustenance, but also live on Bilberry, Cranberry and willows. They pupate and then hibernate on the ground.

Montane Spruce Forests

Jodis putata (Geometridae)

This dainty geometrid has a wingspan of 22 mm and is pale greenish-blue, though old individuals, which have been flying a long time, may be practically white. Across the forewings there is a barely distinguishable, white zigzag line. The tiny caterpillars are light grey, with red spots, and are to be seen in July on Bilberry plants. The chrysalis hibernates and the moths emerge between May and June. This is a common species though it originated in the orient. It occurs in hardwood, as well as conifer forests from northern and central Europe to the north of Italy.

Torula quadrifaria (Geometridae)

An interesting feature of this tiny geometrid is that the pattern on the upper- and undersides of its wings is exactly the same. It has a wingspan of about 25 mm, and is a typical alpine moth, frequently to be encountered above the forest belt from June to August. The brown, light-sided caterpillars, which have a black dorsal stripe and oblique black lateral lines, live on various alpine herbaceous plants. The caterpillar hibernates and does not pupate until the spring. The closely related species *Psodos alpinata,* which is a uniform dark brown with a reddish-yellow lustre, is to be found in similar localities. Both species fly at high altitudes in European mountains.

Hypena crassalis (Noctuidae)

This moth frequents peat bogs and moors associated with spruce woods and sometimes with mixed forests. It is a common species and can be seen in June, July and occasionally in August. Its wings have a span of 30—35 mm. The brown forewings have very intricate markings along their rear edge; the hindwings are light greyish-brown. The caterpillar is basically green, the constrictions between its segments being yellow, and it has three indistinct, dark green lines running down its back. On every segment are four tubercles, each with a protruding hair. In August the caterpillar is to be found on Bilberry plants. The green-headed, black-spotted chrysalis hibernates. This moth occurs throughout the whole of central and northern Europe.

Vapourer Moth *Orgyia antiqua* (Lymantriidae)

Orgyia antiqua exhibits pronounced sexual dimorphism. As in some spring and autumn geometrids, the grey, fat-bodied female has two pairs of rudimentary stumps instead of functional wings. The male (wingspan 30—34 mm) has fully developed, bright brown wings with dark markings and characteristic white or yellow semicircular spots near their posterior margin. These moths are active at or soon after midday, when the males go looking for females. The female lays its eggs on the surface of its cocoon, in which it remains imprisoned for the whole of its short life. Two weeks later the caterpillars hatch and go their separate ways. They are greyish-blue, with red, black and white spots, and have four tufts of yellow hairs on their back. Compared with other species they develop very slowly, not infrequently taking two months. They prefer deciduous trees, but will also live on spruces and on some of the plants in the undergrowth. If the weather is favourable, *Orgyia antiqua* usually produces two generations in a year, but otherwise only one, especially in mountain regions. The second batch of eggs does not hatch until the following year. This moth occurs throughout the whole of the temperate zone of Europe, Asia and North America. It is not confined to any particular altitude, but is commoner in uplands and mountains.

Montane Spruce Forests

Great Puss Moth *Cerura vinula* (Notodontidae)

This large moth has a wingspan of 65—75 mm. In both sexes the ground colour is white and the wings have dark brown (females) or black (males) markings in the form of broken, zigzag lines. The body has spots of the same colour and is extremely hairy. The males have markedly feathery antennae. The moths fly from April to July, according to the altitude. The females lay their large eggs (up to 2.5 mm in diameter) singly on the upper surface of leaves. When fully grown, the caterpillars are green, with a violet saddle mark on the back and a violet scutum on the first body segment. Instead of the last pair of legs the caterpillar has two hollow spines about 1.5 cm long; these are brandished sideways at enemies, and crimson, fleshy, lash-like motile processes are protruded from them. The caterpillar's defence system also includes an evil smelling fluid which is ejected from a gland below its head. These exceedingly voracious caterpillars are capable of stripping shrubs and small deciduous trees completely bare, leaving only short fragments of leaf stalk. Their main hosts are poplars, Aspen, willows and Goat Willow. They pupate at the foot of the tree, after first biting out a pupal chamber for themselves, sometimes in the wood. The resultant waste material is used in the construction of their solid cocoon, which differs very little, either in structure or colouring, from its background and so conceals the almost black, faintly gleaming chrysalis until the following spring. The Great Puss Moth occurs in lowlands, and also high up in mountain areas, throughout the whole of Europe.

Autographa bractea (Noctuidae)

This is a typically montane species, although the moth is also to be seen in uplands. It is rare and appears from June to September. It sometimes flies during the day, especially if the weather suddenly changes, or before a storm. It mostly frequents damp meadows, glades with streams running through them and the banks of mountain streams. The caterpillars live on various herbaceous plants, e. g. Coltsfoot, Hawkweed, plantains and Dandelion. The larvae hibernate and pupate the following spring.

Oeceptoma thoracicum (Silphidae)

This beetle is about 8—11 mm long and being saprophagous, living on the dead parts of plants and animals, it hunts for dead animals and rotting mushrooms. Since it is a scavenger, like a number of other species, it is a very useful insect. It can be found the whole year round, and occurs mainly in Europe, but also in the Caucasus and Siberia.

Four-spot Wood-borer *Anthaxia quadripunctata* (Buprestidae)

The dark brown beetle measures about 5—7 mm and has a slightly domed back. It is a relatively common species, especially in mountainous regions, where it can be found on dry spruce twigs and trunks, or on flowering plants, e. g. Hawkweed. The larvae live behind the bark of dead conifers. It is not in any way a harmful species; on the contrary, it helps to decompose dead wood and thus aids the formation of humus. The beetles swarm from June to September. This species is distributed over the whole of Europe and Asia, except in the more northerly regions.

Montane Spruce Forests

Common Wood-borer *Buprestis rustica* (Buprestidae)
This beetle, which measures 16–18 mm, lives primarily in conifer forests, where it attacks the dead parts of trees. It swarms in June, July and August and lives at high altitudes in various parts of Europe.

Toxotus cursor (Cerambycidae)
This beetle, which is 25–32 mm long, varies greatly in colour and is sexually dimorphic. Its wing-cases are usually either a reddish yellow-brown with black bands, or are brownish-yellow (in the females) and unmarked. Dark individuals may have black wing-cases with a narrow red border, or may be black all over. The larvae live in tree stumps – mainly spruce, but sometimes in other conifers. The beetles can often be seen resting on felled, barked timber, or on various forest plants, such as Butterbur. They swarm from May to August and are most numerous in foothills and mountains. This species occurs both in Europe and in Asia (western Siberia, and western Asia as far as Beluchistan).

Judolia cerambyciformis (Cerambycidae)
This small longicorn beetle measures only 6.5–11.5 mm. It has a brownish-yellow, black-spotted body and yellow wing-cases with black markings. Like the previous species, a large number of colour variants are known, with wing-cases from pure yellow to almost black with narrow yellow bands. Curiously, the host plant of the larva has yet to be discovered, but is presumably a species of deciduous tree. The beetle is usually to be seen on a wide range of flowers from June to August. It is one of the commoner species, in the mountains as well as the lowlands, and occurs in Europe, Asia Minor and Transcaucasia.

Monochamus sutor (Cerambycidae)
This is a moderately large longicorn beetle with a body up to 24 mm long. It is entirely black, except for the yellow spots, arranged in three transverse bands, on its wing-cases, although even these may be absent. Its antennae are more than double the length of its body. This beetle's development takes one year. The beetles swarm on warm days from June to September, when they are very active and are to be found mainly on unbarked timber. When they first emerge they remain in the crowns of the trees, however, where they feed on the leaves for about 15 days until they have finished developing. Later, they transfer their attentions to the new wood, in which the females lay their eggs from June to July. They excavate relatively deep holes in the bark and lay one egg in each. The larvae bite out wide, irregular areas in the bast and sapwood, expelling the splinters and coarse débris through a hole in the bark. They live in the bast for 1–2 months, until they measure about 20 mm. By that time the summer is at an end and the larvae gnaw oval passages in the wood, about 3–4 cm deep, in which they hibernate. In the spring they resume feeding and when fully grown measure up to 40 mm. They pupate in a chamber formed at the end of the passage. The young beetles bite their way to freedom through a round opening in the wood. This species is a pest, due to the damage it causes to timber. It appears mainly after gales have snapped and uprooted trees and attacks conifers – chiefly spruces, but also pines and firs and sometimes Cembran Pine. It is widely distributed over the whole of Europe except Greece, and stretches far into eastern Asia.

Montane Spruce Forests

Pachyta quadrimaculata   (Cerambycidae)

This beetle measures 11—20 mm, the female being larger than the male. In both sexes the antennae are almost the same length as the body. The males have a somewhat shorter body and the sides of their wing-cases are slightly compressed towards the tip. The body is black, while the wing-cases are yellow or yellowish-brown and are decorated with two black spots, one behind the other. The eggs are laid in conifers (chiefly spruces), on which the larvae develop afterwards. The beetles, on the other hand, are fond of flowers, and swarm from June to August. This species is distributed all over Europe and in Asia it extends to the Amur region and northern Mongolia. It is rare in lowlands, but common in the foothills and mountains.

Rhagium inquisitor   (Cerambycidae)

This beetle, which measures 10—21 mm, has a black body and its head and scutum are covered with smooth grey hairs. Its wing-cases are pale yellow, with spotted grey or yellow hairs, and bear two incomplete bands and a few scattered bare black spots. The larvae live behind the bark of conifers or of rotting stumps. There they pupate in a pupal chamber formed of coarse splinters and débris. The beetle emerges in the autumn and then hibernates. In the spring it visits the flowers of various species of plants, or may be seen scurrying over wood. It appears from April to July and again in September. It occurs in Europe, Asia (as far as western Siberia) and North America. It is common in both lowlands and mountainous country.

Otiorrhynchus niger   (Curculionidae)

The beetle, which is 7—12 mm long, has a short snout and relatively slender body. Its scutum is finely granular and its wing-cases coarsely granular, with shallow longitudinal grooves, and its legs are red. The beetles appear in the spring and lay their eggs from the middle of May to the end of August, in piles of about 60, in the soil. The larvae eat the roots of tree (mainly spruce) seedlings. They have a gleaming yellowish white, curved body, a brown head and no legs. While growing they live at a depth of about 2—15 cm. They hibernate in the ground and pupate the following year, from July to September, in an underground chamber at a depth of 5—8 cm. The young beetles also hibernate (in the pupal chamber), dig their way out in the following spring and attack the needles of young spruces less than about 20 years old; in rare cases they may eat the leaves of deciduous trees. They are a menace mainly to conifer seedlings, which, if their roots are severely damaged, die the same year, or at the latest within 2—3 years. This weevil is a typical mountain-dweller.

Pissodes piceae   (Curculionidae)

This weevil, which measures 7—10 mm, is black and has a rust-coloured band on its wing-cases. Its life cycle takes 2—3 years. The larvae attack the bast of firs, in which they gnaw radially diverging passages up to 60 cm long, and ending in conspicuous pupal chambers; the passages barely encroach on the sapwood. The beetle has a predilection for 40 to 80 year old firs and is a serious pest, generally attacking trees already weakened by bark beetles. Its presence is betrayed by escaping sap and by the gaps pecked in the bark by woodpeckers which hunt it.

Montane Spruce Forests

Liparus glabrirostris (Curculionidae)

With a length of 17–21 mm, this is one of the largest weevils in Europe. It is black, with a border of fine yellow hairs on the sides of its scutum, and usually has yellow-spotted wing-cases. On the inner edge of the last segment of its legs (tarsi) it has striking hooked teeth. It frequents mountain streams and torrents and may often be seen sitting on the leaves of Butterbur. In Europe it is abundant at high altitudes from June to August.

Engraver Beetle *Ips typographus* (Scolytidae)

This small, glossy, brown-black beetle, which measures only 4.2–5.5 mm, has a black scutum and head and brown wing-cases which are shorter than the abdomen. Its entire body is covered with fine golden hairs. The beetles swarm *en masse* from the end of April to the beginning of June (in the mountains). They mainly attack fallen or damaged and weakened spruces, but in years when they are numerous will also attack healthy trees. They attain sexual maturity in 2–3 weeks and then mate in 'bridal chambers' behind the bark of trees. These chambers lead into 2–3 maternal shafts in which the female lays the eggs. When the larvae are hatched, they excavate tunnels radiating out perpendicularly to these shafts and widening at the end to form a pupal chamber. Since the larvae eat away the bast, the supply of nutrients is cut off and the tree dries up. The young beetles add to the damage, since they likewise attack the bast of the tree around where they pupated, or move to other trees. The larvae develop in 6–10 weeks. In central Europe there are generally two generations; the summer swarming time is June and July, but in the mountains swarming does not take place until August. Winds and gales uprooting the trees facilitate overproliferation of this beetle in forest growths, but so does the planting of spruce monocultures and the late barking of felled trees. The Engraver Beetle is combated by preventive measures, such as the preparation of special trees left as traps, whose bark is afterwards burnt. Trees attacked during a catastrophe must likewise be quickly stripped and the bark burnt. The Engraver Beetle occurs in Europe and Asia, where it extends to northern China.

Red Wood Ant *Formica rufa* (Formicidae)

This extremely useful ant destroys large quantities of insects and thus helps to maintain the biological balance of the forest. It is a moderately large species, the workers measuring 4–9 mm and the females 9–11 mm. The head and abdomen are brown or black and the thorax is red. In the forest it builds the anthills familiar to us all, usually from dry conifer needles. Its highly developed social life has led to differentiation of the population into females, males (fertile individuals have wings) and workers (which are wingless). The anthill, which may be as much as one metre or more high, contains a colony of up to several hundred thousand individuals. Ants — like bees — hibernate; in the autumn a part of the population dies, but the rest survive the winter inside the nest. Ants are omnivorous and in addition to animal food they also eat sweet juices and berries.

Carpenter Ant *Camponotus ligniperda* (Formicidae)

This ant is almost twice the size of the preceding species and measures 14–18 mm. It builds its nests in old, rotting tree trunks.

Montane Spruce Forests

Common Lizard, Viviparous Lizard   *Lacerta vivipara*   (Lacertidae)

This small lizard seldom measures more than 150 mm, half of which is accounted for by the tail. It has a greyish-brown to blackish-brown, light-spotted body with a bronze sheen. The female has a dingy yellow and the male an orange-red belly. The Common Lizard inhabits wooded slopes at the foots of mountains, where it lives chiefly behind the bark of old tree stumps. It also occurs in damp, peaty meadows and is even to be found in swamps. It is a good swimmer and when in danger will often seek shelter under water. In the mountains of central Europe it occurs up to 1,400 m; in the Alps and Balkans to 3,000 m. It is ovoviviparous, that is to say, it lays eggs from which the young emerge the instant the eggs are laid. The young are almost black and are about 2.5—3.5 cm long. They live chiefly on small insects.

Grass Snake   *Natrix natrix*   (Colubridae)

The Grass Snake is one of the commonest snakes in Europe and is distributed over a wide area. In consequence, there are several geographical races in Europe. The body is usually grey, but may sometimes be greyish-yellow or brownish-grey, and is marked with scattered, irregular black spots. Behind the head there are semicircular yellow and black markings. The eye has a narrow, yellow iris. Their average length is 100 cm, but specimens measuring up to 200 cm have been known. The Grass Snake is to be found in various environments, but in general it requires moisture. It occurs near ponds and rivers, but also inhabits damp meadows. In forests it frequents pools, damp glades and the banks of streams, where it lives on frogs, newts and fish, so that it can often be found in the water, looking for food. The eggs are laid in July in rotting leaves, compost or anywhere where decomposition in the presence of sufficient moisture produces a raised temperature. The young hatch in September and are about 15 cm long. The Grass Snake is distributed from southern Europe to Sweden.

Smooth Snake   *Coronella austriaca*   (Colubridae)

The Smooth Snake is comparatively small; it measures about 50 cm and is seldom longer than 70 cm. It is greyish-brown, with a dark horseshoe mark behind its head and two rows of dark brown spots which sometimes give it the appearance of an Adder. Like all other colubrid snakes it has round pupils. It is very aggressive and mainly catches lizards, slow-worms and young snakes. It frequents dry spots on the outskirts of forests, copses and sometimes damp meadows, especially in the mountains. It is ovoviviparous.

Adder   *Vipera berus*   (Viperidae)

This is the most widespread venomous snake in Europe, although in recent years its numbers have severely declined. Its average length is about 50 cm. Its colouring is very variable; the males are basically grey and the females brownish, but completely black and rusty red specimens are also known. The most characteristic feature is the more or less distinct zigzag black line running down the back. The Adder is to be found at all altitudes and frequents both dry localities and peat bogs and other damp places. It is a very useful snake and destroys large numbers of rodents, though when young lives mainly on lizards. The 5—15 young are born at the end of the summer and are able to use their fangs immediately. The Adder is very shy and retiring, slipping into hiding at the approach of an intruder, and hence favours habitats free from disturbance.

Montane Spruce Forests

Buzzard *Buteo buteo* (Accipitridae)

Next to the Goshawk, the Buzzard is the commonest large bird of prey in Europe (it has a wingspan of up to 135 cm) and is to be found everywhere except in the Scandinavian tundra. It inhabits forests at all altitudes and circles above the neighbouring fields and meadows at great heights in search of prey. It lives mainly on mice and voles, but also takes small birds and large insects, and in the winter eats carrion and sick and otherwise weakened game. The nest, which is made of broken branches, is built high up in a tree, usually right beside the trunk, and is lined with leaves and moss. At the beginning of May the female lays 2—4 white eggs marked with greyish-violet spots and incubates them unaided for about a month. The young, which are covered with white down, are fed by the parents for about 6—7 weeks in the nest and for a further 4 weeks outside it. The Buzzard has very variable plumage, some individuals being whitish and others dark brown with irregular markings down and across their body. In Europe the Buzzard is a resident bird.

Peregrine Falcon *Falco peregrinus* (Falconidae)

The Peregrine Falcon nests all over Europe, Asia and North America, but is now very rare in western and central Europe. It is a little larger than a Carrion Crow and can be identified in flight by its long, pointed wings and short, tapering tail. Its light brown, speckled eggs are laid directly in a niche in a steep rock, in a ruined building or in the derelict nest of some other bird. The 2—3 young hatch after 4 weeks and are fed by the female on food supplied by the male. They fledge after about 40 days and then begin to hunt for their own food — pigeons, jays, crows, Coots and other birds. The Peregrine Falcon always catches its prey on the wing. It seeks a point of vantage from which it swoops, often at 200 k/h, and sinks its talons into the victim's body. These skills are put to good account in the ancient sport of falconry (the use of birds of prey for catching game).

Kestrel *Falco tinnunculus* (Falconidae)

The Kestrel is the best known and the commonest member of the falcon family. It even occurs in towns (where it occasionally nests in towers), as well as in open country with small copses and on the outskirts of large forests. The nest is built in a hollow tree, a niche in a rock or an abandoned crow's nest at the beginning of May. It contains 5—6 brown, speckled eggs from which the young hatch after 28—30 days. The young spend about a month in the nest and are fed chiefly by the female, on food brought by the male — mice, voles and sometimes large insects. Kestrels also occasionally eat sparrows and other small birds. The Kestrel is mainly a resident bird, but sometimes migrates to southern Europe and northern Africa. It is very useful, as it destroys rodent pests, and ought therefore to be afforded every protection.

Tengmalm's Owl *Aegolius funereus* (Strigidae)

This rather small owl (wingspan about 55 cm) inhabits conifer and mixed forests in northern and central Europe, and tends to be sporadically distributed. It nests in holes in trees (often abandoned woodpeckers' nests) or nestboxes. The 4—6 white, spherical eggs are laid in April and are incubated for about 4 weeks by the female. Both parents feed the young for about a month in the nest and for some time after they leave it. Tengmalm' Owl lives mainly on voles, mice, dormice and small birds and their young; it hunts only in the evening and at night. It flies in a straight line and not with undulating motions like the Barn Owl or the Tawny Owl. During the day it remains hidden away in dense foliage or a hollow. Like all owls it is a very useful bird and in view of its local and sometimes infrequent occurrence it ought to be protected everywhere.

Montane Spruce Forests

Golden Eagle   *Aquila chrysaëtos*   (Accipitridae)
The Golden Eagle is one of the largest birds of prey and inhabits mountainous regions in Europe, Asia and North America. In Europe it occurs mainly in the Pyrenees, the Alps, Scandinavia, the Carpathians and the Balkans. It usually nests on a rock ledge, on an inaccessible rock face or in a cave. The nest, which is up to 2 metres across, is made of branches and is always lined with dry grass and fur. The dark brown, spotted eggs are laid in April and are incubated by both the parents in turn for up to 45 days. The female feeds the one or two young for 3 months on food provided by the male. Eagles will catch anything they can, but live mainly on marmots, hares, birds up to the size of a grouse and occasionally the young of deer and Chamois. A cruising eagle, which has a wingspan of up to 2 metres, is a truly impressive sight. The Golden Eagle is now very rare in Europe and ought to be strictly protected.

Capercaillie   *Tetrao urogallus*   (Tetraonidae)
This, the largest representative of the European game birds (it weighs up to 6 kg), is most at home in the conifer forests of Scandinavia and northern Siberia. In western and central Europe it occurs only here and there in spruce forests in the mountains. In April, early in the morning, the male begins its courting display on the branch of a spruce tree and becomes so involved in its song that for a short time it is completely oblivious to everything around it. It then continues its courting on the ground and mates with several females. The female incubates 5—8 light brown, speckled eggs, laid in a lined depression under a tree stump, for about 28 days. The newly hatched chicks are very active and feed themselves on insects, berries and tree buds. Old Capercaillies will also nip off the tops of young spruces, especially in the winter. The Capercaillie is a resident bird and never moves very far from its nesting site.

Black Grouse   *Lyrurus tetrix*   (Tetraonidae)
The Black Grouse occurs primarily in the thin forests of the arctic tundra and the Siberian taiga. In the rest of Europe it occurs in mountain forests and on heaths and moors where there are groups of birches. Black Grouse do their courting gregariously in open spaces at the margin of forests. In April and at the beginning of May, before it is properly light, they assemble on their courting ('lekking') grounds, hop about, ruffle their feathers and utter loud calls. The cocks always mate with several hens, which each lay 6—10 yellowish brown eggs in a depression lined with grass and leaves and incubate them for about 4 weeks. As soon as they hatch, the chicks follow the hen about, looking for food — insects, larvae, worms, berries and seeds. The Black Grouse, which weighs about 1.5 kg, is a very popular game bird and the feathers of its lyre-shaped tail are a coveted trophy.

Hazel Hen   *Tetrastes bonasia*   (Tetraonidae)
This small game bird, which weighs about 0.5 kg, is still very common in Scandinavian forests with sufficient undergrowth. Though it occurs only sporadically in central Europe, it is more abundant in the southeast. It frequents mixed forests with Bilberry, Cranberry and other berry-bearing plants which provide it with food in the winter. In the summer it lives on insects, worms and green shoots. It nests in May, when the female lays 8—12 yellowish brown eggs in a depression lined with leaves and dry grass. The chicks, which hatch after 25 days, begin to look for food immediately, but remain with the hen for several weeks. In central Europe the Hazel Hen is protected by law; in the north and east its tasty flesh makes it popular as game.

Montane Spruce Forests

Great Spotted Woodpecker *Dendrocopos major* (Picidae)
This black and white bird, about the size of a Blackbird, with a red patch behind its head, inhabits the whole of Europe and Asia except the tundra. It is to be found in every type of forest and in parks and large gardens. With its strong beak it hacks a cavity about 30 cm long in the trunk of a tree, in which the female lays 5—6 white eggs. For about 2 weeks, the parents take turns to incubate the eggs. For about 3 weeks after, they both feed the young on insects and insect larvae, found behind the bark. They thus destroy large numbers of insect pests and are extremely useful, but they also eat nuts and the seeds of various trees. In Europe they are mainly resident birds and only northern populations migrate southward. In the winter they roam the countryside in the company of tits and Nuthatches and venture close to villages and towns in search of food.

Black Woodpecker *Dryocopus martius* (Picidae)
The red-capped Black Woodpecker, which is about the size of a Carrion Crow, can often be heard and seen in the forest in the spring, hammering away at broken branches. It inhabits dense mixed and conifer forests all over Europe (except in the south) and in the northern half of Asia. The nest cavity, which is some 50 cm deep, is excavated in the trunk of a pine, Beech or some other tree. Here the female lays 4—5 white, pointed eggs, which it incubates, together with the male, for about 14 days. The parents feed the young for about 4 weeks on ants, pupae and the larvae of insects living in wood. This woodpecker always hacks out several sleeping holes near the actual nest. It is a very useful bird, as it destroys the larvae of longicorn beetles and other insect pests.

Bullfinch *Pyrrhula pyrrhulla* (Fringillidae)
The Bullfinch is a brightly coloured bird a little larger than a sparrow. The male has a pink, and the female a greyish-brown breast. It inhabits the whole of Europe (except the Iberian Peninsula) and the northern half of Asia. It is to be found mainly in montane spruce forests, but also appears in mixed upland forests with dense undergrowth. In the winter it descends to the lowlands, where it roams the countryside together with other Bullfinches from further north. The nest is built at the end of April close to the ground in dense young spruces or bushes. It is made of twigs and lined with leaves, moss and lichen. The 4—5 blue, red-speckled eggs are incubated for about 14 days, mostly by the female. The parents both feed the young for about 2 weeks on small insects. Adult Bullfinches live on berries and the seeds and buds of woody plants. They generally nest a second time in July.

Crossbill *Loxia curvirostra* (Fringillidae)
This crimson and yellow bird, which is a little larger than a sparrow, inhabits conifer forests — mainly in the mountains — over the whole of Europe, Siberia and North America. Its colouring shows up clearly against the snow. It is remarkable for its crossed beak, which is specially adapted for extracting conifer seeds — the main element of the bird's diet — from their cones. The Crossbill nests between January and April, i. e. during the winter, when it has an adequate supply of conifer seeds for its young. The nest is a strong, warm structure with thick walls made of grass blades, twigs, moss and lichen, and is situated high up in a dense network of branches. The female incubates the 4 light green, spotted eggs for about 14 days and, together with the male, feeds the young for a further 2 weeks. In good cone years the forest is full of Crossbills; at other times they fly far afield in search of food.

Montane Spruce Forests

Goldcrest *Regulus regulus* (Sylviidae)

The Goldcrest is the smallest European bird, since it weighs only 6 g and measures about 9 cm. Its whole body is an inconspicuous greenish colour and its main distinguishing mark is the black-edged orange (male) or yellow (female) stripe on its crown. It inhabits the whole of Europe, Asia and North America as far as the northernmost limit of the forests. It occurs at all altitudes, always in conifer growths, though not among pines. High up in the top of a tree, at the end of a branch, it weaves a nest made of twigs, blades of grass, moss and lichen, with a relatively small top opening. Here, in April, the female lays 8—11 tiny, light brown eggs. The young, which hatch after 14 days, are fed for a similar period, by both parents, on aphids, caterpillars and spiders. In the winter, Goldcrests gather insect eggs and pupae concealed behind the bark. Fairly common in central and southern Europe is the Firecrest *(Regulus ignicapillus)*, which is somewhat more brightly coloured and spends the winter (from August to March) in northern Africa.

Dunnock *Prunella modularis* (Prunellidae)

This sparrow-sized, grey-brown bird with a bluish head inhabits dense conifer growths, mixed woods, gardens and parks all over Europe except in the most northerly and southerly parts. Its nest, which is made of twigs and moss, is built among dense young spruces or bushes close to the ground. In April and again in July, the female lays 4—5 glossy greenish-blue eggs, which both parents incubate for some 14 days. The young are fed for 2 weeks on insects. Adult Dunnocks also eat spiders, larvae, berries and seeds. They generally winter in southern and western Europe and return to their northern nesting places in March; in mild years some spend the winter in central Europe.

Dipper *Cinclus cinclus* (Cinclidae)

The Dipper lives beside mountain streams and torrents and also obtains its food — the larvae of aquatic insects and crustaceans — from water. It hunts below the surface, running nimbly over the bottom, and does not even mind a thin, surface film of ice. It is a brown bird about the size of a thrush, with a white breast. Its nest is built under the bank, among roots, in a hole or between stones, and is lined with moss and aquatic plants. In April and July the female lays 4—6 white eggs. The young hatch after 16 days and are fed by the parents for 3 weeks. The Dipper occurs over the whole of Europe and also, sporadically, in northern and central Asia and west Africa. In the winter it occasionally descends to the foothills and will sometimes actually nest there.

Common Treecreeper *Certhia familiaris* (Certhiidae)

This species closely resembles the Short-toed Treecreeper *(Certhia brachydactyla)*. While the latter mainly inhabits hardwood and pine forests, the Common Treecreeper occurs chiefly in conifer woods over the whole of Europe except northern Scandinavia, and is likewise common in Asia and North America. It runs nimbly up and down the trunks of trees looking for food — small insects, larvae and spiders. It nests in April and again in June. The nest, which is made of lichen, moss and grass and is lined with feathers, is built in a crevice behind loose bark or in a woodpile. The first clutch comprises 5—7 white, red-speckled eggs; the second clutch is smaller. The young hatch after 14 days and are fed by the parents on insects for 16—17 days. The Common Treecreeper is a resident bird and not even the severest winters drive it from its home, since there is always sufficient food to be found in cracks in the bark.

Montane Spruce Forests

Fieldfare *Turdus pilaris* (Turdidae)

The Fieldfare is only slightly larger than the Song Thrush and is similarly coloured, but has a slate-grey head and neck. It is commonest in the conifer forests of northern Europe, but also abounds in mixed woods on the hills of central and western Europe. It nests in April, in small colonies. The nest is built on a forked branch, close to the trunk, some 2—3 metres from the ground. It is made of small twigs and grass and is often lined with clay. The female incubates 5—6 greenish grey, finely speckled eggs for 2 weeks; the young are fed on worms for 14 days in the nest and then for a few more days near it. In the autumn, central, southern and western Europe are invaded by migrant birds from the north, which live mainly on Rowan and other berries. Fieldfares were once caught and eaten as a delicacy, but in most countries this is now prohibited owing to the decrease in their numbers.

Redwing *Turdus iliacus* (Turdidae)

The Redwing inhabits the conifer forests of northern Europe and seldom nests in central or western Europe though it is frequently seen there as it migrates to southern Europe and northern Africa for the winter. It is similar to the Song Thrush in size and colouring, but has russet flanks. The nest may be built in a tree, in a bush or on the ground and is made of grass, twigs and moss. The 5—6 greenish-blue eggs are incubated for 2 weeks by the female. The young, which both the parents feed on insects, leave the nest after about 14 days. The largest thrush, which inhabits the whole of Europe, Siberia and northwest Africa, is the Mistle Thrush *(T. viscivorus)*. It prefers conifer forests and in the spring likes to sing perched at the top of a tree; the nest is also built at a considerable height. Mistle Thrushes migrate southwards in October and November and return in February and March.

Ring Ouzel *Turdus torquatus* (Turdidae)

The Ring Ouzel is commonest in the Alps, the Pyrenees, the Carpathians and Scandinavia. It usually nests at the upper limit of the forest belt, often near a stream or a torrent. The nest is made of grass blades and lichen and is built among dense branches. The female incubates the 4—5 bluish eggs for about 14 days. After 16 days the young leave the nest and hide among stones, where the parents continue to feed them for a further 14 days. Ring Ouzels live mainly on insects, larvae and worms and sometimes eat berries. In the winter they migrate to southern Europe and northern Africa. The Ring Ouzel can easily be distinguished from the Blackbird *(T. merula)* by its white bib and the white-edged feathers on its underside. In central and western Europe it also nests occasionally in mountain forests.

Song Thrush *Turdus philomelos* (Turdidae)

In the spring, the Song Thrush can be heard singing almost everywhere — in mixed and deciduous woods and in town parks and gardens. It nests throughout the whole of Europe (except in the extreme south) and parts of Asia, but migrates to southern and western Europe in the winter. The nest, which is made of blades of grass, rootlets and dry grass, and is lined with mud mixed with saliva, is usually built in a tree or a bush. The 4—5 blue eggs are incubated for about 14 days by the female. At the age of 2 weeks the young leave the nest, but the parents continue to feed them on insects, earthworms and caterpillars. There are usually two broods each year.

Montane Spruce Forests

Alpine Marmot *Marmota marmota* (Sciuridae)

In the vicinity of tourist paths high up in the Alps or the Carpathians, one may often hear a piercing whistle. The sound comes from a sturdy little animal like a ground squirrel, which grows up to 70 cm long and may weigh 5 kg. The animal is an Alpine Marmot and its whistle is a warning to the grazing colony to which it belongs. This species lives above the limit of the forest belt in the shrub timber zone, where it excavates burrows several metres long, in which it hibernates from September to April. Alpine Marmots pair in May and after a 6 week pregnancy the female gives birth, in a short summer burrow, to 2—8 young, which it suckles for about a month. During the summer, until September, Alpine Marmots live in small family colonies, subsisting on mountain grasses and herbaceous plants and their seeds. At the end of September, when they attain their maximum weight, whole families settle down to hibernate together, closing the entrance of the burrow behind them. Alpine Marmots are not very numerous in central Europe and they are therefore strictly protected by law.

Forest Dormouse *Dryomys nitedula* (Gliridae)

The Forest Dormouse lives in the shrub timber zone, high up in the mountains of central and eastern Europe, and the Alps in particular. It is about 9 cm long and has a long, bushy tail. It lives mainly on berries, seeds and (in the spring) young shrub shoots, but also eats insects and worms. Its litter usually comprises 2—5 young, which do not open their eyes for about 3 weeks. The Forest Dormouse spends the winter hibernating in a deep underground burrow, where it lies curled up in a neat little ball, while its temperature drops very low and its respiration and metabolic rate slow down. It generally emerges towards the end of April.

Field Vole *Microtus agrestis* (Cricetidae)

The Field Vole is fairly common everywhere in the mountain ranges of Europe and Asia, inhabiting damp spots with thick undergrowth, bogs and marshes. It seldom appears in hills and lowlands, where it is replaced by the closely related, but somewhat lighter, Common Vole *(M. arvalis)*. The Field Vole digs shallow burrows with underground nests in damp ground and in these it produces litters of 4—5 young twice or three times a year. It lives chiefly on grass blades and the seeds of plants growing near water. At high altitudes — often in the shrub timber zone — one can frequently find the greyish-brown, Snow Vole *(M. nivalis)*, which occurs in the Alps, the Carpathians, the Pyrenees and the mountains of inner Asia. It is one of the largest voles and can measure up to 14 cm. It spends the greater part of the year in deep underground shelters.

Pine Vole *Pitymys subterraneus* (Cricetidae)

This is one of the smallest European voles and measures only 8—10 cm. It is a typical inhabitant of mountain forests with soft, damp soil, in which it excavates a whole network of underground passages. It also occurs at low altitudes, but in fewer numbers than higher up. In an underground nest, 2—3 times a year, the female gives birth to 2—3 young which attain sexual maturity relatively quickly. The Pine Vole is mainly vegetarian and lives on blades of grass, seeds, the shoots of low shrubs and herbaceous plants. It is distributed over the whole of western, central and eastern Europe and extends into inner Asia, but does not occur in the far north or Britain.

256

Montane Spruce Forests

Wild Cat *Felis sylvestris* (Felidae)
The Wild Cat, now generally rare in Europe, lives mostly in mountain spruce forests or in mixed foothill woods with dense undergrowth. It occurs in the Carpathians, and sporadically in the Alps, western Europe, Scotland and northern Africa, and is still fairly common in Asia. It has a greyish-yellow, grey-striped coat and weighs up to 10 kg. It makes its lair in rock fissures, hollow trees and abandoned burrows. After mating (in February and June), the sexes live separately for the rest of the year. Following a 9 week pregnancy the female gives birth to 2—6 kittens, which are blind for the first 10 days. The mother looks after them carefully and, if necessary, carries them to a safer hiding place. The Wild Cat lives on mice, voles, small birds and lizards, but will occasionally also catch a hare or pheasant. It can be distinguished from similarly marked domestic cats which have gone wild by its more robust build and its rounded, bushy tail.

Northern Lynx *Lynx lynx* (Felidae)
The Lynx is a typical inhabitant of the deep mountain forests of Europe, Asia and North America. It has already been wiped out in most mountainous regions in Europe, however, and the only places where it still occurs in any numbers are the Carpathians and Scandinavia. It hunts mainly by night and lies in wait for its prey — which includes large mammals such as Roe and Red Deer — on a branch of a tree; it also eats rodent pests and ground-nesting birds, however, and in the case of game, primarily attacks sick and weak animals. The mating season is February and March and after a 10 week gestation the female gives birth, under an uprooted tree or in a fissure in a rock, to 2—3 young which are blind for about 10 days. The female suckles them for 2 months, but soon begins to give them flesh. The Lynx is very vigilant and has excellent vision and hearing, with the result that it can see and hear without itself being seen or heard. In most European countries it is now protected by law from huntsmen, and those who would keep it as a pet, so that once again it has started to spread westwards.

Brown Bear *Ursus arctos* (Ursidae)
The Brown Bear, the largest European carnivore, is now to be found in western and central Europe in only a few mountain ranges such as the Pyrenees, the Apennines in Italy and the Carpathians; in Siberia and North America it is commoner. It mainly inhabits mountain forests, where it makes its lair in a cave or under an uprooted tree and hibernates during the winter. Its winter sleep is not very heavy, however, and from time to time it wakes up. During the winter, after an 8 month pregnancy, the female gives birth to 2—4 cubs which are blind for about 4 weeks. They are suckled for 4 months and do not leave the lair until the spring. The Brown Bear lives chiefly on berries and other forest produce, the bark of conifers and carrion, occasional game, sheep and cattle and loves to rob wild bees of their honey. It is strictly protected everywhere and only bears known to have caused serious damage are allowed to be shot.

Wolf *Canis lupus* (Canidae)
The Wolf is the only large carnivore which is sometimes still numerous in the mountainous regions — chiefly northern, southern and eastern — of Europe. It lives in packs which are usually composed of a single family and mainly eats large game — Red Deer, Roe Deer and Reindeer — which are hunted by the whole pack, usually at night. It also attacks sheep and cattle and sometimes eats carrion. Mating takes place in the winter and after approximately 9 weeks of pregnancy the female gives birth to 4—9 cubs which do not open their eyes for about 12 days. They are suckled for about 2 months, but the female soon begins to give them flesh (which at first is partly predigested). The young remain 2 years with the parents before becoming independent. The Wolf is extremely shy and attempts to hunt animals causing losses to game are frequently unsuccessful.

Montane Spruce Forests

Chamois   *Rupicapra rupicapra*   (Bovidae)

The Chamois inhabits the Alps, the Pyrenees and high mountains in Spain, Italy, the Balkans and the Carpathians. Grassy slopes overgrown with stunted conifers are its typical habitat and only very severe winters drive it down into the mountain forests, where it lives on tree buds, moss and lichen. Its chief summer foods are herbaceous plants growing at high altitudes. Chamois, which live in small herds, are famed for their surefootedness on sheer and rocky mountain slopes. Both sexes have permanent horns. Rutting takes place in November and December and the gestation period is 6 months. There is usually a single calf, which the female suckles for over 2 months.

Ibex   *Capra ibex*   (Bovidae)

The Ibex lives in small herds high above the forest belt in the Alps. It lives on herbaceous plants and in the winter eats moss and lichen. Rutting takes place in December and January. Usually one calf is born in the shelter of stunted conifers and the female suckles it for a whole year. The young are very active and soon after they are born can climb the rocks with the other members of the herd. The males have heavy, recurved horns up to one metre long and weighing 15 kg. The female's horns measure about 30 cm. Ibexes are strictly protected by law and are now gradually spreading right across the whole of the European Alps.

Red Deer   *Cervus elaphus*   (Cervidae)

Although best known as an inhabitant of European deep mountain forests, this deer also occurs at lower altitudes, for example in riparian woods in central and eastern Europe. Its several European subspecies include the Central European Red Deer, which is distributed over the whole of Europe as far as the Carpathians, and the Carpathian Red Deer, which lives in the mountains of the same name. The Central European Red Deer is reddish-brown in the summer, weighs up to 170 kg and has relatively thin antlers, while the Carpathian Red Deer is grey, may weigh as much as 300 kg and has thicker antlers. The Asian Maral or Caspian Red Deer and the Wapiti of North America are also considered to be Red Deer subspecies. The deer's chief adornment are its antlers, which weigh 8—12 kg. They begin to grow in its second year and every year they grow thicker and the number of branches (tines) increases. Their growth depends on inherited factors and environmental conditions. The antlers are shed between February and April (old deer shed them sooner) and new ones begin to grow immediately afterwards. These are covered at first with a furry skin (velvet), which the deer rubs off on the bark of trees in July. From the middle of September to the middle of October the males (stags) wage fierce battles for a herd of females (hinds). Rutting takes place in a clearing or a forest meadow and the hunter, by imitating the deer's 'roar', can attract it within range. This is practically his only chance of weeding out weak specimens unsuitable for further breeding, since Red Deer remain concealed in the deep forest undergrowth and come out to graze only at night. They live mainly on grass, the twigs of trees and bushes, herbaceous plants, acorns, beechnuts, field crops and bark. In the winter they strip the bark from half-grown conifers, causing considerable damage, since the trees either dry up or yield inferior timber; the number of deer must therefore be kept within certain limits. The gestation period is 33—34 weeks and the young (calves) are generally born in June. The usual number is one, two being rare. The female often suckles them well into the winter, although as soon as the second month they begin to take solids. The hinds and calves live together in small groups for a whole year and do not separate until the next calves are due to be born. Old stags usually live solitarily and join the hinds only at rutting time.

Subarctic and arctic forests (tundras)

Moving further north, the temperature falls steadily, the forest thins out and becomes stunted and increasingly acquires the appearance of brushwood. In time, groups of stunted trees appear and lastly the trees are replaced by a short, sparse brushwood formation interspersed with spaces overgrown with grasses, mosses and lichens, which constitutes the most northerly vegetation cover — the typical tundra of arctic Europe, Asia and America.

The decisive factor determining the formation and character of the tundra is therefore the climate, while the soil is of lesser importance. The southern limits of the tundra coincide roughly with the line joining places with an average July temperature of 10°C. These regions are characterized by a long summer day, strong winds, damp air in the summer and a dry winter with severe frosts. The total annual rainfall is small and does not exceed 200—300 mm, but because evaporation is negligible the ground often becomes marshy. Below a certain depth the ground is permanently frozen and even in summer it never thaws out completely. Consequently, bushes, as well as trees, are absent from the tundra and where they do occur they are short and squat and close to the ground, while their roots are correspondingly long and near the surface. The commonest are various types of creeping willows and the Dwarf Birch *(Betula nana)*. Plants naturally grow very slowly under such conditions. For instance, shrubs grow about 1 cm a year and a Juniper *(Juniperus communis)* whose trunk measures 8 cm across at the bottom may be up to 500 years old. It is interesting to note that while the flowers of arctic plants are large and very brightly coloured, they are scentless.

The vegetation cover varies with the ground relief. Depressions, which are partly protected from the winds, are muddy, but are generally overgrown with shrubs. Such localities occur most frequently in the southern parts of the tundra. Flat ground is more or less dry and is overgrown with grasses, while very dry areas (which occur mainly in the northern parts of the tundra) generally do not possess a coherent vegetation cover and lichens are practically the only plants that grow there.

Rivers have a very marked effect on the appearance of the tundra, since trees penetrate far into the north along their valleys and their banks are often overgrown with dense clumps of tall grass. The rivers thus enable the forest to extend far beyond its normal limit. These belts of forest have a specific character, since the trees are short and shrubby in habit. Very often the harsh climate causes such woods to dry up, giving the landscape a sinister appearance. As a rule, the dry plants remain standing for a long time, since decomposition is very slow in the cold tundra.

One would think that such inhospitable surroundings would have no attraction for animals. Appearances are deceptive, however, and during its short summer the tundra is alive with innumerable species of birds and mammals. Of course, most of the birds fly south before the long arctic winter sets in, to spend the winter in warmer regions, and the mammals retire to the spruce forests along the southern margins of the tundra. The best known inhabitants of the tundra include the Redpoll *(Acanthis flammea)*, Brambling *(Fringilla montifringilla)*, Waxwing *(Bombycilla garrulus)*, Rough-legged Buzzard *(Buteo lagopus)*, Hobby *(Falco subbuteo)* and several species of geese and ducks which are regular visitors to central Europe in the winter. Among the more permanent inhabitants, which only migrate to the margin of the forests in severe winters, are the Snowy Owl *(Nyctea scandiaca)* and the Ptarmigan *(Lagopus mutus)*. The tundra also has its own typical mammals, such as the Blue Hare *(Lepus timidus)*, Arctic Fox *(Alopex lagopus)* and the lemmings which form the main food of birds of prey, owls and the Wolverine *(Gulo gulo)*. The most important animal of the tundra, however, is the Reindeer *(Rangifer tarandus)*, whose uses are so many and varied that they enable Man to live even in the northern parts of the tundra, despite the almost intolerably harsh climatic conditions.

Subarctic and Arctic Forests (Tundras)

Cladonia sylvatica (Cladoniaceae) ❶
This resembles the closely related *Cladonia rangiferina* with which it is often confused. The thallus is also biform: the lower part is closely attached to the substrate, the upper part bears the fruiting bodies. Its clusters attain a height of 5—15 cm and are extremely variable in colour — from straw-yellow through yellowish-green to grey-green. This variation is related to the age of the plant, and to external environmental factors. The terminal branchlets of the clusters hang to one side and are pale brown. This lichen grows on strongly to moderately acid soils poor in nutrients. It requires plenty of light and can tolerate long periods of drought.

Cladonia coccifera (Cladoniaceae) ❷
The base of the thallus is covered with leathery squamules and is yellowish to greyish-green on the outside. From it grow broad, cup-like structures up to 5 cm high, with notched margins, bearing minute scarlet dots on a yellow to yellow-green background. *Cladonia coccifera* occurs from lowlands to alpine elevations on both humic and sandy substrates, and is abundant even on moss-covered rocks. It never forms extensive growths — sparse groups at most — and usually grows singly. It is absent from very dry localities.

Peltigera canina (Peltigeraceae) ❸
This has a conspicuous thallus bearing lobes as much as 5 cm in size, which are soft and flexible when dry. Its upper side is greyish-white or brownish, covered with fine down, while the underside is white and attached to the substrate by numerous runners which may grow up to 1 m long. This conspicuous lichen grows from lowlands to highlands, on moderately rich to poor soils. Though it prefers shady and moist localities, it is also found in open spaces.

Parmelia furfuracea (Parmeliaceae) ❹
The phylloid thallus of this lichen gradually develops into a fruticose form. Its antler-like lobes may attain a length of 10 cm. The upper surface of the thallus is grey to greyish-brown, while the lower surface is light violet to almost black. It ranges from lowlands to alpine altitudes living on dead wood, rocks and boulders. The reproduction of lichens is extremely interesting, the plants themselves being dual organisms, each composed of an alga and a fungus. They reproduce sexually after an initial asexual or vegetative phase. The alga and the fungus multiply synchronously, and every fragment of the thallus may develop into a new plant, provided that conditions are favourable. The lichens multiply with the help of special formations containing both the alga and the fungus. These are in fact aggregates of algal cells enclosed in fungal hyphae. The thallus produces large quantities of these corpuscles which are distributed by the wind, and, under favourable conditions, grow into a new lichen.

Subarctic and Arctic Forests (Tundras)

Lycopodium selago   (Lycopodiaceae)   ❶

The erect stem of this lycopodium branches from the base and grows up to 25 cm high. The branches are glossy, dark green and bear tough linear, acute leaflets, approximately 9 mm long. Visible sporiferous spikelets are absent in this lycopodium: small sporangia are located on the upper surface of the fronds, at the stem tips. It also multiplies vegetatively through deciduous buds formed in the frond axils at the tips of branchlets. It is an important species of shady montane spruce stands and occurs up to the timberline, and in the north, as far as the edge of the tundra. It thrives on substrates rich in humus, and also on purely organic substrates formed from putrescent wood.

Forked Spleenwort   *Asplenium septentrionale*   (Aspleniaceae)   ❷

This is a small, sun-loving fern, 10—30 cm high. The frond blade is furcate, composed of linear leaflets of unequal size. It is extremely fecund, its sporangia usually covering the entire underside of the fronds. In Europe it occurs especially in the mountains in rock fissures; in the north it spreads into the tundra. It avoids lime-rich soils. Ferns play a significant role in forest communities. For the most part they are shade-loving plants and are generally confined to shady, moist, humic forests, in particular to coniferous and mixed stands. Dense fern growths protect the soil against excessive desiccation and their withered leaves contribute to the formation of forest humus. Their roots loosen and aerate forest litter and on dying they enrich the lower layers with humus. Rock species such as the Spleenwort also play an important part as pioneers of colonization. Their dense root systems retain humus in rock fissures so that the seeds of higher plants can take hold there. They are of use also in clearings where they are usually the only protection for tree seedlings against frost and desiccation.

Cloudberry   *Rubus chamaemorus*   (Rosaceae)   ❸

This small, low shrub, which attains a maximum height of 20 cm, opens its white flowers in June. Its fruits are orange-red to brown drupelets. It is a rare arctic species which appeared in Europe during the Ice Age, i. e. towards the end of the Tertiary and the beginning of the Quaternary. A substantial fall in temperature led to the formation of a European glacier which forced the northern flora to retreat southwards. This brought arctic species to central Europe where some of them remained even after the subsequent retreat of the glacier. Such plants are called glacial relicts. The sites in which they survive are often separated by hundreds of kilometres.

Bearberry   *Arctostaphylos uva-ursi*   (Ericaceae)   ❹

The Bearberry is a low, prostrate shrub with spreading branches. The leaves are densely arranged on the twigs and are leathery, obovate, entire, and glossy on both sides. Strong veins mark their lower surface. A raceme of 3—12 urceolate flowers with white or rosy corollae blooms in April. The fruits are scarlet berries containing 5—7 uniseminal pips. The Bearberry is of considerable significance as a pioneer species, colonizing rocks and ravines, both in the mountains and in the northern tundra.

Subarctic and Arctic Forests (Tundras)

Dwarf Birch *Betula nana* (Betulaceae)

The Dwarf Birch is found in the tundra of northern Europe and Asia, and has also survived in submontane and montane peat bogs in central Europe as an Ice Age relict. It is a low, decumbent shrub with erect twigs, reaching a height of 50–70 cm. Its leaves are rounded, often larger in breadth than in length, about 1 cm long, with coarsely serrate margins. They have a minute stalk and 2–4 pairs of veins. Its short amentaceous flowers appear towards the end of May. The cone-like fruit structures are cylindrical, erect, and 10–12 cm in size. This shrub may live to be 50–70 years old. In the far north it is used as fuel or as pasture for Reindeer.

Marsh Tea *Ledum palustre* (Ericaceae)

Marsh Tea is a typical plant of the tundra where it inhabits peat bogs and swampy sites whose soils are permanently frozen in the lower layers. It is absent from the coastal regions of the tundra but appears in the peat bogs of central and northern Europe where it often develops extensive growths. It is an erect, wide-branched shrub 70–100 cm high. It has narrow, linear leaves, 2–5 cm long but only 2–4 mm broad, with revolute margins. Their upper surface is glossy, and dark green; the underside is covered with a rusty-coloured pubescence. Its strongly smelling white flowers, borne on long petioles, are arranged in densely clustered umbels and bloom in June. Its fruits are pentalocular capsules attached to drooping stalks. The Marsh Tea is tolerant of moderate shade and requires damp, at best peaty soils.

Least Willow *Salix herbacea* (Salicaceae) ❸

This is a low decumbent shrub not exceeding 20 cm in height and penetrating into the far northern tundra where moss and lichen predominate. It also appears high up in the mountains of central Europe, in stone fields above the timberline. This shrub has circular leaves, 1–2 cm long, with finely crenate margins and pale green undersides with reticular venation. Both flower catkins and fruit catkins are very small – 1 cm at most.

Another willow abundant in the tundra is the Woolly Willow – *Salix lanata*. It attains a height of 20–100 cm and has a globular crown. Its leaves are elliptically orbicular, 2–7 cm long, with entire margins, covered on both sides with silvery pubescence. The veins on the undersurface of leaves protrude markedly. The flowers make their appearance after foliation in June. It occurs in the European and Asian tundra, particularly in damp places in the vicinity of streams.

Male flowers (3), female flowers (3a), seeds (3b).

1

♀

3a

♂

2

3

3b

Subarctic and Arctic Forests (Tundras)

Green Hairstreak *Callophrys rubi* (Lycaenidae)
This is one of the smallest lycaenids in Europe (wingspan 28–30 mm). As distinct from other species, the underside of its wings is a shining green and in some individuals is decorated with small white spots; the upper surface of the wings is plain brown. The only similarly coloured species is *C. avis*, which is confined to just a few places in southwestern Europe. *Callophrys rubi* has a wide area of distribution comprising Europe and Asia and stretching across Siberia as far as Sakhalin. In the north it extends to the Arctic Circle, where we find the subspecies *borealis*, whose wings are yellow on the underside. The butterfly flies early in the spring and in Europe produces only one generation. In the mountains it ascends to altitudes of up to 1,800 m. It chiefly frequents the outskirts of forests, clearings and glades where Bramble and wild raspberries grow; these, together with Cranberry and Gorse, are its main sources of food. The eggs are green as are the caterpillars, which have a white (sometimes yellow) dorsal stripe and pale lateral stripes. The short, compact chrysalis is brown and lies on the ground under leaves.

Pearl-bordered Fritillary *Clossiana euphrosyne* (Nymphalidae)
This butterfly is also widely distributed, occurring from the Mediterranean to the Arctic region, where the subspecies *septentrionalis* is found. In Europe it is a common butterfly, even high up in the Alps, for example, where its markings are more distinct and darker. Normally it produces two generations each year, but in the mountains and the far north only one. The males have a wingspan of about 40 mm, the females slightly more. The eggs are yellowish-green at first, and are laid on Dog Violet. The caterpillars hatch in the summer and hibernate; in the spring they complete their development and pupate near the ground. The related *C. selene* also occurs in Europe, while in the far north, above the Arctic Circle, we find other similar species, e. g. *C. titania*, *C. characlea* and *C. freija*, some of which also appear in Greenland and North America.

Small Heath *Coenonympha pamphilus* (Satyridae)
This butterfly, which has a wingspan of 28–34 mm, is not only one of the commonest species in Europe, but is distributed across north Africa, Asia Minor, Lebanon, Iran, Iraq and Turkestan and possibly eastern Siberia also. It is equally at home in lowlands, high mountains and the far north and is becoming common in towns as well as in the country. From spring to October it produces 2–3 generations, the last of which hibernates over the winter. The caterpillars hatch from yellowish-brown eggs and are green with a double white dorsal stripe; they live on various species of grass. *C. tullia*, which extends as far as the Arctic Circle, and *C. arcania* and *C. glycerion*, whose most northerly populations are in Finland, are related species.

Dicerca acuminata (Buprestidae)
This beetle is a typical member of the arctic fauna, but also occurs in central Europe, although it is not common there and occurs primarily in small areas with large numbers of birches which assure it of an adequate food supply. The beetle, which measures 12–18 mm when fully grown, swarms in May. Its wide area of distribution includes Europe, Siberia and northern China.

Subarctic and Arctic Forests (Tundras)

Redpoll   *Acanthis flammea*   (Fringillidae)
This small bird, about the size of a small sparrow, inhabits the southern margins of the Asian, European and North American tundra, the mountains of central and western Europe and hilly country in the British Isles. In the north it nests chiefly in low bushes, birches and alders and in the mountains in the shrub timber zone. Its nest, which is made of thin twigs, grass and moss, is situated 2−3 m above the ground. The Redpoll nests twice a year and the 4−6 bluish, brown-speckled eggs are incubated for about 12 days; the young leave the nest at the age of 2 weeks. In the nesting season Redpolls live on insects and their larvae; in the autumn and winter they eat alder, birch and spruce seeds. Redpolls from the north spend the winter (October to March) in central and western Europe. The northern tundra, which is characterized by stunted willow and birch growths, is inhabited by the Arctic Redpoll *(A. hornemanni)*, which lives chiefly on seeds, is a ground-nester and likewise migrates southwards in the winter.

Nutcracker   *Nucifraga caryocatactes*   (Corvidae)
The dark brown, grey-spotted Nutcracker, which is about the size of a pigeon, inhabits conifer forests in Scandinavia and northern Siberia and mountain forests in central and western Europe. It usually nests at the beginning of March, high up in a spruce tree − in the north as much as 3−4 metres above the ground. The nest is a tallish structure made of brushwood and lined with moss, lichen and dry grass. The single clutch comprises 3−4 light green eggs, which are incubated for 17−18 days by the female. Both parents feed the young on insects for 3−4 weeks and sometimes also rob other birds' nests. The adult birds live mainly on conifer seeds, beech- and hazel-nuts. In Europe the Nutcracker is a resident bird, but in the winter it descends to mixed upland forests. Large flocks of Nutcrackers from the north and the Siberian taiga occasionally appear in central Europe during the winter.

Water Pipit   *Anthus spinoletta*   (Motacillidae)
In Europe and Asia the Water Pipit inhabits high mountain meadows and in Scandinavia also occurs on stony, unwooded slopes at lower altitudes. The nest, always on the ground, is hidden below a clump of grass or under a low bush. It is made of grass, moss and lichen and is very roomy. In May the female lays 4−6 brownish eggs and incubates them for about 2 weeks. The parents feed the young on insects, spiders and worms for the same length of time. In the winter, Water Pipits descend to the lowlands, where they live on seeds, or migrate southwards. Birds from the far north fly south in large flocks across the whole of Europe, but in mild winters some remain in central Europe; by April most have returned to their usual nesting places.

Brambling   *Fringilla montifringilla*   (Fringillidae)
The Brambling, which is about the size of a sparrow, inhabits the far north of Europe, and Asia, where it nests in conifer and birch woods as far as the limit of the tree belts in the tundra. The nest, which is built on a tree or in a bush, is made of moss, grass and lichen. The 4−6 grey, brown-speckled eggs are incubated by the female for about 2 weeks. The young are fed on insects, caterpillars and insect larvae. From October and November, large flocks of Bramblings from the north can be encountered in central and western Europe, where they roam the countryside gathering alder and birch seeds and Rowan and other berries, and may even be seen at feeding boxes in villages and towns. At the end of the March and in April they return to their nesting places in the north.

Subarctic and Arctic Forests (Tundras)

Waxwing *Bombycilla garrulus* (Bombycillidae)

In central and western Europe, from November until March, one may occasionally see large flocks of brightly coloured Waxwings — small birds about the size of a Starling — which have come from northern Scandinavia and northern Asia to spend the winter in Europe. Their true home is in conifer forests and wooded tundra with isolated groups of trees and shrubs. The nest, which is built in a tree, is made of lichen, grass, moss and small twigs and contains an average of 5 bluish, dark-spotted eggs. The female incubates these for about 14 days and is kept supplied with food by the male. Both parents feed the young on insects, mainly mosquitoes and their larvae, for just under 3 weeks. In October Waxwings gather in large flocks and migrate southwards. Their winter diet consists chiefly of seeds and the berries of woody plants, in particular Rowan, Guelder Rose and Elder.

Merlin *Falco columbarius* (Falconidae)

The Merlin occasionally appears in central and western Europe during the winter, but usually it migrates to southern Europe and northern Africa. In the summer it inhabits the tundra of Europe, Asia and North America. It prefers to nest beyond the limit of the unbroken forest, in places where there are only isolated groups of small trees and bushes. Here it builds its nest, made of dry twigs and grass, directly on the ground or on a rock, although sometimes it uses the abandoned nest of a crow or some other bird of prey. The female incubates her 3—6 brown eggs for about 4 weeks and both parents feed the young for 25—26 days more. In summer the Merlin lives mainly on small birds nesting in the tundra; in the winter it catches sparrows, finches and sometimes mice and voles. It is the smallest European bird of prey, with a wingspan of only 60 cm, and can be identified in flight by its typical falcon silhouette; its long, pointed wings resemble a Swallow's.

Rough-legged Buzzard *Buteo lagopus* (Accipitridae)

The Rough-legged Buzzard, which inhabits the far northern tundra of Europe, Asia and North America, usually nests on the ground or on a rock, and seldom in a tree. At the end of March it builds a tall nest made of twigs on a grass foundation several centimetres thick. The female usually lays 3—7 eggs, but in years in which there is a dearth of lemmings — the bird's chief food — there may be only one or two young. The female incubates the eggs for about 4 weeks. The young leave the nest after 5—6 weeks, but the parents continue to feed them for several weeks more. Rough-legged Buzzards live mainly on lemmings and other small mammals; from October to March, in central and western Europe, they eat mice, voles, rabbits and — in severe winters — small game, sometimes causing considerable damage.

Snowy Owl *Nyctea scandiaca* (Strigidae)

This typical inhabitant of the treeless tundra of arctic Europe, Asia and North America leaves its natural haunts only in very severe winters, when it flies southward, occasionally as far as central Europe. Its nest is an unlined depression in the ground, in which it lays 2—8 eggs at the end of May or in June. The number of eggs depends on the supply of lemmings, which are the main food of both the adult birds and their young. After about 2 months the young owls leave the nest and sit on rocks and hummocks which give them a good view of the surrounding country. Since they consume large amounts of food — chiefly lemmings, rats and mice — they are obliged to hunt the whole day, roaming far from their nest in search of food. In other regions, where the tundra is replaced by small groups of trees, we find the Hawk Owl *(Surnia ulula)*, which nests mostly in tree hollows and lives mainly on mice and voles.

Subarctic and Arctic Forests (Tundras)

Greylag Goose   *Anser anser*   (Anatidae)

About the size of a domestic goose, the Greylag Goose is completely grey, with faint ripple marks on its underside and with an orange beak. It primarily inhabits the arctic tundra, from Iceland across Scandinavia and Siberia to the Far East, and nests only occasionally in central and eastern Europe. The nest is made of reeds and is lined with down. In April the goose lays 4—6 white eggs, which it incubates itself, while the gander stands guard. Soon after they are hatched the young follow the parents to the water and within 2 months they are fully fledged. In September and October Greylag Geese form large flocks and migrate to western and southern Europe, returning to their nesting sites in February or March. Their diet consists mainly of plant leaves and seeds.

Bean Goose   *Anser fabalis*   (Anatidae)

The Bean Goose is a typical tundra bird, its breeding range stretching from Greenland across Iceland and Scandinavia to the most northerly parts of Siberia. In central Europe it is seen only between October and April, when it spends the winter there on ice-free water. A little smaller than a domestic goose, it has darker plumage and a black beak with an orange band. The nest, which stands on bare ground, is made of dry grass and is lined with feathers. The goose incubates the 3—4 eggs for about a month and the newly hatched young soon follow the parent birds to the water. Bean Geese feed on various plants. Of the other geese which nest in the tundra, the best known and most numerous are the White-fronted Goose *(A. albifrons)* and the Lesser White-fronted Goose *(A. erythropus)*. All these three tundra species winter by running water in central, western and southern Europe.

Tufted Duck   *Aythya fuligula*   (Anatidae)

The Tufted Duck inhabits the northern parts of Asia and Europe except the extreme northern tundra, but also nests in central Europe. During the winter it can be encountered in western and southern Europe, where it remains from October until March or April. It nests near water, on islands of sedge and among rushes. The duck incubates 6—10 greenish grey eggs for about 4 weeks and when the ducklings hatch out, at the end of June, they immediately follow her to the water, although it is 2 months before they fledge. The northern tundra is inhabited by several other ducks, such as the Scaup *(Aythya marila)*, the Goldeneye *(Bucephala clangula)* and the Common Scoter *(Melanitta nigra)*, all of which winter in central, western and southern Europe.

Ptarmigan   *Lagopus mutus*   (Tetraonidae)

The Ptarmigan is a typical inhabitant of the European, Asian and American arctic tundra, but also occurs above the forest limit in certain European mountains, e. g. the Alps and Cairngorms. In summer the Ptarmigan is chestnut-brown with white wings, but in the winter it is white and only its outer tail feathers are dark. It nests in May or June, under a low bush or in the heather, and lays up to 12 greenish eggs with large brown spots in a grass-lined depression. The chicks hatch after 3—4 weeks. In the autumn Ptarmigans form small feeding flocks, their food beeing seeds, young leaves and buds; in summer they also eat insects. The forests of the north, right up to the edge of the tundra, are inhabited by the similar Willow Grouse *(L. lagopus)*, which has the same colouring and likewise weighs about 0.5 kg.

Subarctic and Arctic Forests (Tundras)

Elk   *Alces alces*   (Cervidae)

■□
□□

The Elk inhabits the southernmost parts of the tundra and thin arctic forests of Europe and North America and the Siberian taiga. The North American form is known as the Moose. Strict protection has enabled it, in recent years, to spread further south, occasionally as far as the Baltic and central Europe. Male Elk weigh up to 450 kg, the females less; the huge palmated antlers weigh about 20 kg. Elk prefer open, swampy forests with an abundance of aquatic plants, which constitute their main food, but they also eat twigs, foliage and bark. In the rutting season (September and October) the males wage fierce duels. The antlers are shed after rutting and begin to grow again in the spring. The gestation period is about 250 days and in May or June the females give birth to 1—3 calves, which they suckle for some 4—6 weeks. In the autumn, large herds of females and young move south in search of food, but return in the spring.

Reindeer   *Rangifer tarandus*   (Cervidae)

□■
□□

This best known inhabitant of the inhospitable arctic tundra is also to be found in the forest belt and the mountains of the north. In the far north it is kept in huge herds, often in a semi-wild state, since it provides meat, skins, and high fat milk. A bull weighs up to 150 kg. In both sexes the antlers curve forwards. The rutting season falls in the autumn, when the males wage fierce duels to collect a harem of several females. The young are usually born in June; as a rule there is only one but very rarely twins and triplets may be born. Reindeer live in large herds the whole year round and only old bulls live solitarily. They eat mainly grass, herbaceous plants, twigs and leaves, but in the winter have to resort to lichen, which they dig up from under the snow. In the autumn and spring whole herds numbering thousands of animals wander hundreds of miles along fixed routes in search of food, often crossing difficult natural obstacles like rivers, lakes and mountains. The greatest danger for Reindeer are packs of Wolves.

Wolverine   *Gulo gulo*   (Mustelidae)

□□
■□

The Wolverine is the largest European mustelid; it weighs up to 30 kg and is over 1 m long. It inhabits the forest belt and the forest tundra zone in the north of Europe, Asia and North America. It lives mainly on lemmings, but also hunts large mammals, catches birds and fish and is not afraid to attack solitary Reindeer. The gestation period is about 120 days and the female gives birth in its lair to 2 (sometimes up to 4) young, which take a long time to open their eyes. The Wolverine is prized for its coat, especially in Canada and northern Siberia.

Norway Lemming   *Lemmus lemmus*   (Cricetidae)

□□
□■

The Norway Lemming inhabits northern Europe, occurring high up in the mountains and in low-lying tundra with dwarf birches and shrubs. It measures 13—15 cm, has a short tail and is prettily coloured, its back being dark brown and its underside yellowish-brown. It is one of the rodents whose numbers increase enormously from time to time and when that happens the tundra literally swarms with lemmings. Its spherical nest, which is made of leaves and grass blades, lies among stones or below the roots of trees, close to the surface, or on the ground itself, or under the snow. Lemmings are vegetarian and in winter can still find food under the snow. They produce up to four litters of 5—6 young (and sometimes more) in a year. Lemmings are an important component of the arctic fauna, since the abundance of the other animals and birds which live on them (Wolverines, Arctic Foxes, owls and hawks) depends on the size of their populations. If there are too many of them, lemmings travel en masse in search of food and many die on the way. Lemmings are wholly nocturnal animals.

Man and the forest

Since time immemorial the forest and human society have been interdependent and various mutual bonds have formed between them; the forest has influenced the economic and cultural development of society whilst society has had a very decided effect on the face of the forest. In the thousands of years during which this reciprocal relationship has developed, several stages can clearly be seen. The first, when the forest provided food and refuge, was succeeded by a period of unscrupulous exploitation, until slowly and unwillingly, Man was forced to recognize that if he wants to utilize forests, he must be prepared to invest in them. The realization that the forest has other useful functions signalled a great advance in the development of society and resulted in the gradual establishment of national parks and reserves and in some forests being set aside for the purposes of recreation and nature conservation. Finally, we are at last starting to appreciate the supreme importance of the forest in maintaining the oxygen content of the atmosphere.

Let us more closely examine the various attitudes of Man towards the forest. To primitive Man, forests were a source of food, fuel, building material and medicines, and places where he could take refuge from enemies. In the Neolithic age, when agriculture began to develop, his influence on the forest increased. Since then, fields and pastures have spread at the expense of forests with ever-increasing rapidity as human populations have grown in size and the organization of society has become more complex.

The next phase began about halfway through the present millenium, when villages flourished, handicrafts developed and forests became important as suppliers of wood, pitch, ash and charcoal. In this age of exploitation of the forest's products, large sections of the population were dependent on the forest for their living. The archives contain records of handicrafts completely unknown today and in addition to foresters and hunters, they speak of shingle-makers, spoon-and scoop-makers, charcoal burners, pitch-makers and ash-makers. In addition to raw materials, developing industry also required energy, which at that time could only be obtained from burning wood and running water. Every region had its own specific conditions for the development of its industries and these naturally left their mark on the forests. Unscrupulous exploitation of forests continued until the middle of the eighteenth century, when people came to realize that the forest's resources were not unlimited and that one cannot forever take without giving. The concept of planned forest management can be regarded as a revolutionary turning point in Man's attitude to forests, and to natural resources in general.

There are many countries in which the depressing heritage left by the era of exploitation can still be seen. For example, in the USSR, a country with an otherwise illimitable wealth of forests, the forests of the Ukraine were felled on a tremendous scale under the Czars and the inconceivable erosion which followed has in many places made even agriculture impossible. In the USA, vast areas of forest were also cut down at the end of last century and in a comparatively short time more than 150 million ha of land were ruined by erosion. The mountains along the whole Adriatic coast of Yugoslavia were similarly devastated to obtain timber and pasture; they are now completely eroded and the government of Yugoslavia is being forced to spend enormous sums on their reforestation. Special terraces are being built on the rocks to

Fig. 19 — A treeless landscape ruined by galley erosion caused by water reminds us of the consequence of reckless deforestation.

provide a base for the soil, which is brought from other parts of the country. Another classic example of such devastation is Spain, which, despite its wonderful climate, is today one of the poorest countries of Europe (Fig. 19). For the past 500 years it has been paying the price for the policy of its 15th century rulers, who allowed the forests to be cut down to provide grazing land for sheep; they have turned practically the whole of inland Spain into a barren rocky steppe.

History provides abundant evidence to show that where forests were destroyed, deserts have taken their place and cultures have been doomed. The more drastically forests are devastated, the sooner society begins to realize the error of its ways, but unfortunately often too late. Bitter experience has taught Man that the production of timber cannot be pursued to the detriment of the forest's other functions, in particular its role in the conservation of water and the protection of the soil, and its climatic, recreational and health benefits, the recognition of which constitutes the fourth stage in Man's developing relationship with the forest. Today considerable attention is being paid everywhere to the importance of forests for health. For instance, a forest catches up to 60 % of the dust in the air and also keeps back radioactive fall-out; there is 32 times less radioactivity in a forest than in an open space. The forest also damps sound, and a strip of trees 100 m wide will weaken noise by as much as 15 decibels. A knowledge of these benefits provided those who were trying to rouse society to protect forests with an effective weapon, and today all civilized countries are beginning to set aside large areas for national parks, reserves and nature conservation.

The increasing desire of town dwellers to spend more of their spare time in the woods is another matter to bear in mind. Advances in human society are often accompanied by serious problems, the chief one being pollution of our air and water by industrial waste. In all industrial regions throughout the world, Man's environment has severely deteriorated and if he is not to destroy himself, he must learn to harmonize technical progress with the requirements of nature, including plants in general and forests in particular. After all, plants are the sole source of oxygen on our planet and our oxygen requirements are constantly increasing. Wherever something is burnt, oxygen is needed. Motoring is a good example. An adult human being breathes about 350 kg of pure oxygen in a year and a combustion engine uses roughly the same amount in burning 100 l of petrol. A jet plane, during one hour's flight, consumes as much oxygen as 3,000 ha of forest produce in a day. The oxygen in some industrial centres would have been used up long ago if it had not been supplemented by air flowing in from surrounding areas.

This effect of trees on our health makes them absolutely invaluable. To take an example: a 100 year old Beech 25 m tall, with a crown 15 m in diameter has about 800,000 leaves, with a total area of 1,600 m^2. The inner surface of the leaves (the total area of the photosynthetic cells) is about 100 times greater. During its growth such a Beech takes up 12.5 million cubic metres of carbon dioxide from the atmosphere and enriches the air with the same amount of oxygen; in other words, each hour it produces 1.7 kg of oxygen, an amount sufficient for three adults for a whole day.

Other green spaces play an equally important role and should not be neglected either. They include parks, orchards, avenues, gardens around houses, schools and hospitals, sports grounds, the strips of green beside roads and rivers and the protective green belt planted round factories, farms and isolated technical structures for cosmetic reasons. Neither should we forget the greenery which beautifies the countryside and is important for hunting and water conservation. It has been proven that vegetation is absolutely indispensable to modern Man's mental and physical well being. It has a beneficial effect on human physiology, on nervous stability and on the town dweller's mood in general. Inadequate contact with nature causes deterioration of vision and hearing, upsets emotional and nervous balance and produces a tendency to depression. Even a short walk in a park can therefore be of great benefit.

It can be seen from the few examples given above that the importance of forests for the whole of society will increase still further and that forest conservation must be one of mankind's major interests. A progressive society must therefore not only protect its forests, but care for every single tree, whether growing wild or standing in a park (Fig. 20).

The forest as a resource

Both in the past and today, Man has relied on the forest to supply a number of natural products. As the Earth's population grows (at the time of the Roman Empire

283

Fig. 20 — In present-day Europe mountain forests are the best preserved and most extensive part of the natural countryside.

it numbered 250 million and today 3,500 million) and as living standards rise, increasing demands are made on the forest as a source of raw materials despite the many substitutes for wood provided by modern technology.

Man's dependence on the forest is well expressed by the saying that he is accompanied by wood from the cradle to the grave. Many thousands of years have gone by since the first primitive hut was built from the branches of a tree, but in the meantime one improvement has followed another culminating in the splendid, artistic wooden houses of today. The modern craze for weekend chalets heralds a return to wooden architecture. Although houses are no longer built of wood, the building industry still cannot do without it and the consumption of wood as an auxiliary material in building interiors is steadily increasing.

Coal mining in deep mines is still impossible without timber. Wood has a property invaluable in mining, since as soon as the pressure on the pit props approaches the critical limit, the wood begins to creak. Miners say the props are warning them. Wood consumption in coal mines is relatively high, 25 m^3 of timber being needed to each 1,000 tonnes of coal extracted. The American Indians nicknamed the railway engine the 'iron horse'. While it is true that there are hundreds of tons of metal in a train, the rails on which it travels are laid on wooden sleepers. Although concrete sleepers are used today as a substitute, they are not nearly so satisfactory as the original wooden type, which are resilient and absorb shocks better. Concrete sleepers cause jarring, which increases the wear and tear on locomotives. Consequently, of all the world's railway sleepers, only one in 19 is made of concrete, the other 100,800,000 being made of wood. Wood is also essential in ship building, for telegraph poles, for controlling rivers, mountain streams and fishponds, and in the construction of certain types of bridge and pier. In the furniture industry and in match production it is the most important material of all. Even packaging technology needs it for the construction of barrels, crates and wood wool.

Since time immemorial Man has tried to refine wood in various ways and to give less valuable kinds the appearance of rare woods. Veneering (the application of a thin layer of a fine wood to the surface of furniture) was known as long as 5,000 years ago. During excavations in Thebes, a 3,600 year old relief illustrating this process was found. Veneer is a layer of wood from a few tenths of a millimetre to several millimetres thick. In the case of valuable woods it is cut away, while with other woods it is peeled off the trunk like a roll of paper.

Attempts to utilize poorer quality woods has led to the production of various types of composite board, which today have a wide variety of uses. The chief of these is plywood, which, apart from its other advantages, resists warping. Plywood is composed of an odd number of thin layers of wood stuck together so that their grains cross at right angles to each other. Such a board has the same strength as plain wood of treble the thickness. Further types of composite board are made from wood shavings or blocks, bound together with glue.

One of the basic components of important substances like xylolite and bakelite is sawdust. There is no need to describe their wide variety of uses here, but they introduce a further important use of wood, and one that is expanding worldwide — the use of wood as a raw material in the chemical industry. The chemistry of wood is such that, except for coal tar, we should look in vain for a basic raw material from which so many different products could be made. The principle of wood chemistry is apparently simple, since it merely involves separating the cellulose from the lignin, the wood pulp proper, the proportion of these two substances being almost the same. However, the technology required to do this is fairly complicated.

Paper is a product without which modern life would be unimaginable. It was invented (in the year 105 AD) by Tsai-Lun, an exalted official of the Chinese court, who made it out of crushed Mulberry bark and fabric. However, since the Chinese kept the making of paper a secret for centuries, his name fell into obscurity.

Cellulose — the principal carbohydrate component of the cell walls of all plants — has the advantage that it combines relatively well with various other substances and the resultant compounds may be used as the initial raw material for a multitude of commodities. The entire production of man-made fibres is based on this principle, 85 tonnes of cellulose fibres being needed to make 100 tonnes of artificial fibres.

The forest is also useful in many other ways, and particularly today, when attempts are being made all over the world to save raw materials, new ways of utilizing all its products more thoroughly are being sought and tried. For instance, there is increasing interest in resin, the initial raw material for turpentine, which is indispensable both in medicine and in the paint and dye industry, and is also an important raw material in the production of petrol. One example of the benefits of research is the finding by the US Forest Service Research Institute in Florida that the chemical weedkiller Paraquat stimulates resin production by the American Lodgepole Pine *(Pinus contorta)*. The wood of this pine normally contains about 1.5 % resin, but if the tree is sprayed with Paraquat, the resin content rises to 40 %. Economists have estimated that an annual yield of four thousand million kilograms of resin (a production within the realms of possibility) would provide two per cent of the USA's yearly petrol requirements.

It seems therefore that poor quality wood and forest waste products, that until now nobody has considered using, may have potential uses in solving the world's energy problems. Sweden has paid considerable attention to this potential and already has whole plantations of fast-growing trees. The best results are anticipated from poplars, whose shoots, which are about 2 m long and 2 cm thick, can be cut every year. They are cut in the autumn, after the leaves have fallen, and produce a yield of 3 kg/m^2. These plantations are known as 'energy woods'. Various chemical processes are being considered to obtain energy from the wood produced. In one, chopped and crushed wood is heated in the presence of catalysts (substances which accelerate chemical reactions, but are not consumed themselves) to 300—400°C, to produce benzine, oils, waxes and various other substances from which glycols and polyethylenes can be made. Another possibility is to ferment the wood, to produce ethanol and methane, which again are the raw material for other products. The last possibility is pyrolysis, i. e. the decomposition of wood by heat to its gaseous components, which could be distributed in the same way as coal gas. In this way up to 4,500 calories can be produced from each kilogram of wood.

There are still other, previously unthought of ways of utilizing forest products, such as using its green material for the production of vitamin meal. The crowns of felled Aspen, spruces, birches and pines, or whole young trees removed during thinning operations could be used for this. Vitamin meal is an important component of cattle fodder and is given mainly in winter and early spring, when the animals tend to suffer from vitamin deficiency. The needles from the trees felled over an area of one hectare provide as much vitamins as the hay obtained from an area of 3—4 ha. Forest produce may, therefore, help deal with the worldwide fodder shortage.

Tannin, an important raw material, especially for the leather industry, is present in large amounts in the bark of spruces. Waste bark can also be used to make high quality composts for tree nurseries. In addition, the forest can offer us good things to eat — mushrooms, wild strawberries and raspberries, blackberries and hazelnuts. Some of its products are less well known to the general public, such as Juniper oil, which is indispensable in medicine and the foodstuffs industry, digitalis, which comes from the Foxglove, belladonna, a useful drug obtained from the Deadly Nightshade. Everybody, however, is familiar with one forest product: the Christmas tree. There is not a single branch of industry, not a single aspect of life, on which the forest does not leave its mark, directly or indirectly. It provides employment and a living for millions of people, most of whom are concerned with the processing of wood and other forest products, as well as those directly engaged in forestry.

Let us return for a moment to herb, fruit and mushroom picking and also discuss another activity not previously considered — hunting. Both these activities are recreational, being a pleasant way of doing something useful. Forest fruits are quite an important economic consideration. We do not know their consumption per head of the population, but there is no doubt that vast amounts of these fruits are bought and bottled in central Europe every year. This is particularly true in Poland, where some 30,000 tonnes of bilberries are bought yearly.

Hunting has a special place in forestry. Its economic importance is considerable, yet, it is also a sport and adds to the recreational value of the forest. Many thousands of tonnes of game are caught or shot in European forests every year. This figure may seem at first glance to be high, but in relative terms it is very small, since the average annual consumption of game per head of the population is less than half a kilogram. Game meat is not the hunter's only contribution to society, of course, since hide and skins are no less valuable than the flesh, although the profits made from the sale of weapons and ammunition, hunting equipment and charges for licences, etc. are estimated at double this amount. On the other hand, the negative aspects of hunting such as damage to trees and other plants should be borne in mind. Despite this, however, hunting is important both culturally and recreationally.

Apart from its purely economic significance, the forest has many other useful 'non-productive' functions. First and foremost, forests protect the water supply and the soil, and generally affect the character of the climate. Water is an important part of all living organisms, necessary to every vital process. Plants alone, throughout the world, require 650 trillion tonnes of water for their growth every year. We do not realize the value of water until there is a shortage. In central Europe, until quite recently we did not give much thought to the subject, but now Mankind is faced with the problem of whether or not the Earth's water supplies, which cannot be increased, will be sufficient to meet the growing needs of the population. Once, all a man needed was a bucket of water a day. By the beginning of the present century water consumption per head in industrial countries had risen to 50 l a day and now, in big cities, this amount is over 1,000 l a day. We must therefore learn to economize and to manage our water supplies better. History has shown that where forests are felled, flourishing country becomes a desert. This is because the forest not only stops rainwater from draining away too quickly and causing flash floods, but it also helps the soil store more water so that in times of low rainfall water remains in the system.

It used to be claimed that forests strongly influenced the rainfall and there is even

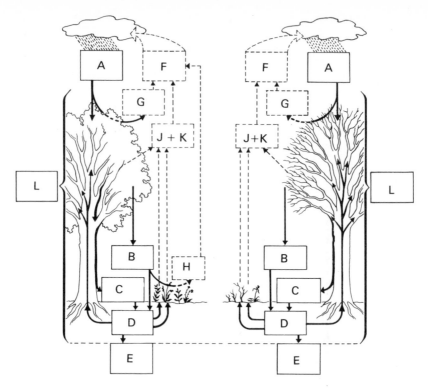

Fig. 21 — The circulation of water in a deciduous wood in the growing season (left) and in winter (right): A — rainfall, B — the rain trickles and drips through the foliage or, C — runs down the trunks and D — soaks into the soil; E — underground drainage, F — evaporation from the soil + transpiration + evaporation from the surface of the plants, G — evaporation from the surface of the trees, H — evaporation from the surface of herbaceous plants, J — transpiration, K — evaporation from the soil, L — water retained in plants and soil.

a saying that forests attract water. This is only partly true, since the effect of forests is confounded with that of mountains (rainfall increases with altitude). The influence of the forest on the circulation of rainwater is much more pronounced, since when it is raining the water does not fall to the ground all at once, but some is caught on the twigs and leaves. This prolongs the period over which rain reaches the ground, with the result that the soil can absorb it better. Some of the water naturally evaporates from the ground, as well as from the crowns of the trees, and some which drips to the ground from the branches trickles away, but the rest filters down to considerable depths to form a reserve against periods of drought. Some of this ground water is taken up by the roots of plants and their leaves transpire it back into the atmosphere (Fig. 21).

The figures for the water balance of a beechwood are very interesting. Of the water that falls as rain, 20 % evaporates from the tree crowns, 22 % drains off underground, 33 % is transpired, 15 % evaporates from the soil surface and 10 % drains off over the soil surface. The loss by surface drainage should be reduced to

Fig. 22 — The dense root system of riparian growths reinforces the banks and prevents them from being undermined.

Fig. 23 — Stone spillways on mountain streams provide very effective protection against erosion and slow down torrential currents.

a minimum, to prevent the soil from being washed away and erosion channels from being formed. However, not all forests conserve water equally well. Only healthy ones, whose soil is covered with decomposing humus, can function properly, since it is the soil covering which exerts most influence on drainage. Surface drainage over bare ground is up to twenty times greater than in a forest, and on denuded hillsides even a little rain will cut a channel in the soil. The channel grows deeper and deeper as it rapidly drains off water from the surrounding area, developing from a tiny stream into a torrent which may undermine river banks and cause floods (Fig. 22). The speed of natural streams, and their erosive power, may be reduced by spillways (Fig. 23).

Apart from its direct influence on the regulation of rainwater, forests benefit the water regime in other ways. In summer, the crowns of the trees prevent water from evaporating from the soil and in spring they prevent the snow from melting too quickly, so that the soil has plenty of time to absorb the melt water. The roots also have an important function, since they bind the soil and prevent it from being washed away. This brief account of the favourable influence of the forest on our water supply ought to underline the importance of its role in the national economy as a whole. Consideration of the forest water interaction very clearly illustrates the dangers of a one-sided evaluation of forest economics. As we shall see in the next chapter, simple tracks (rides) are often cleared in forests, to make it easier for tractors to take the timber from the felling site to the road. In doing this a wide lane is cut through the trees and the ground simply evened out with a bulldozer, naturally taking care to keep costs as low as possible. When building such a ride, however, proper drainage should be arranged, thereby preventing the erosion which would otherwise inevitably occur. Water would run down the ride, carrying loosened material with it. The ride would become a permanent watercourse carrying silty water and blocking up the beds of lower-lying streams and rivers. In other words, the whole of society would have to pay for the 'cheap' transport of timber — usually with soiled and contaminated water.

The beneficial effect of the forest on human health has long been acknowledged and confirmed by statistics. Investigations carried out in Switzerland showed that mortality was highest in industrial areas and lowest in the wooded mountains, while according to studies in West Germany, one third of all deaths may be accounted for by the unhealthy climate of the cities. In our modern, over-industrial and over-technological society, it is essential that people spend some time in the woods, particularly town-dwellers. The type and degree of this therapeutic effect is determined by the type of trees, by the age of the forest and by the surrounding country, and is mediated through the various aromatic substances and pollen in forest air. The different volatile and essential oils are important, since they are good for the airways and make a walk in the woods a kind of inhalation cure. They also reduce the amount of ozone, so that the ozone concentration in forest air is much lower than in open country. The favourable influence of the forest is enhanced by its specific microclimate, which is characterized by greater humidity and a more balanced temperature than elsewhere. During the daytime the crowns of the trees prevent overheating, and in the night excessive cooling, in relation to the external environmental temperature. These two factors both have a beneficial effect on one's mental state. In more open woods, such as pinewoods, which can be penetrated by direct sunlight during the day, but whose crowns prevent the heated air from escaping, we may find the reverse conditions. On hot summer days such woods are stifling, despite the high saturation of the atmosphere with aromatic substances. In this case the forest has a negative effect on the nervous system, but a positive effect on the respiratory system. The silence of the forest, or the gentle rustling of the trees, is another important component of its beneficial effect. The light climate is also different. Light passing through the crowns becomes richer in yellow and green wavelengths and weaker in the red wavelengths — an important factor from the medical aspect, since green soothes the nervous system, while red excites it. The high relative humidity within the forest is not only mentally beneficial, but also aids the respiratory processes; it keeps the mucous membranes of the respiratory tract moist, so that they are better able to trap any solid particles which happen to be inhaled. A further characteristic of the forest is that it damps sounds (in this respect it is ten times more effective than the open country). The extent of this effect is naturally associated with the type of trees present. The best sound-dampers are conifers, while the best deciduous trees are those species with felty leaves or whose leaves, when dry, remain on the tree for a long time (e. g. oak). The forest also catches wind-borne dust particles. As the wind drops, the dust settles and is not stirred up again. Measurements have shown that one hectare of spruce woodland catches 32 tonnes of solid particles each year. To sum up, we can claim that most of the above factors have a beneficial effect on Man's mental state and that they play an important role in the treatment of certain diseases. That is why so many sanatoria and similar institutions are built in wooded country.

From the discussion so far one may justifiably wonder how forests can possibly fulfil all these different functions. Forestry boards divide forests into commercial forests, where the main aim is timber production, and special purpose forests, whose management is determined by the purpose for which the forest is reserved. For example, forests round spas or sanatoria are usually kept specially for the use and benefit of the patients.

One of the most recent special uses of forests is for recreation. Forests reserved for recreation require special facilities and are run with the aim of creating the best possible recreational conditions. After the Second World War, people flocked to the forest as never before, escaping from the over-technical and monotonous life of the town. The advent of motoring brought forests much closer and allowed people to spend a few hours communing with nature even on working days. Again, the figures speak for themselves. In the USA, in 1940 some 16 million persons visited forests, by 1970 the number had risen to 200 million and by the year 2,000 it is expected to reach the 600 million mark. The degree to which each forest is used for recreational purposes naturally varies. It depends on the size of the local population, the forest's area and on the distribution of forests near industrial centres. In the Netherlands, where only 8.1 % of the country is wooded, practically two thirds of it are used for recreational purposes. It has been estimated that the amount of forest allocated for recreational purposes ought in future to be calculated on the basis of 50 m^2 of forest per inhabitant of a town with a population of over 20,000.

With the increasing use of forests for recreational purposes, new conflicts are bound to arise between visitors to the forest and the forest management. In the first place, visitors will have to be taught more about nature and must be made aware that unless nature is kept healthy, their own lives cannot be healthy either. On the other hand, it is necessary to know what visitors want and expect from such recreation. Many countries have therefore carried out opinion surveys using questionnaires. Wherever this has been done, those questioned were all agreed that forests were essential for recreation and — most surprisingly — that they were willing to pay for the maintenance of these facilities by increased taxes or special charges. Spring and autumn were the favourite seasons for forest recreation. Criticisms of facilities included a shortage of litter bins, benches, public lavatories and water. A large proportion were against the use of transistor radios in forests. Mixed woods comprising all the elements of forest beauty were the most popular. The nature of the ideal recreational forest varies according to its specific purpose. Most important are the woods directly attached to towns, which can be reached by means of public transport in 20—30 minutes. Then come woodlands in the vicinity of big cities and woods belonging to spas or sanatoria. National parks and nature conservation areas have a special value. The way in which these woods are run is naturally adapted to suit their specific purpose as places of recreation. In the first place, various facilities must be provided. Woods near towns need car parks, snack bars, sand pits for children, benches, shelters, footpaths and information boards (Fig. 24). Regarding forest management, certain changes must be planned; these include the introduction of mixed stands while leaving some parts of the wood in their natural state. The wood can also be made more picturesque by planting exotic trees along the roads and footpaths. The general appearance of the wood must likewise conform to its future purpose. For instance, woods in the vicinity of towns, which are likely to be visited by mothers and children, ought to be free of undergrowth, so as to allow

Fig. 24 — Forests are becoming increasingly popular as places where people can find rest and recreation in a healthy natural environment.

a clear view, and should have some grassy spaces. Very often the authorities go to considerable expense to convert urban and suburban woodlands for recreation purposes. For example, flat country near Paris is being transformed into more attractive gently undulating hilly country with new woods, avenues and lakes. The experimental introduction of selfservice sale of Christmas trees in West Germany is an interesting project. For children living in cities, it is an unforgettable experience to go into the woods with their parents before Christmas and cut down their own tree. Such a scheme must obviously be carefully prepared. The plantations in question must be made accessible to public transport, car parks and places of refreshment must be provided and the choice of trees must be supervised by an expert, who at the same time can talk to the children about the forest, thereby rousing their interest and broadening their outlook. Those who spoil the forest for others include the litterbugs, who leave their refuse behind them and are sometimes impudent enough to dispose of household rubbish in the woods. Others pollute the water by dumping waste oil or washing their cars there. Forest fires caused by carelessness are a particular danger. The aesthetic appeal of the woods has been repeatedly stressed. It is part of the forester's job to enhance this by cutting down old trees and plants and planting new ones. It is in everybody's interest to support his efforts by behaving in the woods in a civilized manner and by helping to protect them.

Forests are therefore no longer managed for timber production alone and must be cared for with a variety of purposes in mind. Today the countryside changes more in ten years than it used to do in a hundred. Built-up areas are spreading, industry is expanding and new technologies, often very divorced from nature, are being used in agriculture. Not unnaturally, these developments embody much evil as well as good. They cause a decrease in green areas, pollution of the air, soil and water and the accumulation of refuse — factors all detrimental to the environment. The value of forests is therefore more important than ever before and will increase still further. They provide refuge for many animals driven out of their former natural haunts by Man's encroachment on the countryside and they produce wood which in the future will become an increasingly important raw material both as timber and as a source of nutrients and energy. And most important of all, forests play a role in public health for which there is no substitute. Modern forestry practice must therefore aim at harmonious relationships between timber production and the social functions of forests.

Forest management

Scientific and technical progress in mechanization and automation has affected every branch of the national economy of countries everywhere. Profound changes are also taking place in forestry, not only in production techniques, but also in recognizing further uses for forest products, although throughout the world forestry is still mainly directed solely towards producing wood and various minor raw materials to meet the needs of the manufacturing industries. Although forests have long been regarded in central Europe as an important part of the environment and the scenery, this aspect has not so far been included in discussions of forest economics. It will no doubt not be long before the non-productive benefits of forests are accounted in the same way as their present productive functions. For the moment, however, demands for multiple use of forests have brought foresters face to face with a number of problems. Not only are new unfamiliar activities, such as recreation, involved, but the economic implications of these have yet to be resolved. These other uses of the forest must be evaluated and placed on the same financial footing as actual timber production.

One of the most important problems facing forestry today is the cost of production. Manpower is not only expensive, but its capacity and output are inadequate for present day requirements. The best solution is full mechanization and in this respect the greatest advances of recent years have been achieved in felling and haulage; that is actual felling, transport of the timber to the nearest road and its subsequent transport to the customer or to a timber yard, where it is sorted and cut into the required sizes. The days when groups of woodcutters, armed with heavy handsaws,

axes, strippers and other implements worked in the forest are past and gone. The modern forest worker works alone and instead of the axe his principle tool is the portable chain-saw, which is far more efficient, lighter and easier to handle, and can also be used for lopping off branches. While more productive and less fatiguing, these methods of working require more training and the worker must not only know how to use his tool and how it functions, but must also be able to perform minor repairs.

The organization of the work as a whole has also altered. For instance, groups of workers used to sort the timber and cut it into lengths, ready for transport to the customer, in the forest. It was stored in the forest either in piles, if it was destined for use as fuel or pulp wood (for the production of cellulose), or in stacks (commercial wood suitable for the production of small objects). Then there was round timber (rough, untrimmed trunks), destined for sawmills, and mine timber for pit props. Modern practice reduces work in the actual forest to a minimum and processing now takes place in mechanized timber yards at railway stations or beside navigable rivers, or in wood processing factories. This means that the only work done in the forest is felling and bark-stripping. Production teams equipped with a vehicle and tackle — usually a tractor and a winch — represent a higher grade of mechanization. The team, generally of 5—6 men, is transported to the site to be worked. Its task is to fell marked trees and drag them to the road. The highest forms of mechanization in present use are the forestry combines and lopping machines, which fell the trees, lop off the branches and cut the trunks to the required lengths. The degree to which such equipment can be used naturally depends a great deal on the character of the terrain and on the way in which the work is organized (Fig. 25). The work of dragging the felled trunks to the road used to be done by horses. In mountainous country the timber was then taken down to the valley in a very laborious and dangerous manner — on a sledge driven by a single woodcutter. Today this method is hardly ever used. Horses have likewise almost disappeared from the forest and are still employed only in difficult mountainous country or where the trees in question are scattered (i.e. for the transport of single — usually uprooted, snapped or diseased — trees). This brief survey of the development of felling and haulage practice shows what a marked change has taken place in the work of the woodcutter, who has been transformed from a manual worker to a highly skilled mechanic. The efficiency of timber output is also affected by the accessibility of the terrain, in particular the ease of establishment of slipways (simple routes for sending timber down to the road) and the construction of durable forest roads along which timber can be transported by heavy lorries fitted with various mechanical loading devices.

Successful mechanization of cultivating, planting and growing trees (silviculture) is far more difficult. It includes the selection of seeds for the production of suitable seedlings, the care of nurseries and young growths, the planting out of seedlings, the removal of unsuitable individuals and similar treatment of older trees (thinning). This branch of forestry remains partly mechanized, although considerable successes have been achieved here since the end of the war. The problem is again how to replace manpower and do away as far as possible with the seasonal character of cultivation. The first task is the cultivation of good quality seeds. Seedlings used to be cultivated in small nurseries where it was impossible to use mechanization and all the work was done by hand. The seeds were even sown by hand. When they germinated the seedlings were tended for a whole year and it was not until the second year that they were transplanted to open beds, in spaced rows, in a proper nursery, where they were kept for 1—3 years. Before planting out into the woods they were again dug up by hand. Collecting the seeds was laborious and dangerous, since it meant climbing the trees to get them. Obviously such work could only be done by young people, nimble and physically fit. Today seeds are collected from 'seed plantations'. These are composed of selected grafted plants which fruit after a few years, so that the seeds can be gathered comfortably from the ground or collected from low grafts without any danger of injury. To make full use of mechanization, large nurseries are equipped with mechanical sprinklers (Fig. 26). The seeds are sown in flat cold frames covered with plastic sheet. The advantage of this method compared with sowing in the open is that it prevents losses caused by drought, birds and rodents. Furthermore, sowing time is not dependent on the weather and the seeds can be sown early in the spring. The plastic sheet is not removed until the seedlings are well established. These seedlings can be transplanted to nurseries in the autumn or the following spring. Another way of growing trees from seed is the Finnish method, in which the seedlings also develop in a glasshouse, but in special tubs, in which they are planted out directly into the woods. The advantage of this method is that planting can be carried out practically the whole year round and is no longer dependent on the seasons. The greatest advantage, however, is that seedlings in tubs do not suffer shock when transplanted to a forest clearing, and continue to develop normally, so that wastage is very low. The entire process, from the filling of

Fig. 26 — Tree nurseries form the foundations for reforestation and are the guarantee of healthy forests in the future.

the tubs with peat to their planting out is fully mechanized. Where the terrain allows, modern sowing machines are used for planting out both tub-grown plants and normally grown seedlings, whose roots are first stripped of soil. One of the most difficult operations to rationalize is the thinning of young stands and it is best to try to avoid it altogether. This can be done by planting seedlings out at such wide intervals that their crowns do not close for about 30 years. The first thinning then yields timber sufficiently thick for the production of cellulose. A smaller number of good quality seedlings can thus be planted out, and their care and fertilization can then be mechanized. Areas marked for afforestation very often need to be reclaimed, i.e. the quality of their soil needs to be improved. This is usually done be draining or by ploughing over in various ways. Reclamation is a special form of cultivation involving complicated biological processes, whereby devastated areas such as rubbish dumps and slag heaps are forested once again. The afforestation of such places is very difficult indeed, and they must first be planted with 'pioneer' species, such as birches, alders and Aspen, etc. These provide protection for the main trees, which are chosen with regard to local natural conditions.

Forest protection is an important part of the forester's work. During its development the forest is threatened by many types of pests, the chief ones being insects and fungi which attack wood, although snow, frost and wind may likewise do considerable damage. The damage done by the elements is exacerbated by the fact that such disasters leave ideal conditions for the calamitous proliferation of insect pests (e.g. the spruce bark beetles) in their wake. Since it is part of the forester's job to control insect populations, he must monitor the levels of pest populations. Plagues are dealt with using chemical pesticides, but these kill useful animals as well as pests. Chemicals are also used to control weeds in nurseries. It must be emphasized, however, that the problem of the use of chemicals in forestry is far more complicated than in agriculture, since in the latter, harvests are reaped after a few months, whereas a forest takes 100 years to mature. We must therefore be very cautious concerning the use of chemicals in forests and employ them only where it is absolutely necessary.

The forest growth cycle, i. e. the period between the time when the trees are planted and when they are ready for felling, takes 100 years and needs very careful planning. Consequently forestry was the first form of industry or exploitation in the world to be run according to plans (forestry management plans) lasting for over 100 years. These plans are based on a knowledge of timber reserves, growth increments and acreages, so that the forester knows how much timber can be felled every year, and can aim at a steady, continuous annual yield. Such plans contain a textual part with the technical data which the forester needs, and also a graphic part, with forest maps showing the ages of the individual stands indicated by different colours.

As in other fields, international cooperation has proved invaluable in solving forestry problems. On October 16, 1945, in Quebec in Canada, representatives of 42 countries founded the Food and Agriculture Organization (FAO), which is a part of the United Nations. Its aim is to improve the level of nutrition of the Third World and to organize the production and distribution of foodstuffs and other agricultural, fishery and forestry products. It has the task of supporting the development of an international economy, of protecting water resources and soil, of propagating progressive agricultural methods, of fighting epidemics and of providing qualified aid. In other words, its main task is to assure, by a series of different measures, future harmony between the increase in the size of the world's population and the production of foodstuffs and raw materials. The FAO also includes forestry within its remit. The original stimulus came from Franklin D. Roosevelt, the former American president, who, while flying over Lebanon at the end of the Second World War, saw below him a desert instead of the legendary cedars. The forestry section of the FAO was created in 1946. The organization's approach to forestry problems is based on evaluation of the significance of the forest as one of the components of the environment. The forestry section has also predicted the relative sizes of both wood production and wood consumption up to the end of 1985. The FAO naturally also concerns itself with problems of hunting and gamekeeping, forest recreation and the establishment of reserves and national parks, in conjunction with the International Union for the Conservation of Nature (IUCN).

Fig. 27 — Forest reserves are the last remains of natural forest communities where the forest flora and fauna still live together in perfect harmony.

In addition to the FAO there is an International Union for Forest Research (IUFRO), which cooperates very closely with information centres in Great Britain, the GFR, Czechoslovakia and the USSR.

The above data show that forestry will soon become a very important profession, whose worthy aim will be to assure balanced relationships between timber production and the social benefits of the forest.

The Conservation of Nature

The preceding chapters have shown how society's view of the environment has undergone a great change, and how the need to plan the use of our natural resources is now more widely appreciated. Our increasing understanding of the complex relationships between ourselves and the world we inhabit provide the basis for constructive management of the environment. No longer need civilized countries merely plunder and devastate the fields and forests. The way is clear for positive intervention by which we may enhance the yield of productive systems while still retaining a diverse and viable countryside in which every species of plant and animal may prosper. The need for nature conservation was first realized only at the beginning of the nineteenth century. At first these ideas took the form of romantic and sentimental appeals to save a few isolated but outstanding natural phenomena. People soon came to realize, however, that there is no point in protecting some rare plant or animal if the environmental conditions necessary for its survival are not conserved at the same time. They therefore began by protecting small or large areas in which the relevant ecosystems (communities of living organisms) could be preserved and protected. These regions were termed 'nature reserves' (Fig. 27, 28). The first 'national park' was created in 1872 in the USA. However, Man's increasingly ruthless interference with nature has made it necessary to protect the environment as a whole. As well as protecting individual natural phenomena, it is essential to control human activity wherever the integrity of the environment might be endangered. Modern nature conservation must be viewed as a series of measures allowing and ensuring the reasonable enjoyment of the gifts of nature, thus fulfilling Man's economic, cultural and aesthetic requirements. At the same time, the needs of future generations must also be taken into account. Attention must likewise be paid to changes in environmental conditions, whether of natural origin or caused by Man's activities.

The need for international cooperation implicit in this concept of nature conservation led to the formation of the International Union for the Conservation of Nature (IUCN) in France in 1948. This originally semi-private institution has developed into a vast international organization uniting and coordinating the efforts of many state, voluntary and international authorities concerned with conservation of the natural environment and with the rational utilization of natural resources. The members of the IUCN today comprise 35 states, 291 national organizations from 84 countries and 18 international organizations. The union has its quarters at Morges in Switzerland. The activities of the IUCN are conducted through the work of commissions composed of leading international specialists. Six commissions have so far been formed — for the protection of species, for ecology, for national parks, for the

Fig. 28 — In forested regions protected by law, the plant and animal communities are left intact.

environment, for politics, legislation and administration and, lastly, for education and information. Teams of specialists help the commissions with their work. The controlling authority is the executive committee, headed by the president: it is composed of eight members from European countries and three each from North and South America, Asia and Africa. The IUCN has implemented a whole series of proposals for nature conservation such as the convention for limiting the trade in skins of rare mammals, or the agreement on protection of the Polar Bear, and has played a decisive role in the steady increase in the number of protected areas — particularly national parks and reserves — throughout the world. In recent years the IUCN has been active in cooperation with the relevant agencies of the United Nations, whose activities are being concentrated more and more on the protection of nature and the environment. It likewise plays a prominent role in the development of methods for explaining and popularizing nature conservation and for coordinating legal changes and conservation policy in individual countries. This organization also played an active part in the English TV series 'Will they survive the year 2000?' This popular question does not apply only to exotic ecosystems and big game, however, since Man's increasing encroachment on the countryside endangers the existence of many species of animals, often far more than if they were persecuted directly. This destruction of habitats affects not only large and obvious species, but also the small, inconspicuous ones and, no doubt, even some of whose existence we at present know very little.

In the case of some species the attempt to save them has come too late. Others can still be saved, however, and here the IUCN has already done a great deal of useful work both in providing large numbers of reserves and through programmes such as the artificial breeding and reintroduction of individual species. Two of the best known examples are the rescue of the European Bison in the USSR and Poland, and of the Przewalski Horse, the largest herd of which can now be seen in the zoological garden in Prague. Among birds, the rescue of the Hawaiian Goose is a recent classic example. The publication of the IUCN's 'Red Data Book', a list of endangered species, was another important step. This book not only tells specialists which species require special attention, but also enlightens those engaged in planned development of the countryside on the consequences their work may have in regions where an endangered species has its habitat.

Another nature conservation organization — the World Wildlife Fund (WWF) — has been working in Switzerland since 1961. Its aims are similar to the IUCN, i.e. the protection of the environment and natural resources and support for all those working in this field. The two organizations have divided their practical tasks, however, so that the IUCN deals with questions related to research, planning and legislation, while the WWF, through its national committees, educates the public on the need for the protection of nature in general, and of certain species in particular, where the pressures of civilization have left practically no more room for their existence. The WWF also collects funds for international support of these projects.

Many of these conservation problems could not be resolved without international cooperation. This is borne out by one of the latest forecasts on the recovery and utilization of natural raw materials and pollution of the environment. For example, about 10 million tonnes of crude oil and oil by-products find their way into the sea every year. One tonne of oil forms a thin, air-proof film over an area of 12 km^2, so that today about one fifth of the surface of the Pacific is covered with such a film, with all the inevitable consequences. Another example is the seven-fold increase in water, soil and air pollution in the USA during the past 30 years. For instance, the water of the Mississippi, even diluted 100-fold, will kill a fish in a single day. By the year 2000, the amount of carbon dioxide in the atmosphere will have risen by 25 % compared with 1970, owing to the burning of solid fuel, and may have an extremely harmful effect on the climate. Without modern techniques it will obviously not be possible to resolve the problems associated with protection of the environment. The use of ERTS (Earth Resources Technology Satellites) for determining damage produced by sulphur dioxide in Canada is one example of the benefits of high-technology. The latest way of determining the purity of air is with lasers, so far the ultimate in sophistication. The above examples show that scientific and technical achievements can also be used for the protection of the environment, but only close international cooperation, crossing frontiers and linking continents, can guarantee that nature will remain healthy and that future generations will still be able to enjoy the woods and forests which make up such an important part of our countryside.

Suggestions for further reading

Aichele, D. *A Field Guide in Colour to Wild Flowers* Octopus Books, London, 1975

Bramwell, M. (ed.) *The International Book of Wood* Mitchell Beazley, London, 1976

Černý, W. *A Field Guide in Colour to Birds* Octopus Books, London, 1975

Christensen, C.M. *The Molds and Man; an Introduction to the Fungi* Oxford University Press, Melbourne and London, 1951

Clapham, A.R., Tutin, T.G. and Warburg, E.F. *The Excursion Flora of the British Isles* Cambridge University Press, Cambridge, 1981

Corbet, G.B. and Southern, H.N. *The Handbook of British Mammals* Blackwell, Oxford, 1977

Darlington, A. *The Pocket Encyclopedia of Plant Galls in Colour* Blandford, London, 1968

Douglass, R.W. *Forest Recreation* Pergamon, Oxford, 1977

Earl, D.E. *Forest Energy and Economic Development* Clarendon Press, Oxford, 1975

Edlin, H.L. and Nimmo, M. *Trees* Orbis, London, 1978

Fitter, R., Fitter, A. and Blamey, M. *The Wild Flowers of Britain and Northern Europe* Collins, London, 1980

Gorer, R. *Illustrated Guide to Trees* Kingfisher Books, London, 1980

Novák, I. *A Field Guide in Colour to Butterflies and Moths* Octopus Books, London, 1980

Owen, D.F. *What Is Ecology?* Oxford University Press, Melbourne and London, 1974

Pennington, W. *The History of British Vegetation* English University Press, London, 1969

Polunin, O. *A Field Guide to the Flowers of Europe* Oxford University Press, Melbourne and London, 1969

Street, D. *The Reptiles of North and Central Europe* Batsford, London, 1979

Simms, E. *Woodland Birds* Collins, London, 1971

Spurr, S.H. and Barnes, B.V. *Forest Ecology* Wiley, New York, 1980

Svrček, M. and Kubička, J. *A Field Guide in Colour to Mushrooms and Other Fungi* Octopus Books, London, 1979

Toman, J. and Felix, J. *A Field Guide in Colour to Plants and Animals* Octopus Books, London, 1974

Van den Brink, F.H. *A Field Guide to the Mammals of Britain and Europe* Collins, London, 1977

Vedel, H. and Lange, J. *Trees and Bushes in Wood and Hedgerow* Methuen, London, 1960

Zahradník, J. *A Field Guide in Colour to Insects* Octopus Books, London, 1977

Index of Common Names

Index of Scientific Names